THE KING KOBRA OF SIN STRIKES WITHOUT WARNING PREYING ON THE YOUNG AND THE WEAK "PREDATOR BEHIND THE MASK"

ALVIN WALLACE

Predator
Stay
Away
From Me

ISBN 978-1-957582-62-7 (paperback)
ISBN 978-1-957582-63-4 (hardcover)
ISBN 978-1-957582-64-1 (digital)

Printed in the United States of America

According to the Holy Bible, EPHESIANS 6-10-18; and I quote, Finally, my brethren in the Lord and in the power of his might. Put on the whole armor of God, that you be able to stand against the wiles of the devil. For we do not wrestle against flesh and blood, but against, but against principalities, against powers, against the rulers of the darkness of this age, against spiritual hosts of wickedness in the heavenly places. Therefore take up the whole armor of God, that you may be able to withstand in the evil day, and having done all, to stand. Stand therefore, having girded your waist with truth, having put on the breastplate of the righteousness, And having shod your feet with the preparation of the Gospel of peace. Above all, taking the shield of faith with which you will be able to quench all the fiery darts of the wicked one. And take the helmet of salvation, and the sword of the Spirit which is the word of God; Praying always with all prayer and supplication in the Spirit, being watchful to this end with all perseverance and supplication for all the saints; unquoted.

This is a story from the heart of burning love about children between the age of 12 to 18 living healthlessly beyond the rein of despair seeking only to live within the boundary of trust, freedom, safety within, and of course love from their parents. With that being said taken into consideration what we now know about people around us and strangers, What does we need to do different in the name of safety whether we are with our parents or alone? The question was asked by a young lady that I spoke to on the street, a very dear friend no doubt; she asked why should we live in fear? I first thought that was a very strange question especially coming from her. But to my surprise she asked the question again. To be honest I didn't know what to say to her at first. I then remembered watching a movie where someone asked the same question. He said and I quote, never ever should you live in fear. I strongly agreed. If anyone should live in fear, Mr. Predator, it should be you.

The seekers I would say has the power, sagacious, strength, mold, and grow their mind into young adults. This I must add should be wisdom coming from within the heart of many as human beings so to speak lifting knowledge, experience, and learned matters that attracts the minds of those so dearly who depends on us to structure and guide them. We as parents are our children guardian angles from the time they're concerned and born given the breath of life. We therefore especially mothers should take such responsibility very serious. We lay the ground and path way for our children once they are born. The foot print if you will structuring their life introducing them to unfamiliar surroundings. But as the child grows, matures, and become of age they take on a bridge, and a path way of their own. We called this now the learning stage where the child begins to recognize, and understand who their parents are, and others around them.

Even at this age group children are targets of predators and they could be anyone. Therefore parents needs to be very careful, and on the alert for whatever will happen to their child. It doesn't stop there from what I understand but instead goes beyond the river and mountains educating our future of tomorrow and they of course are called children. We must therefore protect them from whatever seek their immaturity, and lack of understanding trying to penetrate their small brain until they are mature enough to know the different between friends, non-friends, predators, and strangers. They must therefore learn and understand words that will protect them throughout life especially now at a tender young age between the age of 12 and eighteen.

Hopefully this story will be that for them the "rock" looking down on them protecting them from the hands of evil. Children wait for me. Predators awaits; so please don't leave. That could mean pretty much anything. But most importantly its telling you simply be safe. What am I saying? do I mean? Time will tell my child and will let you know. The world is not something that you don't know. Listen to your parents and do what they say. They will love you my child and take care of you everyday. I know that you don't understand. So let me make myself clear. We're trying to keep you safe if that makes senses. Children, your parents are telling you that they realize that you are too young to understand the danger around you. Children you don't understand that being outside, at school, or even in the park that something can happen to you.

We were once children not so long ago. I understand that you're young and your brain needs to grow. So give your parents a chance and learn as you go. Your parents, your parents, you asked who are they. They are your guardian angels keeping the bully man away. Children, your parents are your security blanket watching over you, stuck you into bed, and seeing you off to school in the morning. Your parents plays an important in your life. But most importantly they keep you safe and out of armsway. They're there when you need them and a phone call away. So don't cry my child they have not gone astray. They're always with you in spirit and in sight so open your eyes my child at the beautiful light. Let it shine down and give insight.

Knock, knock, whose there I wonder, whose at the door? This is a question naturally asked by everyone when someone knocks on their door. But for the purpose of this story; it relates to family safety and the safety of their children. It teaches a child what to do when someone comes to the door. Whether or not to open the door. Whether or not to hide. Whether or not to call the police. Knock, knock whose there; should not be taken for granted. Think of it as a safety net for your child. Be ware my child know what to do. Don't open the door if you're not sure. Why did you say that? What does it mean to you? Be safe my child bully man awaits you. The word bully man is ok for children between the age of 5 to 10, but should be translated out to a smarter word for children between 12 and 18, such as bully man – danger, danger - predator, predator – peril, peril – threatening, danger – harm.

Your little brain can only understand so much. So let me say this and saying it I will. Reach out to your parents and do no wrong. So they will guide you safely all the way home. Their home, your home, which one should I go? If your confused my child listen to what I say. Trust yourself, trust your mind, but when in doubt just turn around. Look up at the sky it's not so hard. Although it may be for you being a child. There is a lot that you don't understand. We your parents we know that's true. But whatever you do don't feel blue. Help is always there at your side. So don't be weary and please don't cry. Just be aware of strangers that's the smart thing to do. Strangers I say who are they? Strangers might mislead you far, far away. Know your house and where you live. Write down your phone number and cell at will. This is something that parents needs to teach their children. It's an important way of keeping them safe. It's not something a child is going to think of doing on their own. Children for the record don't focus on safety. Their too busy focusing on other things depending on the age group fun, and the opposite sex.

A stranger child is someone that you don't know. Stay away from strangers and don't open the door. If they force you scream, scream, scream as loud as you can. Because they will take you against your will. If that should happen let me say this. My child scream out loud and run away as fast as you can. Hide, hide, hide, the best that you can. Don't let them find you whatever you do. They will cut off your head and put it in a shoe. This is not to scare you or your child. But it is something that happens in real life. You cannot be too careful these days. Too many children has gone missing and never heard from again. Don't take what I say for a joke. It could be your child. You could be in a supermarket and when it's time to leave your child is no where to be found. Your child could disappear just that fast. There is so much as a parent you need to teach your child. My child, my child, don't let that happen to you. If someone says to you come with me what will you do? If you are a stranger don't force me to come with you. Let me go home and home I will. You are a stranger and not my friend.

You will hurt me and I now that's true. I don't want to be hurt by someone like you. I love myself, my life, and my parents. So stranger leave me along and bother me no more. For it is written right is right and wrong is wrong so stranger whatever you do just leave me along. I live my life and yes I'm young let me live my life without harm. I want to grow up and live a long life. Stranger please don't take that away from me. Let me live, live, live, as tall as a tree. I look forward to my very first date and marrying the man of my dream making him my mate and wearing a beautiful ring. I look forward to going to college and having my first child being the lifeline of a bride and a wife. I hope this is not asking too much of you.

I thank you stranger for sparing my life letting me live my full life. You know stranger the Bible speaks of people like you having a heart and feelings to. It goes to say that you were once a child then why should you take my life. Can't you see I'm only 10 years old I need my parents to learn and to grow old. I am a beautiful young child Mr. Predator don't you agree? What would your parents say Mr. Predator if you made me scream? What would your parents say to you abducting and kidnapping me, sin, sin, sin, that's what they would say; leave me along and go your way. Mr. Predator, do you not agree; your parents would be happy even in their dream. My parents Mr. Predator lives in a beautiful house. They watch over me day and night. They don't ask for much although I don't know why. So, please Mr. Predator don't make me cry. Mr. Predator, whoever you are please don't touch me. I know that you have a heart and knows right from wrong. Please don't torture me or tie me up but let me go home. I will not tell anyone anything about you. I just want to go home to be with my parents. I will not tell them Mr. Predator where I was, and nothing about you listen to what I say this will be our little secret please believe me.

https://www.nytimes.com/2017/12/19/magazine/what-makes-someone-a-predator.html
What Makes Someone a Predator'? by Michelle Dean; and I quote, years ago, I was out very late in Brooklyn at a restaurant whose name I was too drunk to catch. I arrived there with a clutch of people who had lingered until closing at a publishing party nearby. I wasn't particularly young, but I was still new to this world of writing and people who care about it, and a little star struck by most of the people in attendance. I think I was hoping their status as official literary figures real writers, real editors might rub off on me. One of them was someone I'll call a Powerful literary Man. We had never spoken, and I was no one of importance, but he sat down next to me. We ordered drinks. I don't remember what we talked about, if we really talked at all.

The only memory I have crystallizes at the moment I became aware of a hand stroking the inside of my right thigh, under my dress. I turned and looked at the Powerful Literary Man, Who, seated beside me, was the only one eligible to be owner of the hand. His half crouch indicated that indeed, yes, it was he stroking my inner thigh without invitation. He smiled at me. I think I remember—this is the part that shame me—smiling back. I have no explanation except to say that ever since I was a child, it's the tic I've had in awkward situations. I smiled, or even laugh, to smooth something over. I looked back around the table. No one betrayed any sign of having noticed anything. After silently reviewing my options, I excused myself and went to the bathroom, and then I left. As we get our bearings in this new post-Weinstein age, a lot of women have spent time returning to experiences like this one—holding them up to the light, considering what we might have missed. It's the

similarities that are trickier. The most arresting thing about Harvey Weinstein, for me, was how methodical he was, how consistent in modus operandi, when he decided to go after a woman: The call from a talent agent to arrange the meeting, the reassuring female assistant in the lobby, the hotel-room door closing, the bathrobe, the incongruous request for a message. There was a ritual sameness to these stories, one that said to us: This was a result of consideration and planning, of practice. This treating of the hunt like a craft, the carefulness of it, is one mark of what we often call a predator. People like that word because of its certainty, the way it rules on the case all by itself. A predator naturally lives outside the herd, and because of that, he can be very easy to ostracize. The shaming, the firing, the possible criminal prosecution: All of that seems a logical consequence for predators. Now the word comes up everywhere, and many of the cases are easy: Weinstein; Roy Moore, reportedly chasing teenagers around an Alabama mail; Russell Simmons, accused of taking women up to penthouses and keeping them there against their will. But then there are the other instances—when the behavior is unquestionably wrong and invasive, the consequences are justified and yet the word "predator" doesn't quite comfortably apply.

There are all sorts of men who do all sorts of things they should not be doing, but who believe themselves exempt from this moment because, well, they're not that bad. That Powerful Literary Man, it occurs to me, could read this sort of essay and not think, not the word "predator" might apply to him. In ecology, a predator is an animal that kills and eats other animals, and the threat it poses is relatively clear-cut. There is very little ambiguity when the mountain lion eviscerates the rabbit, or the leopard rips apart the gazelle. A scientist, of course, might point out that from the standpoint of the whole ecosystem, a predator is necessary: It has a role in balancing populations, in preserving biological diversity. But when people talk about human predators, they're looking at them from the standpoint of the gazelle. In 1981, early in his first term, Ronald Reagan stood before the international Association of Chief Of Police and railed about "utopian presumptions about human nature" in what he characterized as the age of "the human predator". He liked to carve the world into good and evil this way, conjuring the criminal and an irredeemable cancer on society, evil as a matter of his nature rather than his situation. But outside the question of racial bias in identifying evil people, and policy arguments about how to deal with them. What few people to question is the notion that there are people who are just fundamentally dangerous. We are even, in the face of our own dismay, fascinated by them.

"To catch a Predator" aired for three seasons on MSNBC; true crime has of late been a highbrow obsession, making a kind of intellectual game out of trying to detect a gleam of murder in Robert Durst's placed expression on HBO's "The Jinx". The fantasy of predator is that they are watching us, always hunting, always about to strike. We watch them in turn because we have a fantasy of ourmarting them, of turning tables. The rhetoric of the predator has been wrapped up for so long with a brutal reading of human nature—a Dar winian vision of hunter and game and cold, remorseless victimization. But what about those who harm other people carelessly, thoughtlessly drunkenly, ignorant of the consequences?In life, these people seem harder to avoid than the absolutely evil ones. They are a stranger reminder that words like "predatory" were used to refer to people before they were used to classify animals. The Latin root of "predatory" is not, as you might assume, the word for "hunt", venari. It's actually praedor—-to plunder. Which you have already conquered, by right, like a pirate taking a ship's treasure.

Answers.yahoo.com/question/index?qid=20071029042656AAiL3V
Should parents teach their children not to talk to "strangers" by YAHOO ANSWERS. Everyone according to Yahoo Answers has heard the child safety advice of "don't talk to strangers" however, it occurs to me that children need to learn and be comfortable with approximate social etiquette such as asking for assistance to stores, ordering food in restaurants, making small talk and being generally polite. Best answer: Telling children not to talk to strangers is not the best way. I think that teaching children how to approximately talk to strangers would

be a better idea. They need to be comfortable in order to approach strangers if the need arrives. Sg. Seeking assistance if they are lost or in trouble. They also need to know when not to talk to strangers. We don't approach people in the streets or someone who pulls over in a car. Children also needs to be taught to trust their instincts. If they do not feel safe. To go somewhere or to approach someone that could help. Not to accept food or gifts or random people.

According to Asker's rating, and I quote, Teaching children to be open and polite to strangers is just plain dangerous. I think for me it's more a case of teaching children about approximate boundaries with strangers. I think it's more important though to put more emphasis on protective behavior, rather than a blanket "don't talk to strangers" statement. I also think children should be aware of the danger that come from people they actually know, considering that the majority of child abuse happens with relatives or family friends. And by all means, practice, practice, practice, with your children to yell "STRANGER," if someone tries to take them. That if a car pulls up next to them on the street/sidewalk that they should walk into the yard and then up onto someone porch. And.....if someone that you don't know, or your child don't know, start talking to them and they act shy and don't answer. You need to be their advocate and stick up for them and your teaching and be comfortable saying, My kids have been taught that it's OK not to talk to people they don't know well. Child need to have some kind of "PASSWORD" agreement so that they will know that the adult who claims to be representing the parents really IS representing them. The trouble with "don't talk to strangers" is a child does not have the ability to determine what a stranger is.

https://www.parent24.com/Child-7-12/Development/health-safety/12-facts-on-childaductions-20080808
12 Facts on child abduction – how to avoid every parent's nightmare-a child going missing
Sometimes kids are never found, and I quote, as in the case of Etan Patz who was abducted in New York in 1979. His father spoke of "the crime that had a beginning, but no end". Here are some facts on kidnapping and abductions. And also some hints on what parents can do to prevent happening.

1. There are three types of abductions
   • When a stranger takes a child away for criminal purpose (such as sexual assault or ransom-the latter would be classified as a kidnapping in South Africa);
   • When a child is stolen to be brought up by the abductor;
   • When a parent removes a child from the other parent's care.

2. What make it kidnapping?

The following things classify an abduction as kidnapping: the child is detained, taken away some distance from where it was abducted, and is held for ransom money. Or the child is taken in order to keep it permanently.

3. Kidnapping or abduction?

According to the law in South Africa, kidnapping is a separate crime from abduction. Abduction is defined as the unlawful taken of a person for a long period of time.

4. Ransom

Kidnapping for ransom (of both children and adult) is most common in countries with a high crime and corruption level, a poorly resourced police force, a weak judicial system, and a history of social or political instability, according to a study conducted in South Africa for the institute for Security Studies.

5. Dozen of kidnappings

The Gauteng Police deal with over a dozen kidnappings for ransom each month, according to the study mentioned above. Most of these kidnappings involve children.

6. Parental abduction

In the case of parental abductions, the parents are usually involved in a custody battle. Children are almost never harmed in these abductions, and according to studies, the vast majority of them are returned to the rightful parent within a week.

7. The outcome

When children are kidnapped, statistics reveal that over 40% of the incident end with the death of the child.

8. Who is the kidnapper?

53% of non-family abductions are committed by people known to the victim, according to NISMART (National Incidence Studies of Missing Abducted, Runaway and Throwaway Children -an American organization). A study of theirs also found that three-quarters of non-family abductions are committed by men. These men often had brief contract with the child, such as delivering something to the house, or doing minor repairs.

9. Locations

71% of non-family abductions occurred in outside areas, such as a wood, a park or in the street, according to NISMART. Very few abductions take place from schools grounds or shopping centers.

10. The usual suspect

The average age of a male abductor is 27, and he is usually unemployed, working in a low-skilled job, living alone, or with his parents, according to a study conducted by OJJDP (THE American justice Department's Office of Juvenile and Delinquency Prevention).

11. Run-away or abducted?

The vast majority of children who are reported missing have run away, or there has been miscommunication with the parents about where they should be.

12. Girls more than boys

About two-third of stranger abductions involve female children with an average age of 11.

CHILDREN MAY INTERPRET: 1. someone I never saw before, 2. someone I think is strange/weird looking 3. an adult I don't know 4. someone ugly 5. only someone I need when I'm alone (no parent about). CHILD PREDATORS ARE FREQUENTLY: 1. someone your child sees regularly 2. pleasant, nice, funny, kind, generous 3. use another child as a lure 4. Normal looking 5. can take a child right from under a parent nose if they so desire! htps://www.ortv.org/Charter/17 lures predators may use.htm; The 17 Lures Predators May Use to Exploit Children; and I quote, 1. The Affection Lure: Most children are abused by someone they know and trust. Pedophiles exploit these relationships and are experts at taking advantage of normal tensions between teenagers and parents as well as youngsters who face issues at home like divorce, substance abuse or neglect. 2. The Pet Lure: Children love animals and may be asked to help look for a "lost puppy." Remind children, "There is no lost puppy!. 3. The Assistance Lure: This appeals to the helpful nature of children when predators ask for directions or a helping hand. Tell children that, generally speaking, adults should ask other adult for help. The best defense against this lure is pretending not to hear, then quickly leaving the area. 4. The Authority Lure: Pedophiles take advantage of their positions as coach, clergy, scout leaders, relative, etc, to intimidate or force youngsters into abuse or worse.

Stress that it is illegal for any adult to touch a child in the Bathing Suit Zone. 5. The Bribery Lure: Children are offered candy, toys, CD, drugs, money, etc. to persuade them to go willingly with a potential abductor or as a reward for tolerating abuse or keeping it secret. 6. Ego / Fame: Youngsters are offered an immediate audition or private tryout and told to keep it a secret from parents. 7. Emergency: By faking a crisis, predators trick youngsters into going with them willingly. "Example: "Your mother was in a car accident and has been taken to the hospital! I was sent to take you to her". 8. Fun and Game: Games that include the use of handcuffs, ropes, duct tape or other restraints prevent children from protecting themselves or escaping. Advise children not to participate in these "games". 9. The Hero Lure: Predators exploit their" status, or individuals they admire like favorite teachers, coaches, relatives or local celebrities, to abuse youngsters. Children may endure repeated abuse in order to maintain the "friendship" or keep their hero out of trouble. 10. The Job Lure: The offered of a high – paying, interesting or fun job may be just a trick to abuse or abduct children and particularly college students. Phony interviews are often scheduled in secluded locations or advertised with only a post office box. 11. The Name Recognition Lure: Well-meaning parents often mark backpacks, clothing and other belongings with name-tag. Predators call the child by name, creating a false sense of familiarity and trust.

12. The Playmate / Companion Lure: Pedophiles may youngsters to their home with a party atmosphere, providing toys, sports equipment, use of a swimming pool, etc. They may promote an "anything goes" attitude that can be very attractive to adolescents. 13. The Threats & Weapons Lure: Predators may blackmail or threaten youngsters into cooperation or silence. "It's my word against yours, and who's going to believe a little kid?" 14. The Pornography Lure: Pedophiles routinely introduce pornography to set the stage for abuse. Children of all ages are curious about sex, and it is not difficult to hold their attention with this material. 15. The Computer Lure: Predators successfully lure children through the use of anonymous chat-rooms and e-mail to learn a child's personal information and to arrange private, in-person meetings. 16. The Drug Lure: Drugs, especially alcohol, can be used to incapacitate, seduce or lure youngsters into abuse. Keeping a clear head at all times is critical to a child's safety. 17. The Hate and Violence Lure: This lure results in untold bullying and harassment in schools across America. Repeated cruel, belittling or sexual comments can have a profound effect on sensitive youngsters, sometimes leaving deep scars; unquoted.

I asked the question same as many of you; although it feels uncomfortable, cold hearted, and scary. The feeling remain alive warning you and others to stay away. We sometime wonders why such feelings occurred at that particular time. So I asked the question; What causes an adult to abduct children? A lot has been said but what has been learn? Only time will tell. One thing we know for sure is that kidnappers and abductors are people like ourselves but with the wrong purpose in life. They have set aside what matters the most the right to live freely without harm and having to look over your shoulder watching your every move. Why, because no one should live be force to live in fear. You should not be the product of an assault being prey on like an animal target for the beast of the unknown eating away our flesh, sole, peace of mind, and propriety. Why should you as a human being having equal rights to walk the streets day or night force to undue just to satisfy the wrong doing of others. Please repeat these words; ENOUGH IS ENOUGH, ENOUGH IS ENOUGH! Stop bothering me. Stop stalking me. Stop following me. Stop hunting me. Stop preying on me like an animal. let your message be heard. let your message be clear.

Address to the public that your not to be touch by predators in way shape or form. Do not touch me. Do not tied me up. Do not gab me. Do not rape or forcefully rape me. Do not kill me. Do not hurt me. Do not abduct me. Do not kidnap me.
All of which you have heard become FEAR. Being in fear can cause many things to happen within you. Because living in fear you will never be the same. Fear to go outside, fear to go outside your house/resident, fear to walk along, fear to go to school and to public establishments, fear going out at nights, fear of being on the internet /social media, fear of driving along, fear simply of doing normal things. So much has been said but when you really think about it kidnappers and abductors has only thing in mind and that is to control you through fear. Because being in fear can make you obey their commands. And, they know that you will do nothing to bring harm on yourself and others. How smart is that? Fear has a way of taking advantage of people. Fear will make you give in to your captures. Fear will make you give them what they want. Fear will make you beg for mercy. Fear will make you beg for your live. Because kidnappers and abductors know that they have the power over you. Why do Predators do such things; to name a few but not inclusive; to help a family/love one, pleasure, sex, money, sickness, no fear of getting caught, prostitution ring, for sale to others -the very rich, to family that cannot have a child of their own, and because they can.

Whatever the reason is its criminally and against the law. We know that words is knowledge. Money is power. Merging those words together means we got problems. Because kidnappers and abductors feed on knowledge. They know that. The question is; do you? Your life to them is expendable. No end is too great in term of victory. Therefore to stop kidnappers and abductors you need to think like them. You need to feel what they feel. You will understand why they do what they do. You then will know how to stop them. Isn't that what you want to do? To observe is to watch, to watch is to look, to look is to anticipate what will happen next. Let them come. But don't let them leave. But if they must leave let them be dead. Predator, predator, what do you want? Be smart Mr. Predator and leave them along. We now know more about you can't you see? Predator leave us along and let us be. I must be able to go outside without living in fear. So please Mr. Predator don't come after me. I need to live in peace without you trailing me. I wouldn't hurt a fly or a fruit on a tree. Mr. Predator please let me walk in peace. Please don't take my life or my sole.

Mr. Predator please let me live until I'm old. I know that you have the upper hand of knowing who you are. Well, that's fine Mr. Predator, you see that I'm no threat to you. Mr. Predator please consider what has been said because I look forward to sleeping in my bed. Mr. Predator I know that you're not a bad person and that you have a heart. So please whatever you do don't kill or take my life let me live Mr. Predator hoping you feel the same so that together we can once more cross ease other way this very moment another day. I hope that's not asking too much from you Mr. Predator I don't mean to. It's just that Mr. Predator I don't want anything to happen to you. I know that people can change and so can you. I believe that Mr. Predator. I really do. Please turn yourself into the law. Surely that's not asking too much of you after all Mr. Predator "Your" human to. Do you not feel the same way, if so why not? Please act quickly Mr. Predator time is near. You don't want to wait too long because of the danger there is. It's whispering afar in the wind waiting for you to say yes or no stands ready to grab you up without warning don't you understand? You think you're smart Mr. Predator, I suggest that you think again, the police will soon come and arrest you and that will be the end. To help me understand I sought help from these following articles as follows:

https://www.nytimes.com/200208/27/science/who-would-abduct-a-child-previous-cases-offer-clues-html#-text=Sometimes%2C children are abducte…

The New York Times
Who Would Abduct a Child? Previous Cases Offer Clues, By Mary Duenwald, August 27, 2002, and I quote, Child abduction by strangers, the experts continue to say, is not a growing menace. The number of cases – 115 or so a year, according to the most recent federal statistics – has remained steady. Yet, the crime has been prominent this summer because of a few startling cases. In one, Elizabeth Smart, 14, was reportedly led from her bedroom in Salt Lake City on June 5 and has not been found. On July 15, Samantha Runnion, 5, was pulled screaming from a courtyard near her town home in Stanton, Calif., and abused and murdered. Two 10 – year-old friends in Soham, England, disappeared on Aug. 4 and were found dead in the woods two weeks later. Similar atrocities have occurred in recent months in Missouri, Texas, Virginia, Oregon, and Wisconsin.

What kind of person does such a thing? After studying hundreds of cases, scientists can provide at least a partial answer. The broad population of child molesters, most of whom do not abduct their victims, is too diverse to fit a single psychological profile, but the far smaller group of those abduct and keep children for sexual abuse share common traits. At least 95 percent are men, and they tend to be unmarried and have few friends. In general, as everyone suspects, these people are losers," said Kenneth V. Lanning, a retired Federal Bureau of Investigations Agent in Manassas, VA., who is a consultant for the National Center for Missing and Exploited Children. "They are the seedier, more unattractive, socially outcast kind of individuals, "said Dr. David Finkelhor, a professor of sociology at the University of New Hampshire. Many abductors harbor sexual fantasies that involve children, and may exercise these fantasies by using child pornography. Many others pick on children only because they may be easier or more convenient, said Mark Hilts, a supervisory special agent for the F.B.I who specializes in Child Abductions for the National Center for Analysis of Violence Crime.

"Their preferred partner might be an adult female, "Mr. Hilt said. But because of their poor social skills, they may not feel comfortable with that. Or they have to restrain an older woman but were unsuccessful, so they progress until they're finally able to find someone small enough to bring into their vehicle." Abductors usually have very little, if any, contact with children in their daily lives. That distinguishes from a great majority of child molesters who are able to coerce victims by winning their trust and friendship.

"Why do these particulars child molesters abduct?" Mr. Lanning asked. "Because they lack the interpersonal skills to attract, befriend and seduce their victims." For that reason, they are more likely than other molesters to use guns, knives or other force to commit their crimes. About 40 percent of the time, abductors who take children for sexual purpose kill the victims, said Dr. Finkelhor, who complies child abduction statistics for the Justice Department. In 32 percent of the cases, the children are seriously injured.

A fourth of abductor—molesters are sadistic, deriving pleasure from their victims' suffering, You according to a study by Dr. Robert A. Prentky, of F&P Associates, a forensic psychology practice in Boston. Eight percent of child molesters over all considered sadistic. No statistic exist to show how many abductors are repeat offenders, but based on his observations, Dr. Finkelhor said, he suspects the number is significant. Socially bereft, sexually fixated on children and willing to use violence, the portrait is clearly incomplete, the experts acknowledge. What makes such men dream up their schemes in the first place? What leads them to be so callous about the welfare of children? Why are they violence?

The answers are more likely to be found in the psychological characteristics of individual abductors. "What motivates these people are their thoughts, their fantasies, Dr. Ann W. Burgers, professor of psychiatric nursing at Boston College, said. "They have it in their heads that they want to have sexual contact with children, and they look for the opportunity to get that. What we aren't so clear on is, Where do there fantasies come from? And now you have to look at the individual person." Most abductors are not actually pedophiles, Dr. Prentky said. "Pedophile is a very technical term, "he explained, "And it literally means love of children. Pedophiles would be just for sexual gratification, but for social companions, us well. A pedophile would be mortified at the thought that his actions would be harmful to the child."

Because most abductors are not sadists either, but commit violence only because they are so desperate to abduct a child, they are able to rationalize the violence, Dr Prentky said. Because the abductors feel so compelled to force themselves on children, they are able to convince themselves that their victims wanted to have sex or that some other forced them to use violence. Some abductions may begin as less complicated crimes, more like the thousands of child molestations each year in which victims are lured into cars or alleys for such short times that they are never even really considered missing, Mr. Lanning said. But in some cases, events go wrong. Someone interrupts the crime, perhaps, and the molester panics. "What can happen then is analogous to the story of Lennie in 'Of Mice and Men; "Dr. Prentky said. "If a powerful 200—pound man is trying to subdue a frightened, screaming 40—pound child, he may seriously injure the child unintentionally." Even those abductors who are sadists exhibit differences. Some men abduct children for sexual purposes and end up killing them, Mr. Lanning said, while others abduct children for the thrill of killing them, and end up having sex with them. It is often said that abductors are people who themselves were abused as children. A study by Dr. Prentky found that 71 percent had experience with sexual assault in childhood or adolescence. Yet the percentage of nonabductor molesters who were abused as children approached 100 percent, Dr. Prentky said.

One—third of abductions are carried out for a purpose other than sexual, Dr. Finkelhor said. Sometimes, children are abducted for ransom or because they are caught up in another crime like carjacking, when an abductor drives off with a child in the back seat. On othere occasions, children get trapped in gang violence, sometimes as acts of revenge. Last month in Philadelphia, Erica Pratt, 7, was abducted by men who demanded $150,000 in ransom. The police suspected that the abduction might have stemmed from a feud between drug dealers. Erica escaped after chewing through the duct tape that bound her hands and feet. Each year, about 10 abduction s are committed by women who desire children of their own, Mr. Lanning said. One case occurred two weeks ago, when as 1-month-old girl was taken from her mother in a Wal-Mart parking lot in Abilene, Texas. The child was returned the next day.

Women who abduct babies usually do it to preserve a relationship with a man, Mr. Lanning said. "Woman will try to convince the man that the baby she suddenly has is his," he said. A boyfriend of the woman suspected of committing the abduction in Abilene reported that she brought the baby to him and told him it was his. Psychologists often warn against focusing on the small number of crimes in which children are abducted by strangers, because it draws attention away from the larger problem of child sexual abuse—by family members, priests and others. "A couple hundred thousand cases of sexual abuse of kids are reported to authorities every year", Dr. Finkelhor said. "and more are not reported.

In particular, the public tends to focus on cases involving children under the age of 12, only about a third of the total abductions by strangers. "These stories tap into the primal fear in human beings that somebody's going to take their kid, "Mr. Lanning said. "But it's a voice that keeps calling us back from the reality that 90 percent of child abuse is committed by family members and acquaintances." The larger issue of missing, exploited and runaway children will be the subject of a dying conference on Oct. 2 at the White House; unquoted.

REASON WHY CHILDREN AND YOUNG ADULTS ARE POTENTIAL TARGETS FOR ABDUCTION AND KIDNAPPING:

- Their young
- Their innocence
- Companionship
- Spouse can't get pregnant or have a baby
- To take care of a love one
- Black market – to be sold
- Prostitution
- They can be control
- Easy targets
- Shy – can't get a girl friend
- Make fun of as a child
- Mental illness
- Sickness
- Attraction
- Miscarriage
- Child dies at a young age
- Something happened to him /her in the past
- Sex / sexual pleasure
- Maybe the person is attracted what one who called (the red light district), sexual activities
- Maybe addicted to sex
- Maybe the person was mistreated by women as a child
- Maybe he loves how it make him feel
- Maybe he see women / girls as toys – something idealism in nature
- Maybe he has a problem entertaining a relationship with females
- Maybe in his mind their evil
- To raise as their own
- Might have psychological problems
- To exploit the child / children
- Forced labor
- Ranson – is an obvious reason but not in all cases (some just wants publicity) to be notice
- Child custody battle
- Fail pregnancy
- Fail marriage

- Stress due to the loss of a baby
- Desperately for a child
- Human organs
- Spouse too poor to care for the child / children
- Boy friend / girl friend abusing the child
- Divorce
- Religious belief / sacrifice
- Kidnapped out of love to help the child
- Death of their own child
- You don't need a reason
- Just don't like children
- Just don't like females
- Psychologically impair
- Maybe alcohol and drug related problems
- A crating for sex after being in prison locked away from society
- About family
- Desperate for money
- Desperate
- Black mail
- An eye for an eye
- vengeance

https://www.usmarshals.gov/news/chron/2020/082720.htm
U.S. Marshals Service Find 39 Missing Children in Georgia during 'Operation Not Forgotten', by Justice. Integrity, Service, and I quote, Washington, D.C – The U.S. Marshals Service Missing Child Unit, in conjunction with the agency's Southeast Regional Fugitive Task Force, the National Center for Missing and Exploited Children (NCMEC) and Georgia state and local agencies, led a two-week operation in August in Atlanta and Macon, Georgia, to rescue endangered missing children. "Operation Not Forgotten" resulted in the rescue of 26 children, the safe location of 13 children and the arrest of nine criminal associates. Additionally, investigators cleared 26 arrest warrants and filed additional charges for alleged crimes related to sex trafficking, parental kidnapping, registered sex offender violations, drugs and weapons possession, and custodial interference. The 26 warrants cleared included 19 arrest warrants for a total of nine individuals arrested, some of whom had multiple warrants. The U.S. Marshals Service is fully committed to assisting federal, state, and local agencies with locating and recovering endangered missing children, in addition to their primary fugitive apprehension mission", said Director of the Marshals Service Donald Washington. The message to missing children and their families is that we will never stop looking for you".

These missing children were considered to be some of the most at-risk and challenging recovery cases in the area, based on indications of high-risk factors such as victimization of child sex trafficking, child exploitation, sexual abuse, physical abuse, and medical or mental health conditions. Other children were located at the request of law enforcement to ensure their wellbeing. USMS investigators were able to confirm each child's location in person and assure their safety and welfare. The Justice for Victims of Trafficking Act of 2015 enhanced the U.S. Marshal's authority to assist federal, state, and local law enforcement with the recovery of missing, endangered or abducted children, regardless of whether a fugitive or sex offender was involved. The Marshals' authority established a missing Child Unit to oversee and manage the implementation of its enhanced authority under the act. In 2019, the USMS helped recover 295 missing children based on requests for assistance from law enforcement and has contributed to the recovery of a missing child in 75 percent of cases received.

Additionally, of the missing children recovered, 66 percent were recovered within seven days of the USMS assisting with the case. Since its partnership with NCMEC began in 2005, the agency has recovered more than 1,800 missing children. "When we track down fugitives, it's a good feeling to know that we're putting the bad guy behind bars. But that sense of accomplishment is nothing compared to finding a missing child,' said Darby Kirby, Chief of the Missing Child Unit. "It's hard put into words what we feel when we rescue a missing child, but I can tell you that this operation has impacted every single one of us out here. We are working to protect them and get them the help they need ". This initiative was the culmination of several months of planning and coordination between the USMS, NCMEC, Georgia Bureau of Investigation, Georgia Department of the Attorney General, Georia Department of Family and Children and Children's Healthcare of Atlanta; unquoted.

SOME MOSE LIKEFUL PLACES TO ABDUCT AND KIDNAP CHILDREN / YOUNG ADULTS:

In the yard   toy store   side walk
Left along when in a dressing room   public park   pool area
Super market   left along when in the bath-room   neighborhood store
Department store   mall   going to the neighbor house   social events
Walking to and from school   walking to and from a party   walking to and from church
Walking along in the woods   simply walking along   airports   at the beach
Boat dock   restaurant   along in a parking lot   left along in a vehicle
When you are distracted   at a place of work   at a theater   when on a trip
When the child walks away from you   on a country road   music events-concert
Walking to hang out with friends   at a lake   walking in isolated areas   at a cook out
Along at nights   at a bus stop   at sport events   on school property   at a play ground
What follows next an event based on a true story about a family of four living in Romanian, husband, wife, brother, and daughter. This story brings me to think hard about motherly love. It's shocking to say the least when you read and understand the abusive treatment and turning your back on someone so precious "your own daughter" in the name of the all mighty dollar. Why would a mother do such a thing? It's bad enough when the father does the unspeakable thing kidnapping and abducting his own daughter to be marry to a 2nd cousin. I guess you're wondering what's in the hail this guy is talking about. Without further ado I presents to you a story called forced marriage. It's about this young girl, a family of four, who was abducted and kidnapped by her father at the age of thirteen (13) years old, and taken first to Sidney, and later to Australia forced marriage to her 2nd Cousin. She was hidden from the people of that country for awhile living in run-down buildings and move around a lot to avoid being notice by others. She was dressed in clothes rickrack her from head to feet showing only her eyes. She was forced to stay with other women of the family to avoid suspicious and local authorities. She ate whatever was available although it wasn't much. She slept on broken down bedding surrounding by beaten down floors and paint pilling from the walls.

Some of the places where she was moved to smelled badly and had no windows. She lived in fear of her father not knowing what was going to happen next. She moved back to Romanian with the help of her brother escaping the hands of her father. Her mother Marighan was happy that her daughter was back home. But it was only for a short while. Her father shortly thereafter got wind of her returned to Romanian and sought to capture her again but this time through trickery using his wit and smart convenient his son to bring her back to Australia. Her mother Marighan who I thought was the more concern parent had blinders over her eyes, a brain of stone, and a mouth that wouldn't stop. She represents herself as a woman who cares about her daughter but in reality its all a ghostly misunderstanding. The father calls home to Romanian asked to speak to his wife Marighan. He told his wife that he wants her back. He said don't you dare try to (F) me over. He said I don't give a (F) what you think. Send her back now. His wife Marighan said; I didn't have anything to do with her returning here. He said if you don't send her back; I will killed you, and burn down that (F) house. He said that you don't has to talk that way to me. She's only thirteen years old. She said have you thought about how she feels? She's too young to marry. He got very pissed off and told the wife to shut the hail up and send the girl back now. He said you have three days. The wife face swelled up with tears and anger.

She was shaking bitterly with anger, passed out and fell to the floor. Her son ran into the room hearing the fall, yelling mother, mother, what is wrong? He shook her, gave his mother something to drink, and assisted her to stand. She said your father called threatening to take back your sister. He said mother no, don't let him take her. He held his mother tightly and she started crying. Her daughter Marie awaken heard her mother crying, and quickly went to her yelling mother; what's wrong, why are you crying? She lied and said nothing. Her daughter Marie said mother I know something is wrong, please tell me the truth. Marighan looked at her daughter and said that your father called and wants you back. Marie said why? I don't want to go. Her mother said I don't want you to go but if I don't send you to him he will kill me, maybe you too. Marie said mother, mother, please don't, make me go. "Please don't make me go". They both started crying. Her mother said I'm sorry but I must. I must sent you back. You know your father. He will stop at nothing to get you back. Her mother out of fear made plans to send Marie, their daughter back to Australia. Days later Marie was taken by her brother back to Australia as demanded by the father to carry out the father wish, and that wish is for her to marry her 2nd Cousin. Her father met them at the airport with another man and a woman.

The woman was fully dressed in dark color clothes from her head to her feet. He took control of Marie and told the woman hold onto her. "You hear me"? "You hear me"! She said yes. They drove to the city, a very crowed city as people were seeing walking in every direction wearing dark color clothes despite the heat. It was a very hot day but it didn't seem to matter to them.

The city looked like a cue of stones and bricks a place only fit for animals. The father took his daughter to a building up high above looking down upon the streets. If you could call them streets being that they looked more like dry land. There were other women inside. He asked his daughter is she a virgin? Marie didn't say anything. He had her examine by the women. She was shock and quiet. She could only stand there like a rock as the other women took off her clothes. Marie wanted to scream but knew it was forbitten. She asked her brother why did they do that? He told her if you were not a virgin father would had kill you. Day later the father takes his daughter to Jordan to be marry to her 2nd Cousin. She is placed in the hands of other women living together in a small building. They watch over her like a hawk not letting her leave or to be seen by strangers. The building was an open floor surrounding by four walls and two windows. There was no private bathroom setting nor private sleeping areas provided. Noise could be heard from the street as people walk throughout the night. One of the women told her about a lady that she knows that works at the American Embassy.

She approached Marie introducing herself out of the blue looking her into the eyes. She said I know someone that can help you. She said just trust me. Marie said O' my God. Who is she? Who is she? She said look keep your voice down. She said I've let you know more tomorrow. Marie said please hurry. My father has gone to tell my Cousin about me. She said I know I know. The woman met with her friend in question the next day

explaining to her that she know someone, a woman in need of her help desperately. She is being held against her will by other women pending the return of her father here in Jordan visiting the girl 2nd Cousin whom she is being force to marry. The woman agreed to help and told her to tell the girl to meet her at an disclose location. Marie met with the woman later the next day and was given papers, boarding papers, and other documents. Marie was told by the woman to meet a man in one hour and that he will take her to a private airport to board an airplane for home. When the father found out hours later hail marry was not an option because Marie was already on her way home. He was very pissed off and angry like a barking dog being bitten by fleas.

https://www.google.com/search?q=Romania+law+on+forced+marriage+&aqs=chome..69157j3313.662797j0j1... Although there is no formal prohibition of early (child) or forced marriage in the Romanian Constitution, and I quote, it brings guarantee for the protection of children. Early and forced marriage in Roma communities in Romania; Under the Civil Code 2009 the minimum legal age of marriage is 18 years. However an individual can marry at 16 with parental consent, on the basis of a medical certificate or with authorization from the tutelary authority. Romania – Child Marriage Around The World. Girls Not Brides Search for what is legal age to marry in Romania? In what country is forced marriage legal? Fully 96% of countries have laws that specify when people can legally marry. Only six countries – Equatorial Guinea, Gambia, Saudi Arabia, Somalia, South Sudan and Yemen – do not specific a minimum age for marriage. Many countries allow child to marry Pew Research Center. What is a forced marriage called? Sometime called servile marriage, forced marriage also occurs when a wife is forcibly transferred to another for some type of payment or when a widow is given no choice and inherited by one of her husband's male relatives.

Forced Marriage Trafficked Through Marriage – End Slavery Now
What are the consequence of forced marriage? Risk. One serious consequence of forced marriage is marriage faces an increased risk of rape and sexual abuse as they may not wish to consent, or not be the legal age to consent to a sexual relationship.

Forced Marriage – Procedures Online
There are no residency requirement to get married in Romania, however you must wait 10 days after submitting the paperwork before you can marry, and the ceremony must take place before the expiry of the medical certificate.

Of the 25 countries with the highest rate of child marriage, almost all are affected by conflict, fragility, or natural disasters.

Top Countries For Child Marriage

Chad – 67%
Bangladesh – 59%
Mali – 52%
South Sudan – 52%
Burkina Faso – 52%
Guinea – 51%
Mozambique – 48%
India – 47%

Untying the knot: 10 worst places for child marriage: World Vision: What country can you marry your daughter? Parliamentarians in Iran have passed a bill to protect the right of children which includes a clause that allows a man to marry his adopted daughter and while she is as young as 13 years.

Forced Marriage – what are the signs? Flick Learning

Romania law on force marriage:

How many marriages are sexless?
How can we stop forced marriages?
Who is involved in forced marriage?

What is force marriage protection?
Under the Family Law Act 1996 (FLA1996), the court can make a forced marriage protection order (FMPO) that can be used to protect who has been, or is being forced into marriage against their will by imposing restrictions against the effecting of marriage and requirements such as the surrender of passport.

Estonia, now has the lowest marriage age in Europe with teenagers able to get hitched at 15 with parental approval. Globally, the average legal age of marriage for boys is 17 and 16 for girls but many countries permits them, particularly girls, to marry much younger. There is no legal restriction on the marriage of first cousins. You may not marry your Grandmother or grandfather.

What religion has forced marriage?
Arranged marriages are commonly associated with religion, a few religions that practice this form of marriage include Islam and Judaism.
The problem with arranged marriages. I haver an issue with arranged marriages …However, so often we come across people who are married purely by merit of caste, community, religion, family connections, etc, without getting to know the partner, simply because the families insisted on it and have lived to regret it. What are the problems with arranged marriages?
In arranged marriage - both the bride and the groom consent to have their marriage arranged (with varying degrees of choice about when to wed); in a forced marriage, one or both of them is coerced into the marriage and does not give full, free, informed consent; unquoted.

https://en.wiki/Romani_society_and_culture
Linguistic and phonological research has traced the Roma people's origin to places in the Indian subcontinent, specifically linking proto-Romania groups to Central India. Many report in extracts from popular literature that Romani emerged from the North-west regions of India, rather than from Central India. The Romania language shares many features with the Central Indo-Aryan languages such as Hindi, Urdu, Punjabi and Rajasthani; it also shares connections with Northern Indo-Aryan languages like Kashmiri, and the language itself contains a cluster of Persian and Arabic words. The Romani people are today found in many countries. Typically, Romani adopt given names that are common in the country of their residence. Seldon do modern Romani use traditional names from their own language, such as Papush, Luludi, Patrin, etc. Traditionally, Roma place a high value on the extended family. Traditionally, the Romania community is highly partriarchal, such that issues like virginity

is considered essential in unmarried women. This practice provides a visible representation of a young women's preserved purity and thereby the maintained honour of her family. As a result, men and women often marry very young. The Romani practice of child marriage has generated substantial controversy across the parties were of legal age in their country of residence.

Bride kidnapping is believed to be a traditional part of Romani practice. Girls as young as twelve years old may be kidnapped for marriage to teenage boys. This practice has been reported in Ireland, England, the Czech Republic, the Netherlands, Bulgaria and Slovaka. Bride kidnapping is thought to be a way to avoid a bride price or a means for a girl to marry a boy she wants but that her parents do not want. The tradition's normalization of kidnapping puts young women at higher risk of becoming victims of human trafficking. The practices of bride kidnapping and child marriage are not universally accepted throughout Romani culture. Some Romani women and men seek to eliminate such customs. Romani mothers breastfeed their children for optimal health and increased immunity. They also view this as a gift from God, and a help to building healthy relationships between mothers and children.

Romana men are allowed to have more sex and express their libido more openly than women. Pregnancy means a woman is impure in the Romani culture. Having sexual intercourse before marriage is considered dirty.

Parts of the human body are considered impure: the genital organs, because they produce impure emissions, and the lower body. Clothes for the lower body, as well as the clothes of menstruating women, are washed separately. Items used for eating are washed in a different place. Childbirth is considered "impure" and affects the whole family of the dead, who may remain "impure" for a period after the death; usually private items of the dead are considered to be impure and are to be buried in his/her grave or given to non-Romani poor people. Romani people believe in ghost and the afterlife. Through Romani ethnic groups have different sets of rules, some rules are common for all. These rules are considered to be the Romani Code, and rules that differ are called "customs". Oral Romani cultures are most likely to adhere to the Romani code, these communities are geographically spread. There are proverbs about the Romani Code and customs, such as: There exist as many customs as there are Romani groups. (Kitsyk Roma, dakitsyk obychaye in Ruska Roma's dialect)

There are many Romani groups, but only one law. (Romen isy but a, a Zakono yekh in Ruska Roma and Kaldarash dialects)

Rules of Romani Code describe relationships inside the Romani community and set limits for customs, behavior and other aspects of life. The Kris is a traditional institution for upholding and enforcing the Romani Code.

https://en.wikipedia.org/wiki/Marriage_Australia

Marriage in Australia, and I quote, is regulated by the federal government, which is granted the power to make laws regarding marriage by section 51(xxi) of the constitution. The Marriage Act 1961 applies uniformly throughout Australia (including its external territories) to the exclusion of all laws on the subject. Australian law recognizes only monogramous marriages, being marriages of two people, including same-sex marriages, and does not recognize any other forms of union, including traditional Aboriginal marriages, polygamous marriages or concubinage. The marriage age for marriage in Australia is 18 years, but in unusual and exceptional circumstances a person age 16 or 17 can marry with parental consent and authorization by a court.

Australian law recognizes only monogamous marriages, being marriages of two people, including same-sex marriages, and does not recognize any other forms of union, including traditional Aboriginal marriages, polygamous marriages or concubinage. A person who goes through a marriage ceremony in Australia when still legally married to another person, whether under Australian law or a law of another county, commits an offence of bigamy, which is subject to a maximum 5 years imprisonment, and the marriage is void. A marriage must be entered into with the full consent of both parties, and it is an offence to force someone to marry them or another person, by the use of coercion, threat or deception, and whether in Australia or abroad. Full consent assumes a mental capacity to understand the nature of a marriage.

Void Marriages

- A marriage entered into in Australia is void if:
- Either party is already married (bigamy, polygamy).
- The parties are in a prohibited relationship: direct ancestor or descendant or sibling (Whether full sibling or half sibling), including those arising from a legal adoption.
- The marriage was not solemnized by an authorized celebrant.
- There is no consent, for example due to duress, fraud, mistake as to identity, mistake as to the nature of ceremony, mental incapacity, or being below the marriage age.

The Family Law Act 1975 (Cth) replaced the previous faults-based divorce system, requiring only a twelve-month period of separation. The 1970s saw a significant rise in the divorce rate in Australia. This change has been attributed to a change in social attitudes: having once been considered acceptable only if there were severe problems, divorce was now widely considered acceptable if it was the of the.

https://lawhandbook.sa.gov.au/ch21s03.php
Legal Help For All South Australians
Home>Family Relationships

Marriage
The law regulating marriage in Australia is contained in the Marriage Act 1961 (Cth)

The Marriage Act 1961, and I quote, sets out who may marry, who may perform the marriage ceremony, how the ceremony is to be conducted and where it may be performed.

Who may marry?
Any person over the age of 18 may marry provided that the person:

- Is legally able to consent
- Is not married to someone else,
- Is not in prohibited relationship (such as that of a grandparent, parent, sibling) with the proposed spouse.

A person who is aged under 18 may marry provided:

- They are at least 16 years of age, and
- The proposed spouse is over 18 years of age; and
- They obtain a court order authorizing the marriage (the relevant court is the Magistrates Court);

- and they have the written consent of the parents or guardians (unless a court has given the consent in place of the parents).

Same and/or Intersex Marriage

Since changes to the Marriage Act 1961 (CTH) on 9 December 2017, it is possible for couples to be legally married in Australia, irrespective of their sex or gender identity. From this date all same and/or Intersex Marriages lawfully solemnized overseas are also able to be recognized as lawful marriages in Australia.

What documents have to be filed before a marriage can take place?

Before a marriage ceremony can take place, A Notice of Intended Marriage Form must be given to the Marriage celebrant, not more than 18 months and not less than one month before the dater of the intended marriage. The notice must give all the required details and be signed by each of the intending spouse in the presence of the celebrant or another person authorized by the Act. Even though it may be legal for a child with dual nationality to marry whilst under the age of 18 in the country of their other nationality, such a marriage will not be valid under Australian law, even once they turn 18.

Marriages performed in Australia according to the laws of another country are generally valid if made in the presence of consular or diplomatic staff from that country and provided they observe the rules about age and prohibited relationships.

Does Marriage gives one party a Right to Sexual Intercourse?

Marriage gives no right to sexual intercourse and a person may be convicted of sexual offences on his or her spouse.

Are There Alternatives To Marriage?

A de facto relationship is recognized in some areas of the law. It is similar to marriage in that it can provide automatic recognition for various legal purpose in South Australia. However, there are two main differences between registered relationships and marriage. The first is that marriage can provide recognition both interstate and internationally. The second is that marriage cannot end as quickly or abruptly as a registered relationship. A marriage cannot officially end unless it has broken down irretrievably evidenced by 12 months separation. A registered relationship, by contrast, can end by application without proof of actual separation, after 90 days cooling off, or sooner by way of marriage of either of the partners.

https://www.girlsnotbrides.org/child-marriage/jordan/#:-:text=During its 2013 Universal Periodic, end child marriage by 2020.

WHAT'S THE CHILD MARRIAGE RATE! HOW BIG OF AN ISSUE IS CHILD MARRIAGE!, and I quote, Child marriage is driven by gender inequality and the belief that girls are somehow inferior to boys, in Jordan, child marriage is also driven by:

- Poverty: Some families, particularly those with multiple daughters, marry girls off in order to reduce their perceived economic burden and the number of months that require feeding.

Emergency Pass Words Parents + children

llat	tall	trohs	short	llams	small RV	
rac	car	kcurt	truck	supmac	campus	
roliart	tractor Trailer	esuoh	house	nrab	barn	apartment
noisnam	mansion	evac	cave			
nam	man	nemow	women	dlihc	child	
nerdlihc	children	yob	boy	lrig	Girl	
loohcs	School	emoh	home	krap	PARK	
robhg	ien	neighbor dneirf	friend	teerts	Street	
roloc	color	door	road	evird	drive	
klaw	walk	sriats	Stairs	roolf	floor	
basement	Themesab	egarag	Garage			
roof	food	knab	bank	enohp	Phone	
yenom	money	egdirb	bridge	kcolc	clock	
esuoh	eraw	warehouse	letoh	Hotel		
letom	motel	enalpria	Airplane			

- Traditional attitudes: A 2014 UNICEF study found that a number of Jordanian, Iraqi, Syrian and Palestinian refugees considered child marriage to be acceptable in "compelling circumstances". These included teenage pregnancy, an abusive home environment and the preservation of cultural traditions.
- Traditional customs: Some families marry off their daughters to provide them with sutra, a concept rooted in Islam but now widely accepted among faiths in Jordan. Sutra generally means a secure life, protection from hardship and safeguarding for a girl's future.
- Religion: Some sheikh and shari'a court judges have expressed acceptance of child marriage, considering it to protect girls from destitution, sexual abuse and honour crimes.
- Displacement: With increasing political instability in the region, child marriage rates among the Syrian refugee population are dramatically increasing. A 2014 report states that as many as one in four registered marriages in Syrian refugee communities involve a girl under the age of 18. Some families marry off their daughter to protect them from sexual violence. UNICEF reports that "opportunists" pretend to be sheikhs and conduct illicit marriages in Za'atari refugee camp, and some older Saudi and Jordanian men reportedly visit the camp to marry Syrian girls as young as 13. The urgent need for security within these camps has undermined the depth of research that Syrian families normally make into the character and qualifications of potential husbands.
- Power dynamics: 2012 statics show that 16 of married Syrian girls aged 15=17 married men who were 15 or more years older than them.
- Resettlement: Some Syrian girls are married off to enable them to move out of refugee camps and into host communities. Among Palestinian refugees in Jerash camp, marriage to a Jordanian spouse is considered to bring greater rights and opportunities.
- Media: Some Jordanian parents marry off their daughters because they are concerned that the internet will expose them to undesirable behavior that may damage future marriage prospects; unquoted.

Pornography impact the chemistry of the brain strengthen and focusing on the need, desire, and wants of the predator from the person being abducted and kidnapped. Pornography itself is an indication of what the predator will do to satisfy his / her sexual pleasure. lets talk about what attract men and women to children and young adults. If you feel that this list is in conclusive and or misleading please let me know. I will not be offended but will take your thoughts and opinion under consideration. I welcome your openness, thoughts and understanding especially when it comes to why things happens. if we know why things happens then we will know how to control and solve the problem. And, maybe stop predators from abducting and kidnapping children and young adults. So please, give me a shout out. Let me know how you feel and what your think. "To know is better than not to know"!

SEXUAL PREDATOR – ATTRACTION

Men	Women
Butt size	Butt/butt size
Face	Face
Long hair	built/muscles
Hair style: long, short, straight hair	height: tall, short
Way they sit (specially) sexually	size matters(penis)
Way they walk(twist) tightness	how well dressed they are
Attire: dress, skirt, pants, upskirt, mini dress,	sharp dresser, uniform
Legs: long, short, nice thighs, big legs	hair: short, long, style cuts (ball)
Bathing suits, bikini, sexual swim wear	friendliness, eyes, voice
How forward she is	intelligent

Smile, laughter, lips, skin tone	smile, laughter, mouth size
Giggle butt, Bouncy (big butt)	helpful
Helpful	shorty shorts, boxers
Breath size	how fresh and clean he smell
How well dress she is(especially) sexually	well built chest(especially) hairy
Petites	how well they dance
How well they dance (total body attraction)	mustache

https://en.wikipedia.org/wiki/Law_of_jordan#:~:text=The legal age of marriage, be married under Islamic law.&text=However%2C under the law applie…

Law Of Jordan, and I quote, is influenced by Ottoman law and European laws. The Constitution of Jordan of 1952 affirmed Islam as the state religion, but it did not state that Islam is the source of legislation. Jordanian penal code has been influenced by the French Penal Code of 1810.

Court System// Religious courts;
Shari'a courts only have jurisdiction over personal matters; including areas of family law marriage or divorce, child custody, adoption, and inheritance matters. Islamic religious courts only have jurisdiction over Muslims. Christians have separate religious courts of the family's religion, but governed by Shari'a principles in all cases.

Personal Status Law
The Personal Status Law is the family law applies to all disputes involving Muslims and the children of Muslim fathers. The legal age of marriage has been increased to 18, but at the chief justice's discretion this may be lowered to 15. All Jordanian Muslims are required to be married under Islamic law. Article 19 of the Personal Status Law allows women to place conditions on their marriage contracts, within certain limitations. As most women are not aware of this right, it is rarely used in practice. Women's rights advocates suggest that a list of possible conditions attached to the contract would serve to inform women of their rights under Jordanian Law. The Jordanian government has elected to adhere to the Maliki school in some matters, which has restricted women's marriage rights. Hanafi Law, which is the dominant influence in Jordan, does not require the consent of a male guardian for a woman to marry. However, under the law applied in Jordan a woman can not marry without the permission of either a Shari'a judge ora a male guardian. A guardian is a person appointed under the law to act on behalf of a minor or other person who does not have a full legal capacity. Any female dependents under 40, who have not been previously married, are subject to lose their rights to financial maintenance if they "rebel" against their guardian; unquoted.

9 September 2011

errc
European roma rights centre

ERRC Submission to the Joint CEDAW-CRC General Recommendation /
Comment on Harmful Practices:
Child Marriages among Roma

The European Roma Rights Centre (ERRC), and I quote, is an international public interest law organization working to combat anti-Romani racism and human rights abuse of Roma. The approach of the ERRC involves

29

strategic litigation, international advocacy, research and policy development and training of Romani activists. The ERRC has consultative status with the Council of Europe, as well as with the Economic and Social Council of the United Nations. The ERRC's extensive research programme has provided reliable data about the human rights situation of Romana since 1996. Some recent and ongoing ERRC campaigns advocate for: effective state response to violence and late speech against Roma; school desegregation; an end to forced evictions and protection of other housing rights; implementation of comprehensive and anti-discrimination law.

INTERNATIONAL LAW ON CHILD MARRIAGE

Child marriage represents perhaps the most prevalent form of sexual abuse and exploitation of children, particularly girls. According to Article 1 of the Convention on the Rights of the Child, a child is defined as "every human being below the age of eighteen years unless under the law applicable to the child, majority is attained earlier. A child marriage is defined as any union in which one or both of the partners is younger than the legal age allowed for marriage. A forced marriage is defined as the union of two persons of any age, at least one of whom has not given their full and free consent to the marriage.

The Convention on the Elimination of all Forms of Discrimination against Women (CEDAW) OR Convention) Article 16(2) bans child marriage, stating: "The betrothal and the marriage of a child shall have no legal effect. It further requires that States enact legislation and other necessary measures to specify a minimum age for marriage and to make the legislation of marriage in an official registry compulsory.

OVERVIEW OF CHILD MARRIAGES IN ROMANI COMMUNITIES

Despite the wealth of international legal provisions banning this practice, and I quote, child marriage continues to be practiced in certain Romani communities around Europe. Although there is insufficient data on the extent of this practice, ERRC research as well as reports by international organisations indicates that child marriages continue to be practiced in Romani communities in Albania, Bosnia and Herzegovina, Bulgaria, Greece, Kosovo, Macedonia, Moldova, Montenegro, Romania, Turkey and Ukraine and in migrant Romani communities in certain Western European countries, such as Italy.

European States generally fails to apply international or national legal protections when Romani women and girls are subjected to such human rights violations. Despite the continuation of this practice in some Romani women communities and the very negative effect of child marriage on Romani girls and women, the ERRC is unaware of any serious Governmental response to issue.

THE HUMAN RIGHTS IMPACT OF CHILD MARRIAGE IN ROMANI COMMUNITIES

In addition to violating the rights of Romani children themselves, in most if not all cases the betrothal and marriages of children in traditional Romani communities in Europe creates the conditions for serial human rights abuses. This includes diminished access to education, resulting in increased illiteracy rates and poorer chances of employment, as well as sexual abuse and exploitation, early pregnancies, muted psychological development, and other negative health effects as a result of early/forced sexual activity.

Domestic Violence

Victims of child marriage face heightened vulnerability to domestic violence. During ERRC research in Italy in 2011 on Romani women's rights, five respondents married below the age of 18 stated that they were forced to marry against their will. Four of these women reported experiences of domestic violence. While several factor influences the high vulnerability of domestic violence among Roma, the powerless position in which

Romani women and girls end up as a result of child marriage and the resulting lack of education and hindered employment opportunities are key factors. Incidents of domestic violence among Romani go underreported for several reasons. First, violence against women is accepted in some Roman families. Secondly, Romani women who experience domestic violence fear being ostracized and shamed by their communities and families. Thirdly, perpetrators of violence against women are rarely held accountable for their acts, which discourage women from seeking help. Fourth, Romani women who experience domestic violence fear further victimization on the part of the police and/or others.

Another consequence of the continuing occurrence of child marriage in Romani communities is the practice of VIRGINITY TESTING in preparation for marriage, which violates young Romani women's human rights and bodily integrity. This practice contributes to continuation of child marriages as some Romani children are required to marry to increased the likelihood that they will be virgin at the time of marriage and pass the public test. There are various modalities of virginity testing but they generally include the practice of observing or even breaking the girl's hymen in way or another in order to prove the girl's virginity. Additionally, Romani women who "fail" virginity tests face DIVERSE CONSEQUENCES. Respondents in Italy for example often noted that punishments were more severe in the past but that nowadays women may be scolded, sent back to their family or otherwise shamed, verbally abused, or suffer from infidelity of the husband, disrespected from the groom's family, or ostracism from the community.

TRAFFICKING IN HUMAN BEINGS
While child marriages do not constitute trafficking in all cases, forced child marriages can result in the trafficking of the young bride and increases her and her children's vulnerability to trafficking. The barriers that Romani women and girls face, namely poverty, discrimination and marginalization, and the human rights violations that stem from child marriage place them in desperate situations which makes them particularly vulnerable to being trafficked.
During research by ERRC, and People in Need on trafficking in Romani communities in 2010, is that they marry too early (often at the age of 14) after the husband "steals the girl "; unquoted.

WHEN YOU IRRITATES A PREDATOR

When you irritates a predator, you irritates a fool, you have better think twice before going to school. He'll get you on the road. He'll get you in he air. He won't stop until he get you where ever you may be. But he will dawn sure get you even in on the sea.
He's not a monster to be wrecks with. He's not a monster to be train. He's not a monster to be ignore or turn your back on. Because he will surely kill you whether you believe it or not. Because he's that that type of monster who will not stop short of the stick. Be smart I say; don't mess with this monster, do not approach him its not safe, you know my friend.

This predator he comes from an unknown land walking around like he's lost trying to fit in kidnapping little boys and girls from within. What should we say? What should we do? This predator we're talking about; do you know him? He's scaring all the children with the talk of death telling their parents he's not lying. Why is he doing this? Why don't he leave?

When morning come this what's we're going to do. You go to the police. I've go to my friends. We'll tell the story so that all can hear giving his description telling who he is hoping that someone will recognize him. But whatever this must be stop even if it means cornering the blocks. We must out smart him. We must not give up. We have nothing more to depend on (no one for help) it's now up to us to do our best.

Whatever that is it must be good. Because we only have one chance to make it right. This predator is no ordinary predator,(he will fight), not only that he will kill us all. trust me my dear; he's no push over (we will fall). We will fall to our death that is true enough so whatever we do; we need to do it now. Before this predator come back and end us all.

I don't want to die. Surely neither do you. Let's get this bitch now and feed him to the zoo. Maybe something is in the zoo will show him whose boss. But believe me that's not all. They will teach him not to PREY on children and to leave their parents alone. But most importantly everyone will go home.

HOW DOES PREDATORS THINK

How does a predator thinks; a predator thinks with his brain like you and me. But does see the world like you and me. He looks out at the sea and wonders what could be. He looks at your child as if she was fresh meat. He hide in the shadow while awaits his prey kneels down on his knees blessing another day. He know soon that one will come to be grab one by one. How does a predator thinks; why do you ask? How does a predator thinks; what does it mean to you? How does a predator thinks; what should I say to you? These questions you asked; what should I say? I am not the predator he sits and wait. If I was the predator but I'm not. I would prey on you around the clock. So, don't ask me questions no more. I will tell you no lie, leave me along before I turn you into a fly. If you value your life than walk away. Should you stick around you will loose your life. I am sly as a fox and deadly as a snake. I will cut your head off an laid it in the sun to bake. Leave me along Mr. Predator before its too late. Hoes does a predator thinks; what if anything should I say? How does a predator thinks; please, please go away. How does a predator thinks; do I have the right to say? How does a predator thinks; should I be asking you? How does a predator thinks; He thinks with his mind same as you. How does the predator thinks; He thinks with his heart for me and you. If that was true; why would he prey on me and you? This predator you say where is he now? He's around so go straight home because he will capture you when your along. Don't think he won't because he is smarter than you.
He has all day to plan his next move. It could be someone else but nevertheless be at your best. Don't let him get the jump on you. I warn you now that you will surely die.

How does a predator think; He thinks with his soul although it rarely stands out. |He thinks with his body that awaits them the next day. How does a predator thinks; He thinks with his little finger threatening the lives of others. He thinks with everything that means so much, standing around watching your children as they pass by, reaching out to kidnap them like a fly in the sky. One would ask but dare not say why does a predator like to play. So now you know their mean and demeanor parents keep your children safe and far, far away from them. He could be anyone even your kin. A cry for help. A cry of death nevertheless parents please do your best. Your child life depends on it this you should know. Please keep them safe from whoever it might be because Mr. Predator might be hiding in a tree. If he preys on them. He will prey on you. If that not true parents what color is blue? Monkey see, monkey do; children are not animals in a zoo. How does a predator thinks; He thinks with both hands planted on the ground. How does a predator thinks; what can I say? He comes here everyday. He come

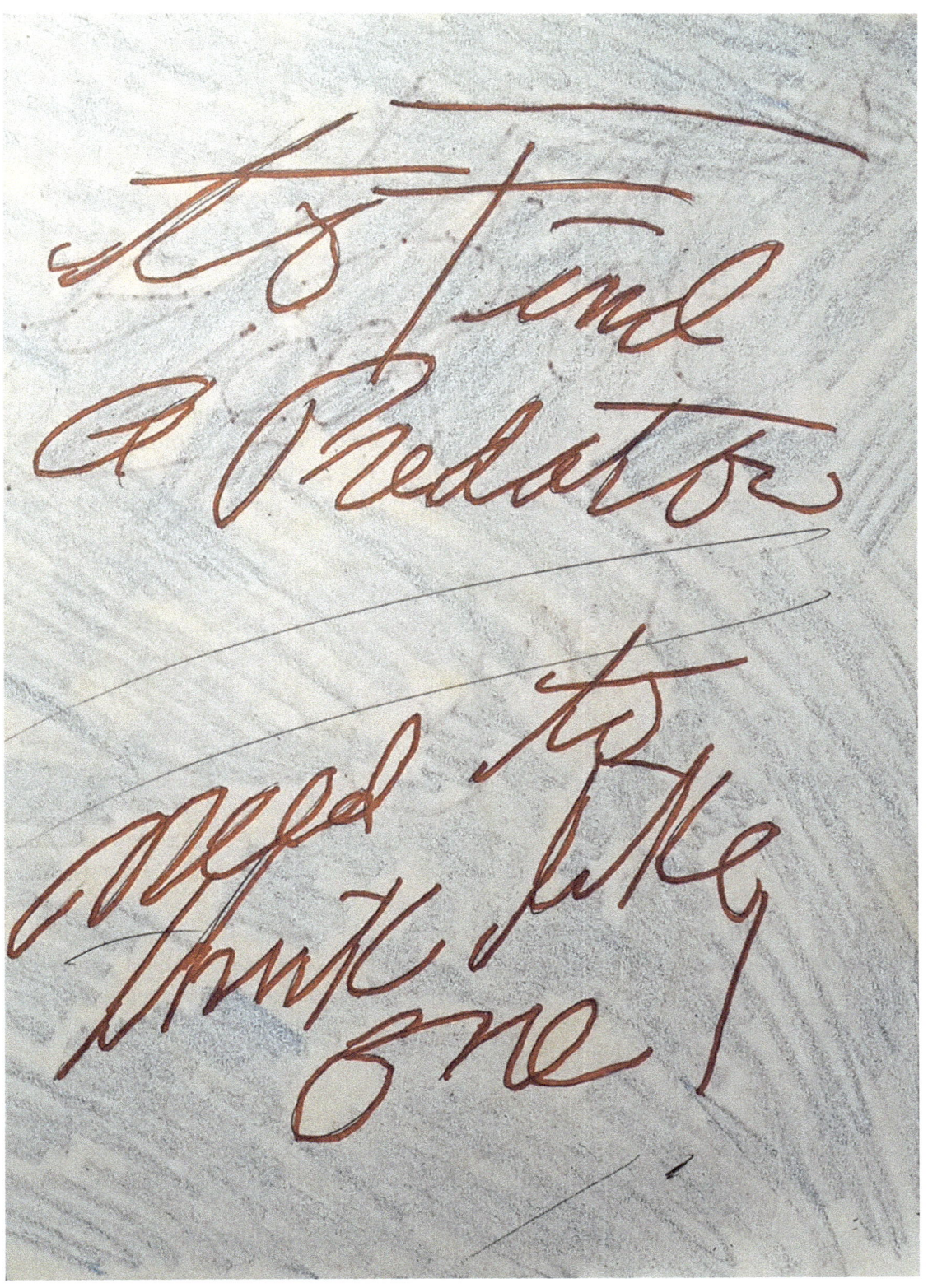

and go as he please. He thinks even in the trees. How does a predator thinks; what does it mean to you? How does a predator thinks; He thinks while walking on both legs and bare feet.

How does a predator thinks; He thinks like a woman, is that not true? How does a predator thinks; He thinks looking staring at you in the face making you his prey tomorrow and today. He thinks in the middle of the night planning his trap and his flight. He needs a way in. He needs a way out, so that he don't get caught like a fox. He's always on the alert avoiding the police for this is what he do but that's nothing new. How does a predator thinks; He thinks while hunting his prey spinning his head around both night and day. How does a predator thinks; He thinks when he opens his eyes I wonder why, making plans to kill. Kill me not I say. I've done nothing to you. Spare my life predator this I ask of you. How does a predator thinks; when he show his teeth and opens his mouth. He preys on his prey putting fear in her heart knowing that she's next to die. Why does he do such a thing; only someone like yourself Mr. Predator would know, I'm not threaten by you Mr. Predator so close my door. I love my child is that not true? Please spare her life and leave us along. You much have feelings and a heart that speaks. There much be kindness within you so please Mr. Predator let her go. Parents would appreciate a sign off good faith giving their children hope of waking up to see another day. O' how it feels putting fear into them all making them my prey and watching them fall. When I finished touching them their body they will feel like cherry pie. I will brain suck them crazy as a fly turning their soul into mud and draining their life. Once I kidnap them no world is safe closing the door not even than will it be safe. Torture you say! O my, O my. I will get your children and that's no lie. You will not know when. You will not know how. But rest assure I'll come by.

Your loving teenagers how safe are they? They will not grow up to see another day. How does a predator thinks; He thinks with fear as he prey staring them in the eyes as he runs away. She runs hard, and fast but know this he will get that ass. How does a predator thinks; He preys hard and greet as he approach your door. You can run but you can't hide Mr. Predator no matter how smart you think you are. One day your luck will run out and you will wish that you were dead. This is not a threat but a friendly warning to you. As parents Mr. Predator we are tired of you. Leave here predator. Leave here while you can. Get that ass you say! That ass might be your own. The police will be coming to your home.

How does a predator thinks; so much has been said. Two wrongs doesn't make it right. But when you go after someone else child parents will fight. How does a predator thinks; a predator thinks with a clear head always knowing what to do. He will transform you like an animal in a zoo. Don't you know if that's not true? He's not afraid of me or you. Why much he be afraid; he's the predator can't you see? A predator knows when and where to get you. So, parents keep your children safe from others. This predator we know so well. He will prey on your children and they will surely end up dead. Parents, if they end up dead you'll have your self the blame. So yield if you must stay ahead of the game. Just keep your children safe whatever you do. Don't be a fool parents and don't turn blue. Keep your children safe if not they will become my prey.

How does a predator thinks; a predator thinks without a meaning of life as the sky turns dark ending life. Don't ask me why. I do not know. This predator is walking around like he has no where to go. Does that sound familiar to you as he lay a trap, preying on them all like a bat, catching them off guard as they go on their way? They take it seriously stalking your child. He's the predator abducting and kidnapping them all. If you mess with me no one will live. I will break into your house and kidnap your kid. I will rape your child. Mess with me and you will die. If you listen to what I have to say. Keep your children safe if not they will be my prey.

How does a predator thinks; a predator thinks with anger and hatred targeting his next prey. a predator thinks with his ass pointed toward the sky hoping for rain to fall from high. a predator thinks while holding hands walking around blessing the land. a fan from high saying good – by hoping for your sake not to die. With a smile on his face he drives away hoping to see another day. If its up to the predator, yes it is, you will not live another day to see your kid. How does a predator thinks; He thinks sitting on his ass wondering how long it will last. You bastard, you bastard, go scratch your ass. You do what you want. You do what you will. You kidnapped our children without mercy and torturing them. Do you really think you're going to get away with this? The Lord will hunt you down Mr. Predator and do you in. He will strike you from high. He will make it rain for 40 days and 40 nights until you Mr. Predator give up the fight. When the Lord speaks the world stands fast. The Lord will get you Mr. Predator singing at last at last. Then everything will be back to normal without a minute to spare. O glory have a hallelujah at last. You now |Mr. Predator can scratch your ass because the Lord come to restore the world, and Mr. Predator this is the end of your world. To hell you must go; and you must go now. Because Mr. Predator, you are dead as a fly.

Marriages and Controversies

Marriage in Romani society underscores the importance of family and demonstrates ties between different groups, often transnationally. Traditionally an arranged marriage is highly desirable. Parents of the potential bridal couple help identify an ideal partner for their child. Parents rarely force a particular spouse on their child, although it is an established norm to be married by your mid twenties.

"WOW"; You just read about children being sexual abuse, exploitation, and runaways.

Sex Trafficking

Wow, Who would think of such a thing? Well, let me open your mind as salt is sprinkled on death ears. People only listen to themselves then wonder why shit happens. What bothers me the most is when you start pointing fingers at others everyone but yourself. What a laugh! Do you really think so? Word of warning; walk softly and avoid leaves and don't forget to look over your shoulder. Because if a snake don't bite you on the ass something else will. It's time for all women to take blinders off while shaking their ass in the middle of the street. Stop shaking your ass because you just might attract the wrong attention. This bring me to the subject at hand; sex trafficking. The event is base on a television movie that I of course kick back watching. Women, its something that you might want to puss, puss, your lips and take notice of. Children very young between the age of 9 and 14 were being abducted and kidnapped in the name of sex and money. To be more clear; they were forced against their will to have sex with strangers.

This one girl in particular she was about thirteen (13) maybe a little bit older. A high school male friend caused her to be abducted and kidnap by two men and a woman. He pretended to be taking her out for some simple fun things that teenagers do. At least that's what he told her parents. Do you get the picture? They knew each other. I believe that he was sixteen (16) years of age. He drove his family car which was German made to an isolated parking area. She asked him; why are we here? What are we waiting for? He ignore her at first tapping the steering wheel. Minutes later two cars pulled up. She and her so-call friend got out of their car and sit in the back of one of the other cars. She didn't even see it coming. Everything was happening too fast. She trusted her male friend thinking that everything was fine. She was offered drinks upon arrival to a party, drinks after drinks. Her so-call male friend never said a word or tried to stop her. He barely look at her while at the party. Why, because he knew what was going on. He set her up to be abducted and kidnap. He told her parents that he dropped their daughter off home therefore she should be there.

Her father believe it. Her father wasn't the least suspicious that something was wrong. His wife had to put her best foot forward telling him that we need to do something now. He finally listen to his wife and called the police. His wife hit the streets looking for her daughter. Their daughter was no where to be find. The mother hard hitting the streets working with the police posted flyers and televise their daughter safe return pleading with the captures to let her go. Naturally that didn't happen but hope was in her corner. Two men and a woman left with the girl before the party ended taking two different cars. The girl drunk and unconscious under the influence of alcohol was put into an Suv. Her cell phone was thrown out of the window by the driver. He drove her to his house and later told her to clean herself up. The next morning she was lying in bed asleep. He awaked her and told her to get out of bed their leaving. He gave her a dress to change into. He told her don't disappoint me. You must be nice to the customers. We make plenty of money.

While in the bathroom changing over a window caught her attention. She tried to open it but without luck. He seeing her trying to open the window came into the bathroom and told her to get out now we're leaving. He drove to a house maybe ten minutes away where three black guys were waiting. One black guy came up to him and said; is the merchandise here? He later looked into the Suv staring down at her. He gave the driver some money not sure how much. The driver said walking off to leave; good luck with that. She was taken into a room which later turn out to be a motel room. There she met two other females. The black female was in charge of everyone. The other girl was white. She was very understanding and tried to help this girl the men abducted and kidnapped in a very nice and patient way. She understood her feelings, pain, and emotions. She said just do what they say and you'll be find. The black girl in charge was told by the men to get her ready. The black girl in charge clean her up in the bathroom combing her hair and pretty up her face putting on lipstick, and ear rings. She was forced to drink beer and take a control substance putting her in the mood for sex and romance.

This went on for at least three to four days always a different man sexually raping that poor girl fulfilling their pleasure of desire. She got lucky one day when one of the black guys left his cell phone on the dresser. She crawled from the bed and used it calling a friend. He was pissed off coming out of the bathroom knowing that she called someone. He grabbed the phone out of her hands and slammed her head to the floor. He said you bitch; your fuck, your fuck now. He's going to have your ass. The other two black guys after hearing about what has happened told everyone to get everything out of the room, hurry. They told the motel front desk manager to give them another room. They were pissed. The person receiving the phone call was unaware that the girl was abducted and kidnapped. He was about to ignore the call until a female came up to him, and asked; who is that? Who called? She said; O' my God; that's the girl who was kidnapped.

The two of them went quickly to the police station. According to the police; the call was no help. No message. But, how wrong can you be? The call lead them to the motel where the girl was being held capture. A tall white woman approached the police (VIP) Status, questioned the police, and asked them; how is the search for the girl going? They look at her like, what search? Shortly after that a search for the girl was in motion with the formation of police officer consisting of four teams, man and ready to engage the motel. They identified themselves as police officers and second thereafter forced in the door going from room to room. Then an all clear was given. She's not here lets go. "That's what they thought"! The main team leader was standing right next to a door, a door that they fail to check. A female officer told the main team leader that the girl must be here. Before the female officer the word "here"; the girl scream, and scream, saying I'm here.

The police officers forced open the door, and grabbed the girl taking her into safe haven. The other two girls were arrested. The black guys were no where to be found. But, two of the abducted and kidnappers were found and arrested. The girl testified against them and that so call friend whatever his name was. But prior to the arrest and everything; the few days their daughter was home things were not the same. Their daughter had flashback and terrible nightmares awakening in her sleep crying and screaming. This ordeal went on for several days and nights although the nights were worse. She had no appetite for food. She would sit at the table holding her head down staring at the floor.

Her mother couldn't take it seeing her daughter in that demeanor emotionally and psychologically hurting and in pain. Their daughter went through a lot. Being tied to the bed. Forced to drink alcohol and consumed drug, control substance, gun to her head, and threaten. Forced to commit to being sexually raped and taken advantage of by others. She felt helpless and dirty. She had no choice. Because the three black guys threatened to kill her and would had if she didn't do what they told her to do. For the record; that movie that I was watching was based on a true story. When you thought it was safe to go back into the water a slap in the face ignominious your private space of trust causing you to think differently when making decisions. Children feed on your feelings and emotions sometime for the wrong reasons to get their way especially when it comes to hanging out with friends. They know how to break you making you feel sorry for them and guilt whenever you say no, your staying home. That may have been a mouth full but hopefully you as parents has learned a lot from what has happened to others. That takes me into the article as follows.

https://en.wikipedia.org/wiki/Sex_trafficking
Sex trafficking
Sex trafficking, and I quote, is human trafficking for the purpose of sexual exploitation, including sexual slavery, which is considered a form of modern slavery. A victim is forced, in one of a variety of ways, into a situation of dependency on their trafficker(s) and then used by the trafficker(s) to perform sexual services to customers. Sex trafficking crimes can involve acquisition, transportation and exploitation; this includes child sex tourism (CST), domestic minor sex trafficking (DMST) or other kinds of commercial sexual exploitation of children, and businesses in the world. In 2012, the international Labour Organization reported 20.9 million people were subjected to forced labour, and 22% (4.5) million are victims of forced sexual exploitation. The ILO reported in 2016 that of the estimated 25 million persons in forced labour, 5 million were victims of sexual exploitation. However, due to the covertness of sex trafficking, obtaining accurate, reliable statistics, is difficult for researchers. Most victims find themselves in coercive or abusive situations from which escape is both difficult and dangerous. Locations where this practice occurs span the globe and reflect an intricate web between nations, making it very difficult to construct viable solutions to this human rights problem. To report human trafficking to the federal law enforcement call: 1-888-373-7888, and to the National human trafficking call: 1-866-347-2423.

Common Misconceptions There are a number of misconceptions about sex trafficking. Sex trafficking and human trafficking are not to be confused with human smuggling. Human trafficking for sexual or other labor may involve transporting victims across international borders, but to meet the definition of trafficking, there needs only to be exploitation of an individual after they have been coerced or deceived, so it does not necessarily involve transportation across national borders. Human trafficking and sex trafficking are often used as synonyms. However, trafficking for non-sexual exploitation may be even more prevalent than trafficking for sexual exploitation, though accurate estimates of trafficking rates are extremely difficult to obtain. Sex trafficking tends to receive more attention from aid organizations and donors due to the greater public outrage that forced sexual labor evokes compared to forced non-sexual labor and thus incidents of sex trafficking are more frequently reported.

Sex trafficking is also commonly conflated with non-coerced sex work criminalized as prostitution. These misconceptions often stem from underreporting of trafficking because of the survivor's fear of their trafficker,

and conflicting views of trafficking and sex work. In addition, some researchers argue that the main research that underscores these debates is flawed for leaving sex workers and survivors of sex trafficking out of the conversation. Other scholars argue the two are commonly conflated because of the inherent link between volitional prostitution and sex trafficking. those who argue this believe that commercial sex trafficking demand for sexual services and consequently increases sex trafficking. Some anti-sex trafficking programs and initiative have been criticized for contributing to these misconceptions because they give non-trafficking sex workers incentives to identify as victims of trafficking, such as gaining access to resources like shelters.

Law Enforcement agencies have been criticized for providing similar incentives, because they threaten suspected prostitutes with jail time if they admit they are working by choice, while those who claim they are trafficking victims get training workshops and social services instead of jail time. Many feminist scholars inflicts on their view of trafficking and sex work. These are two dominant frameworks that demonstrate the divide: the abolitionist discourse, which derives from dominance feminist theory, and the sex work discourse. Feminist scholars in the abolitionist discourse argue that all prostitution is coerced due to the prevalence of Compulsory heterosexuality and social and economic pressures stemming from Neoliberalism and patriarchy. The arguments frame women as victims of sexual slavery and attribute male sexuality as the problem. In addition to ignoring the fact that many men and non-binary people engage in sex work, the abolitionist discourse conflicts with studies conducted by groups and individuals who advocate for the decriminalization of sex work. Decriminalization views sex labor as preferable to poorer paying and inflexible mainstream employment where they are subject to sexual harassment and assault by male employers and colleagues. In 2000, countries adopted a definition set forth by "United Moms". The United Nations Convention Against Transnational Organized Crime, Protocol to Prevent, Suppress and Punish Trafficking in Persons, Especially Women and Children, is also referred to as the Palermo Protocol.

- Trafficking in persons" shall mean the recruitment, transportation, transfer, harbouring or receipt of persons, by means of the threat or use of force or other forms of coercion, of abduction, of fraud, of deception, of the abuse of power or of a position of vulnerability or of the giving or receiving of payment or benefits to achieve the consent of a person having control over another person, for the purpose of exploitation. Exploitation shall include, at a minimum, the exploitation of the prostitution of others or other forms of sexual exploitation, forced labour or services, slavery or practice similar to slavery, servitude or the removal of;
- The consent of a victim of trafficking in persons to the intended exploitation set forth in subparagraph (a) of this article shall be irrelevant where any of the means set forth in subparagraph (a) have been used;
- The recruitment, transportation, transfer, harbouring or receipt of a child for the purpose of exploitation shall be considered "trafficking in persons" even if this does not involve any of the means set forth in subparagraph (a) of this article;
- "Child" shall mean any person under eighteen years of age.

Article 5 of the Palermo Protocol then requires the member states to criminalize trafficking based on the definition outlined in Article 3; however, many member states' domestic laws reflects a narrower definition than Article 3. Although these nations claim to be obliging Article 5, the narrow laws lead to a smaller portion of people being prosecuted for sex trafficking. The United States passed the Victims of Trafficking and Violence Protection Act of 2000 (TVPA) to clarify the previous confusion and discrepancies in regards to the criminalizing guidelines of human trafficking. Though this act, sex trafficking crimes were defined as a situation where in which a "commercial sex act is induce by force, fraud, or coercion, or in which the person induced to perform such act has not attained 18 years of age.

If the victim is a child under the age of 18 no force, fraud, or coercion needs to be proven based on this legislation. The United States took legal measures to define more varieties of exploitive situations in relation to children. The two terms they defined and focused on were "commercial sexual exploitation of children" and "domestic minor sex trafficking. Commercial sexual exploitation of children CSEC) is defined as "encompassing several forms of exploitation, including pornography, prostitution, child sex tourism, and child marriage. Domestic minor sex with a child under the age of 18, who is a United States citizen or permanent resident, for a gain or cash, goods, or something of value.

According to ECPAT USA, the average age of entry into street prostitution is between 12 and 14 years old. The demographic of street prostitutes range from poor women, kids, ethnic minorities, and immigrants. In the United States, sex traffickers and pimps often find their victims in malls or on the streets. Sometimes vulnerable looking girls will be abducted while walking to their cars. Other times the pimp will go up to a victim and convince them to leave with them, often offering a job of some kind and money. Vulnerability increases when girls are young or homeless. Emotional and physical coercion is used in order for the victim to trust the pimp and build a relationship. This coercion often makes the relationships between trafficker and trafficked and pimps and prostitute difficult to identify. Often, the victims are tricked into thinking they will have freedom in the work they are promised along with a large sum of money but instead, they become a sex slave.

After the victims has withholding and / sexual abuse. Girls are often motivated by finances and basic survival. It is very common in the United States for pimps to own a business or store, especially nail salons and massage parlors. It is also very common for sex slavery businesses to be conducted near U. S. military bases, because of the businesses soldiers bring. In order to obtain control over their victims, traffickers will use force, drugs, emotional tactics as well as financial means. In certain circumstances, they will even resort to various forms of violence, such as gang rape and mental and physical abuse. Traffickers sometimes use offers of marriage, threats, intimidation, brainwashing and kidnapping as means of obtaining victims. A common process is for the trafficker to first gain the trust of the victim, called the grooming stage. They seek to make the victim dependent on them.

The trafficker may express love and admiration, make lofty promises, such as making the victim a star. Offer them a job or an education or buy them a ticket to a new location. The main types of work offered are in the catering and hotel industry, in bars and clubs, modeling contracts, or au pair work. Once the victim is comfortable, the pimp moves to the seasoning stage, where they will ask the victim to perform sexual acts for the pimp, which the victim may do because they believe it is the only way to keep the trafficker's affection. Another tactic is for traffickers to kidnap their victims, and then drug them or secure them so they cannot escape. Traffickers may seek out potential victims who are traveling, alone, are separated from their group, or seem like they are depressed, anger with their parents, and having low self-esteem. Traffickers are using social media at an increasing rate to find victims, potential victims, control their victims and advertise their victims.

After the victim has joined the offender, various techniques are used to restrict the victim's access to communication with home, such as imposing physical punishment unless the victim complies with the trafficker's demands and making threats of harm and even death to the victim and their family. Sometime, the victims will succumb to the Stockholm syndrome because their captors will pretend to "love" and "need" them, even going so far as promise marriage and future stability. This is particularly effective with younger victims, because they are more inexperienced and therefore easily manipulated. In India, those who traffic young girls into prostitution are often women who have been trafficked themselves. As adults they use personal relationships and trust in their villages of origin to recruit additional girls.

Gang-controlled trafficking

Gang-controlled sex trafficking and Pimp-controlled sex trafficking run their operation in very similar ways. The largest difference between the two is that gang-controlled trafficking is run by a large group of people whereas pimp-controlled trafficking is run by one person. In general, gang members are expected or forced to participate in tasks that involve illegal and violent activity. Some of these criminal behavioral may include: distributing drugs, robbery, trafficking drugs, extortion, and murder. The gangs can make a larger amount of money quicker by selling other people's bodies, and are less likely to get caught. In certain circumstances, gangs may team up with other gangs in the area, and work together as a sex ring. This gives their client, also known as a john, a greater variety of options to chose from. Clients are often willing to pay a larger price for a sexual experience with someone new. Another reason that gangs will share females is because this makes it more difficult for law enforcement to keep track of the victims, alternately preventing them from making a positive identification.

When people think or talk about sex trafficking a very common question people will ask is, "where do they find people to traffic "? In many cases, gang members will scope girls out at malls, skip parties, online and through social media. In addition, they often will seek out female runaways from their neighborhood. Many of the girls they look for have been physically or sexually abused, having low self-esteem, struggling with drug and alcohol dependency, or are seeking a home / family.

Familial trafficking

In familial trafficking, the victim is controlled by family members who allow them to be sexually exploited in exchange for something of value, such as drugs or money. For example, a member may allow a boyfriend to abuse a child in exchange for housing. Usually, it begins with one family member and spreads from there. Familial trafficking may be difficult to detect because these children often have a larger degree of freedom and may still attend school and after – school functions. These children may not understand that they are being trafficked or may not have a way out. Familial trafficking is considered by some to be the most prevalent form of human sex trafficking within the United States.

Cybersex trafficking

Cybersex trafficking involves trafficking and live streaming of coerced sexual acts and or rape on webcam. Victims are abducted, threatened, or deceived and transferred to 'cybersex dens. the dens can be in any location where the cybersex traffickers have a computer, tablet, or phone with internet connection. Pepetrators use social media networks, videoconferences, pornographic video sharing websites, dating pages, online chat rooms, apps, dark web sites, and other platforms. This type of sex trafficking has surged since the advent of the Digital Age, and the development of online payment systems, and cryptocurrencies that hide the transactors' identities. Millions of reports of its occurrence are sent to authorities annually.

Forced marriage

A forced marriage is a marriage where one or both participants are married without their freely given consent. Servile marriage is defined as a marriage involve a person being sold, transferred or inherited into that marriage. according to ECPAT, "Child Trafficking for forced marriage is simply another manifestation of trafficking and is not restricted to particular nationalities or countries. A forced marriage qualifies as a form of human trafficking in certain situations. If a woman is sent abroad, forced into the marriage and then repeatedly compelled to engage in sexual conduct with her new husband and / or his family, then this is a form of labor trafficking. Approximately 140 million girls under the age of 18, which is about 39,000 a day, will be forced into early marriages between 2011 and 2020. Forced marriage, which is identified by the United Nations as a "contemporary form of slavery," occurs without full consent of the man or woman, and is associated with threats by family members or the bride / groom. Forced marriage occurs not only in foreign countries but in the US as well. There is not one simple factor that perpetuates sex trafficking, rather a complex interconnected web of political, socioeconomic, governmental, and societal factors. The cause of sex trafficking which have been identified lie at the intersections of these factors. There are three types of causes which have been identified: gender hierarchies, migration for work (pull factors), and neoliberal globalization (push factors); unquoted.

FORBIDDEN FRUIT

This Re-cap is base off, of a true story involving a girl, her mother, and her mother's man; who later became her father. This family was living in New York, a very poor area of New York, and where as walking the streets were dangerous. The story starts out in the middle of the night while the family is sleeping. A man comes up from no where and pushed a girl, and forcefully hold her down onto the bed. He is later seen having sex with the girl penetrating her from behind. Upon daylight, the family awakes. A woman named Creitol comes out of her bed room wearing barely nothing telling her daughter to get her ass up out of bed; she's hungry. She said, get up, you fat bitch, and don't you even give me that look. The mother, Creitol does nothing in the apartment in which they lived with regard to cleaning or cooking. Her daughter, Sachi Lauriton, does everything to include all the cooking.

Creitol, treats her daughter like she's the maid. Sachi Lauriton is only 16, sixteen years old. But she's big and very fat. The mother, Creitol is also big and fat but not so much like her daughter. Creitol orders her daughter around. Her daughter, Sachi Laurilton, while in class at school one morning was told by her teacher to go to the Principle's office. The Principle's named was Sylvania. She was a very nice lady and concern about Sachi Lauriton. The principle asked Sachi Lauriton, is she pregnant? Sachi Lauriton became silent and never did answer the question. Base on a no respond; the Principle, Sylvania, suspended Sachi Lauriton from school. Sachi Lauriton mother asked her; why are you home so early? Sachi Lauriton, told her mother Creitol that the Principle suspended her. Her mother loudly said; you dumd ass, fat stinking ass should not even be in school. You are a dumb ass. You can't read. And, you damn sure can't write. You're not going to mount up to nothing. Do you hear me, do you hear me, you fat piece of shit? School, you don't need no school, you're too dumb. You're too fucking dumb to learn. You're just a fat bitch. Get that through your head.

Put that shit down and fix me something to eat. Sachi Lauriton said OK mommy. Her mother thought that her daughter said something negative, and begin yelling at her, and hit her daughter up beside the head several times; and then said, say something else. That same night her mother man forcefully sexually raped Sachi Lauriton again. Sachi Lauriton learned days later that she was pregnant. She had a baby girl. Her school Principle, Sylvania, showed up at the apartment building one day. She pressed the door bell-buzzer several times. Sachi Lauriton thought that it was someone wanting to sale something. Sachi Lauriton pressed the buzzer yelling go away, go away, go away. Then Sachi Lauriton finally asked; who is it? The lady identify herself as the principle. She asked to come up. Sachi Lauriton, said that she could not come up. The Principle, Sylvania, told Sachi Lauriton, there

is an Alternative School. The principle gave Sachi Lauriton the name, and the address of the school. Her mother repeatedly asked her daughter Sachi Lauriton, who is ringing her buzzer? Sachi Lauriton told her mother Creitol, it's the school principle. Sachi Lauriton mother was very pissed off and mad as hail. She couldn't wait for the principle to leave. Creitol told her daughter; how dare you invite that bitch to my apartment. How dare you, how dare you. Are you fucking crazy? Are you loosening your mind? Creitol in anger tells her daughter to tell the principle to leave. Creitol said, tell her to leave now. Sachi Lauriton said OK mommy. Now, I say!

After the principle left the apartment building. Creitol started viciously, loudly, and in anger yelling at her daughter. You bitch, you bitch, how dare you, how dare you! Creitol started slapping her daughter in the face, hitting and beating her down like an animal. A whipping ass sure but brutal.

Sachi Lauriton, after being beaten down by her mother. She was told by her mother Creitol, to go to the social worker office the next morning. Creitol said, you need to go there before they stop paying me my money. Sachi Lauriton said OK mommy.

Morning came and Sachi Lauriton got up out of bed and quickly started cooking breakfast. Sachi Lauriton is a very good cook. She later went to the alternative school. She met with a very nice teacher named Blu-Aboka. She saw Sachi Lauriton sitting in a chair as if she was sick. Sachi Lauriton earlier threw up into the hallway waster container. The teacher, Blu-Aboka, pass Sachi Lauriton going to the soda vending machine. She then headed back to the class room, stop briefly, and asked Sachi Lauriton, is she's coming to class? Sachi Lauriton did not respond but shortly thereafter got up out of the chair, and went to the class room.

There was about 5, five girls in the class room, all of which had problems, and serious issues. But not to say the least even attitudes, and trouble at home. The teacher, Blu-Aboka, had each student introduce themselves (1) name, (2) where are they from, (3) favorite color, (4) what they do best., and (5) what brought them to "ONE TEACHES ONE". Some of the girls had problem with math, English, and general studies. Sachi Lauriton, had problem reading. She was good in math but did not know (1) her A, B, C's and (2) how to read. Remind you of Sachi Lauriton age; she was 16, sixteen years old. Of all the ugly, and bad things (ie) insults, that Sachi Lauriton mother called her she never gave up hope of pursuing her dream of learning how to read, and of course attending college. Which was one thing above all she wanted to do.

Sachi Lauriton finally learned to read with the help, understanding, and patient of her teacher Blu-Aboka, who believe in her. One day the teacher took the class on a field trip. Sachi Lauriton returned home late. Her mother Creitol, was very angry and pissed off, as furious as a hunger lion. Creitol said to her daughter; where in the hail were you? Where in the hail have you been? I'm sitting here hungry waiting on your black ass to come home. Where in the hail were you? Creitol said, get your black ass in the kitchen, "now I say" and fix me some food. Sachi Lauriton said OK mommy.

Despite all of the physical and mental abuse, and insults, by her mother, Sachi Lauriton not once disrespected her mother. That very same night the PREDATOR, her mother's man forcefully sexually raped Sachi Lauriton again. But Sachi Lauriton went to class the next morning as usually as if nothing happen. Because (1) she felt safe, (2) she had nothing to fear, (3) she was at peace, (4) she was away from her mother's man, (5) had others to talk to, (6) chose to get an education, (7) chance to attend college, (8) among friends, (there was kindness, love, and compassion. (9) her teacher believe in her. Sachi Lauriton while walking home after class passed three guys hanging out along side the street corner listening to music. She was pushed from behind by one of the boys as she passed them falling face down onto the street. That same boy, whoever he was pulled down Sachi Lauriton pants, and sexually assaulted her, raping her from behind. When Sachi Lauriton awaken, her face was being slick by a cat. Sachi Lauriton got up and continue on her way home. Sachi Lauriton after returning home was asked by her mother; why are you late? She complained of being sick. Surprisingly her mother Creitol did not get piss off. Sachi Lauriton went to school the next morning with a smile on her face. The teacher asked every student to come up front, and write what has been written into their booklet.

Sachi Lauriton was third. She went up to the front and started to read, suddenly, she fail to the floor. she was rush to the hospital with the quick thinking and help of her teacher Blu-Aboka. Sachi Lauriton gave birth to a baby boy. Incest, sexually assaulted by her mother's man raping her repeatedly, who was also her father.

While in the hospital Sachi Lauriton met a very nice young man who was also a male nurse. He gave her money and flowers. He even spent a lot of free time with Sachi Lauriton whenever possible. It appeared that he was attracted to Sachi Lauriton, and starting to have feelings for her.

Sachi Lauriton went home a few day later but not empty handed. She was carrying her new born child. Shortly after returning home hail started again. Her mother, Creitol, started first acting real nice, and if she cared. She even asked her daughter Sachi Lauriton if she could whole the baby. minutes later physical and verbal abuse by the mother attacking her daughter. Reminder; her daughter Sachi Lauriton was just discharged from the hospital minutes ago after giving birth. Her mother, Creitol, within seconds quickly put down her daughter Sachi Lauriton baby son. The mother, Creitol, started yelling, hitting, and beating down her daughter.

But this time her daughter Sachi Lauriton fought back, fighting like an angry lion, kicking her mother ass. Sachi Lauriton then grabbed her baby and left the apartment, and never not even once look back. Words to remember: ENOUGH IS ENOUGH. The mother started out beating the hail out of her daughter and didn't even care that she had just left the hospital for home. Her mother didn't even embrace the baby. She barely look at the baby. Not one kind word did the mother had to say.

Sachi Lauriton after leaving the apartment was walking the streets in the cold weather carrying her baby. She later board a bus heading for the ALTERNATIVE SCHOOL where she felt safe. She broke a glass of a door entering into one of the class rooms. One of the teachers seeing the damage to the door was frighten, and threatening to call the police. But she put down the phone when Sachi Lauriton teacher Blu-Aboka, told her that Sachi Lauriton broke the glass, and sitting in the class room with her baby.

They allowed Sachi Lauriton to sleep in the class room. The next morning the teacher Blu-Aboka, had one of the students teach the class while she tried to get help for Sachi Lauriton, hopefully help with a place to stay. Her teacher tried desperately but without hope or success of any kind. Her teacher not having too much of a choice allowed Sachi Lauriton and her baby to stay with her.

Days later, Sachi Lauriton went to the welfare office. It was a scheduled appointment, and Sachi Lauriton having another child, and no where to stay. The Social Worker, Nancy Beach, told Sachi Lauriton, that her mother, Creitol, wants to meet with them together, and of course she said, its up to you. Sachi Lauriton had no problem with her mother being at the next meeting. The following week, well, her mother showed up for the meeting. The Social Worker, Nancy Beach, asked the mother, Creitol, about the sexual attacks on her daughter. The mother openly said; it begin at the age of three. The mother, Creitol, said that her daughter Sachi Lauriton, would sleep on one side and her man would sleep on the other side next to her. Creitol said, from time to time while sleeping her man would touch her daughter Sachi Lauriton. She would ask him; what are you doing? She said that; he would say shut up your fat ass mouth. Creitol said, that she wouldn't say anything more.

The Social Worker, Nancy Beach, asked the mother, what did you do to stop it? The mother said; what could I do? He was my man. The Social Worker Nancy Beach, asked, what about now? She said that your daughter is 16, sixteen years old, and has two children by your man. The mother said; he died a week ago. "He's dead". The Social Worker, Nancy Beach, asked Sachi Lauriton, what are your plans now? Do you want to go back and stay with your mother?

Sachi Lauriton stood up and said; I be damn if I go back and live in that apartment. You, you mother treated me and my babies like shit. You pretend to love them when the social worker came to visit. You treated me like a bitch, maid, and a slave. I had to do all the cooking and the cleaning. If I was to get out of line just once you would slap me silly, and beat me down. You yelled and hit me down like an animal. You allowed your man to have his way with me. You allowed your man to touch me. You allowed your man to sexually rape and force himself on you. You didn't even care what happens to me. You didn't even care about my education. You didn't even come and visit me in the hospital. Your no mother. You're a bitch. You're the animal. Respect, you showed me no respect. No love for me or my babies. You treated me like a slave not like a daughter. You have no love for me. Go fuck yourself. Sachi Lauriton grabbed her two children and left.

I AM A TEENAGER

I am a teenager. That's what I am. I am a teenager!. Do you care? That what I am. No, that's not what I'll always be. To say differently that wouldn't be true. I'm just a child anew. I live my life the best that I can. But being as teenager "well", that's win, win. For me its true maybe not for you. I don't live my life in a zoo. Here looking at you as a teenager on the fly. Believe me I will never lie. Am I crying out for help or just telling the truth? I'm just being a teenager that's nothing new. But again only the world can see. What does that say about me.? What does it say about you? One thing for sure I'm no fool. I'm not trying to disrespect you. No, no, no, I wouldn't do such a thing? Who would say who, when, or why? Please mother don't make me cry. But who would give a damn if not me? I'm just as teenager can't you see? This little girl, silly little me. I'm looking down from a tree. This tree believe it or not speaks to me. Sending me secrets from beneath. Don't look at me like that. I'm just a little girl. A girl with many words expressing myself. It's time to party can't you see? I'm thick and thin smoking and laughing in the wind.

Listen to what I say but please don't take me wrong. For the best of two worlds I might go home. But what's in a word "I am teenager can't you see? Leave me alone and let me be. What more should I say! You need to understand me or go away. I am not your little girl anymore out of sight and out of mind. Do you understand what I'm trying to say! What am trying to say to you? I am a teenager is that not true? What can I say! What am I saying to you? Is it making you turn blue? I don't want to hurt you nor bring shame on myself. Because mom and dad I love you to death. I need for you to open the door so that I can pass through. Because growing up is hard to do. Me being a teenager I still need you. If that's not true please tell me more. I have a heart can't you see? In the meantime please open the door. I need to be able to entertain my friends without you being around. I say this with hope that you would understand. I don't want to hurt you although it can. I am still a child that much I know. But I am growing into a woman so pleas don't let me go. Please don't stop me from having fun even if it means having sex one on one. Because this is what a teenager does believe it or not. Hey, why am I telling you this? When its something that you should already know. So mom, dad, what can we do? I need my freedom ain't that not true? I need many things but for now I'll start with this. Some new wheels a care at best. What more should I say? You should know the rest. I can't wait to move out on my own. I can't wait to buy my own home. What a peace of mind "freedom" at last. At least now I can be glad. I can have friends over anytime day or night. I'll be able to party anytime, anywhere, without having to seek permission from my parents. That says a lot and how good it feels. There is nothing like being a teenager hanging out with friends and dancing in the wind. Is this not what a teenager does? Will have fun and so much more. Will even take a bath in the tub. How much fun will that be? Partying, and drinking while hanging in a tree. Huge smile upon our face; laid back, having fun while drinking punch in the sun. I am a teenager trying to be myself. Did you not do the same? Mom and dad can't you understand? I am a teenager soon a young woman to be and that make me glad.

I looked forward to doing the things that a teenager does. Kissing, dating, and crawling around in the mud. Want that be fun or do you not care? Being with your boy friend on a clear sunny day stroking his hair far, far, away. Jumping and playing games having fun one would say. laying out in the sun admiring the view when all of a sudden then came you. I though I was going to throw up, but my stomach held it together. Good night everyone. Sleep tight "don't let the bed bugs bite.

A Word Of Advice To Parents

Parents, its ok for your child to grow up and into a woman.
It's ok for your child to have friends.
It's ok for your child to party.
It's ok for your child to have fun.

But parents, whatever you do, don't let your guard down protecting them. Because you know what can and what will harm them. A mother's love for her daughter is unconditional something that all mothers would understand, die for, and take to their grave. Nothing is more stronger than love for family no matter how young or how old he or she may be. Love for your child doesn't there. Whatever happens a mother still love her child. Missing, gone missing, escape from prison, a mother still love her child. "There is no greater love". That takes lead into this story but with a different twist. In this story the mother is being accused of being too hard and overly protected of her child. That creates problems between them. I believe her daughter is at least fourteen (16) years of age. She doesn't get kidnapped but classified as gone missing. When everyone else gave up her mother did not. My heart goes out to all mothers. The girl, her brother, and mother are home. It is spring break. The mother daughter want to hang out with friends at a beach. First the mother wasn't going to go but later changed her mind. The girl mother called her best friend and off they went to spring break. They first checked into a hotel booking two separate rooms.

The brother unfortunately had to share a room with the girls. "The brother had his own room. Her daughter changed into a beach outfit. The mother told the daughter she's showing too much. Go put on something else. She did and was later seen stretch back onto a pool side lounge chair talking to two guys. Her mother and her best friend observed the three of them. Surely you know what happened next. The mother walks over to where they were seeing a up with beer inside of it tells her daughter to go to her room. How embarrassing do you think that was? "Go to your room" in the present of others. Two guys who were just having innocent fun with no harmful intentions. Her mother didn't see it that way. The mother told her daughter; I can't believe you. You're not eighteen. Those guys were trying to get you drunk. Her daughter said "so what"; if they were trying to get

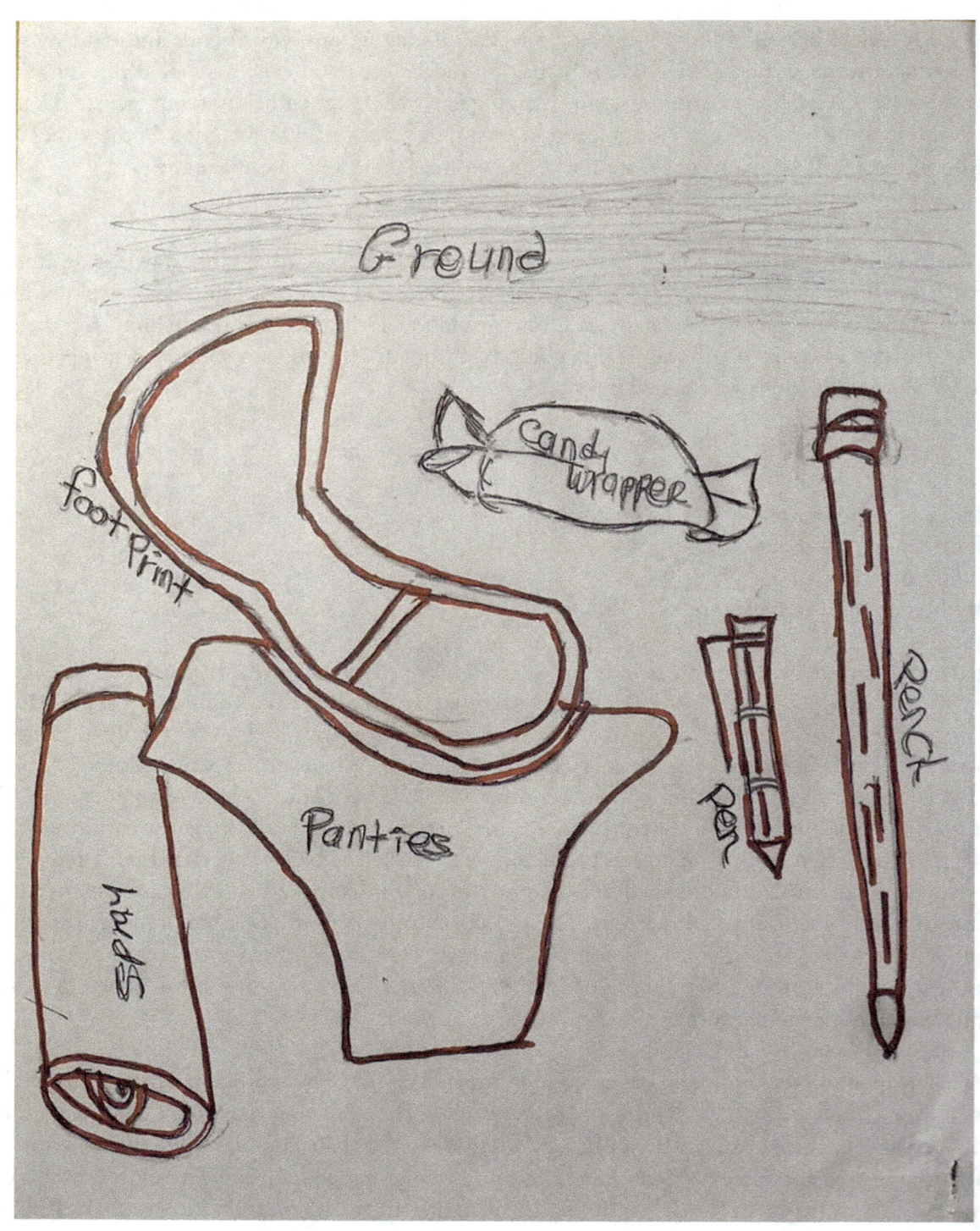

me drunk. I felt that slap and wasn't even there. What a cross left hand her mother have. Her mother last words were "you're grounded".

Can you imagine being grounded on spring break? Her mother was seen talking to her best friend about what has transpired. Her best friend told the mother that she need to start trusting her daughter. This is spring break. Give her daughter some space. The mother told her best friend that her daughter is a virgin and never had a boy friend. That she's worry about her. There were some people down the hall having a party. It happens to be the room of the two guys her daughter met early on. The mother's daughter, and her best friend were hanging out in her brother's room heard music coming from down the hall. They wanted to go and check it out. The brother said; what if your mother come looking for you? Hey, what should I tell her? The sister said call us. She said whatever you do don't tell her. They kicked him out of the room and starting getting dress for the party. The two guys were surprise to see them especially the mother's daughter. They hanged out at the party for awhile. Everyone later left to go to a club. That club was jumping surrounding by so many people wall to wall dancing and having a good time.

The two girls were seen holding hands and being offered a ride with two other young guys. They were completely in control of there surrounding but a bit drunk. They didn't have the slightest ideal of where those guys were taking them. This was in the middle of the night and roads were very dark. Neither of the girls ask the guy where they were going. It turnout that they were going to Mexico. Once the mother's daughter was told that the guys were taking them to Mexico she told them to stop the car. First, they refused to stop the car. She then told them again, and again, repeatedly to stop the car or the police will be call. Finally, they stopped the car and the mother's daughter got out but her best friend did not. They drove off continuing their drive to Mexico leaving her along side the road. The mother's daughter was very pissed off at her best friend. She were seen walking slowly along side the road. It was so dark nothing could be seem. A vehicle shortly thereafter was seen coming down the road. It was a vehicle from the hotel being driven by a white male. The driver at first didn't want to pick her up.

But after she identify herself he changed his mind. The driver and the girl saw someone farther down along side the road. It was one of the guys from the party who also stays at the hotel. But he was very badly drunk under the strong influence of alcohol. He could barely stand nor less walk. She tried to help him stand. It was impossible. She told the driver to help her put him on the vehicle. The driver refused. The driver said no, no, he's too drunk; and drove off leaving them both along side the road. Her mother after realizing the time and that her daughter was not in their room called security. He was very patient and understanding. Security and the girl mother viewed security cameras checking all floors. They were seeing leaving the guys room later that night, and leaving the hotel by taxie. Minutes later, they saw one of he guys that her daughter was hanging out with along side the pool area. He took off running but was caught by security. He confect that the girls were at the party that night and took them to his room. His friend was past out drunk on the floor. He told the mother that's true they did to a club and gave them the name of the club.

The girl mother and her best friend went to the club looking for their daughters. Their daughters were not there. And why is that? They were in a car heading for Mexico. The mother and her best friend returned to the hotel and asked security to call the police. Police conducted search with the help of other and flyers were posted throughout the city. They even telecast a missing person alert. Days pass, nothing. Now, both mothers were starting to worry. No phone calls, no nothing. The search for the girls continued. The mother's daughter was later seen trying to climb over a fence. She dropped her cell phone causing it to fall over to the other side down near some rocks resting in water. She eventually climbed over the fence but fell along side the rock area near the cell phone unconscious hitting the side of her head. Her mother, her best friend, and the police was searching the beach area days later. The girl mother remember something that her daughter told her before disappearing. "The beach clip". She asked police; where is the beach clip? The girl mother saw foot prints along side a fence. When the mother got closer to the fence area foots stopped along side the edge.

The fence itself was push inward. A shoe was on the ground next to the fence. When the mother looked down below toward the beach and rocky area. She saw her daughter. Her daughter was down the clip lying face down on rocks surrounded by water. She was unconscious and bleeding from the forehead. Hopefully all parents will learn something from this story. Her mother never gave up hope that her daughter would be found. She never stop looking for her. What would you had done? Would you had went back home waiting for your daughter to call? Would you had went back home waiting for the police to call? Parents, it's just a question of how well you know your daughter. True or False? Once the trail goes cold. The police will stop looking for your daughter / children unless there is reason to believe that your daughter / children is still alive. BUT, DO YOU KNOW WHO SHOULDN'T STOP LOOKING AND WHO SHOULDN'T GIVE UP? ANSWER: IS YOU, THE PARENT. The whereabout and location of your child, children, boy or girl, starts with you. It's through you that they have hope of one day (soon) they will be home.

https://www.acf.hhs.gov/otip/about/what-is-human-trafficking
WHAT IS HUMAN TRAFFICKING; and I quote
- Human trafficking is a crime and public health

There are two types of a severe form of trafficking in persons:
- Labor Trafficking
- Sex Trafficking

Who is at risk?
- Individuals who have experienced childhood abuse or neglect
- Children and youth involved in the foster care and juvenile justice systems
- People experiencing homelessness
- American Indians, Alaska Natives, Native Hawaiians, and Pacific Islanders
- Survivors of violence
- Lesbian, Gay, Bisexual, Transgender, and Questioning (LGBTQ) individuals
- Migrant workers
- Undocumented immigrants
- Racial and ethnic minorities
- People with disabilities
- People with low incomes
- People with a history of substance abuse
- Communities exposed to intergenerational trauma

Where does trafficking occur?

- Anywhere
- Illicit markets to legal industries like hospitality
- Construction
- Agriculture
- Domestic services

Who are the traffickers?

- Any gender or age
- Strangers
- Peers
- Friends
- Romantic partners
- Family members

What are the signs that someone may be experiencing trafficking?

Physical Health
- Frequent treatment for sexual transmitted infections
- High number of sexual partners
- Multiple pregnancies / abortions
- Exposure to toxic chemicals
- Dental issues
- Bruising and burns
- Signs of self-harm
- Weight loss or malnourishment
- Respiratory issues
- Suicide attempts
- Physical and sexual abuse

Behavioral Health
- Confusing / contradicting stories
- Inability to focus or concentrate
- Unaware of current date, location, or time
- Protects person who hurt them
- Minimizes abuse
- Guilt and shame about experiences
- Suicidal ideations
- Extreme timidity
- Aggressive, antagonistic, or defensive
- Heightened stress response
- Post-traumatic stress disorder
- Withdrawn
- Depressed

Social / Environmental
- Absent from school
- Failing grades
- Sudden increase in substance use
- Change in dress
- Age-inappropriate romantic partner
- Change in friends
- Repeat runaway
- Not able to speak for oneself or share information
- Evidence of being controlled
- Wears inappropriate clothing for the weather
- Lives at worksite

How can we prevent sex trafficking?
- Encourage healthy behaviors in relationships
- Foster safe home's and neighborhoods
- Identify and address vulner abilities during health care visitors
- Reduce demand for commercial sex
- End business profits from trafficking—related transactions

When we think of the Brain, we think of the human head. Because the brain its left/right side is enclosed into the human head. which protect it from damage, diseases, and harm. When we think of the Brain literally feelings, love, pain. When you think about love / pain. You think about others and their problems. When you think about personal problems – You think about what's going to happen next. Ideally we don't know. But by you having a brain that helps to solve the mystery. A knock on your door so to speak. Because the brain is a problem solver. It can think, hate, feel, love, and so on. You can't do anything without the brain. That five letters word. But that five letters word can destroy you.

The brain as we know it has no boundary, no limits, and no define direction. With the help of your bran you can do anything. You can scream, yell, talk, but most importantly you can define right from wrong. Because your brain controls your connection with the rest of the world. When someone tells you to think. It's your bran their talking to. When someone ask you a question. It's your brain their speaking to. Everything you do relates to your brain. Your brain has a left and a right side. Together they get the job done. You cannot live without your brain. You cannot think without your brain. You cannot feel any part of your body without your brain. Protect your brain. If your brain get damage you will never be the same. Your six senses will never be the same. You will not be the same person. You feel like a vegetable. Don't take your brain for granted.

If the brain is so important; how is it that people become human predators preying on others especially children? Without making excuses giving them justification of their actions; you could say that their brain is damaged. A chemistry in the brain leaping out, burn out, or damage in such a way causing them to turn on others criminally and sexually. The question is, can you explain it? Surely there is more than one answer. Surely there is more than one solution to their problem. It has been said, and I quote, the brain is a terrible thing to waste. Therefore to study people you must study the brain. To understand people you must study the brain. Treat your brain with tender loving care. Knowing what we know we should be able to understand people better. We should know

what makes people tick. It's the brain. Therefore, to control what people do we need to understand the brain. The brain therefore should be handle very careful.

Many questions has been asked and still being asked such as follows:
Why did that happened to me, why couldn't you had just stop, why did you have to kill him/her,
Why couldn't you had just let it go, what were you thinking, why did you do that, why do you feel that way, why did you go there, why did you take my child, why are you like that, why did you do that, why are you so angry, why did you kill my child, how would you like someone to do that to you? THINK ABOUT, EVERYTHING YOU SAY AND DO IS ASSOCIATED WITH THE BRAIN. Your talking to the brain because the brain controls the human body. SOMEONE ASKED IN A MOVIE; IS THAT YOUR MOUTH TALKING OR YOUR BRAIN! GO FIGURE.

BRAIN ANIMAL

BLACK BOX

What is their association to each other? Is there an association? The brain controls the human body. What about animals? Does animals have a brain? Yes of course. But the anima in question that I'm referring to is called METALPHOR. The different in distinguish its an animal. Therefore has nothing to do with the human brain. Because a human being is not an animal. Well, maybe not all of us. What about the Black Box? The Black Box is Mechanical. It's more associated with something that can fly. But as your Brain records and store information BELIEVE IT OR NOT so does the BRAN. The only different is; When the Black Box stop recording and storing information the fly object whatever it is can still fly. Mechanically it would be called a Malfunction. But when the Brain stop functioning most times your dead or clinically Brain dead. Therefore you don't go on living. So, I asked the question; how smart is smart? Can we re-boot the Brain? Can we re-boot the Black Box? Most importantly, Predators and the Brain. People and shame. Being who we are human beings and having a brain. What can we do to stop the sin of the world people who are predators preying on others? Can we use our brain to stop them? Can we use our brain to get treatment for them? Can having a brain change them at all? The Tin Man said and I quote, I wish I had a Brain. What about you? Do you have a Brain?

https://en.wikipedis.org/wiki/Human_brain
The Human Brain. Why in the hail would I include articles about the human brain! I'm glad you asked. Why is why. He is he. She is she. First of all. What make us human? The brain. What does the brain do? For starters, it keep up alive. Next to the heart the brain is the next important organ of the body. Why? You have something called "six (6) senses. With that in mind. You can distinguish between right and wrong. In other words your able to think. The brain can tell you what to do and not to do. It can tell you what to wear and not to wear. The brain can tell you when to sleep and when not to sleep. When to get angry and not to get angry. When you happy and not happy. When to kill and when not to kill. When to hurt someone and when not to hurt someone. When to abduct / kidnap someone and when not to abduct / kidnap someone. The brain can tell you what to think and how to think. Today is cold. Today is hot. When the brain stop functioning its over. When the brain stop functioning your life is over. Because you're not the same person that you were before. Your more like a vegetable (lifeness). The human brain is responsible for "what makes us human". The brain causes you to ask questions such as; why did you abduct/kidnapped my child? Why did you overnight abduct/kidnapped my baby? Why did you tortured my child? Why did you do these things to my child? Why, why, why, why? Who made you God?

How would you like someone to abduct/kidnap your child? how would you like someone to abduct/kidnap, and shelter you in an under ground cave?

What if the shoe was on the other foot? Are you or are you not man enough to face the fact that you are acting courageously? Wikipedia; HUMAN BRAIN, and I quote; The human brain is the central organ of the human nervous system, and the spinal cord makes up the central nervous system. The brain consists of the cerebrum, the brainstem and the cerebellum. It controls most of the activities of the body, processing, integrating, and coordinating the information it receives from the sense organs, and making decisions as to the instructions sent to the rest of the body. The brain is contained in, and protected by, the skull bones of the head. The cerebrum is the largest part of the human brain. It is divided into two cerebral hemispheres. The cerebral cortex is an outer layer of grey matter, covering the core of white matter. The cortex is split into the neocortex and the much smaller allocortex. The neocortex is made up of six neuronal layers, while the allocortex has three or four. Each hemisphere is conventionally divided into four lobes – the frontal, temporal, parietal, and occipital lobes.

The frontal lobe is associated with executive functions including self-control, planning, reasoning, and abstract though, while the occipital lobe is dedicated to vision. Within each lobe, cortical areas are associated with specific functions, such as the sensory, motor and association regions. Although the left and right hemispheres are broadly similar in shape and function, some functions are associated with one side, such as language in the left and visual-spatial ability in the right. The hemispheres area connected by commissural nerve tracts, the largest being the corpus callosum. "In other words; the human brain controls the body". Therefore, you know right from wrong. It all comes down to common sense. When you don't do something. You have yourself the blame. When you do something. You have yourself the blame. (Your brain is processing) what your thinking, feelings, desires, and wants. Blame who? Blame your brain. Blame who? Blame yourself. My personal comments and of course everyone has one.

The cerebrum is connected by the brainstem to the spinal cord. The brainstem consists of the midbrain, the pons, and the medulla oblongata. The cerebellum is connected to the brainstem by pairs of tracts. Within the cerebrum is the ventricular system, consisting of four interconnected ventricles in which cerebrospinal fluid is produced and circulated. Underneath the cerebral cortex are several important structures, including the thalamus, the epithalamus, the pineal gland, the hypothalamus the pituitary gland, and the subthalamus; the limbic structures, including the amygdala and the hippocampus; the claustrum, the various nuclei of the basal ganglia; the basal forebrain structures, and the three circumventricular organs.

The brain protected by the skull, suspended in cerebrospinal fluid, and isolated from the bloodstream by the blood—brain barrier. However, the brain is still susceptible to damage, disease, and infection. Damage can be caused trauma, or a loss of blood supply known as a stroke. The brain is susceptible to degenerative disorders, such as Parkinson's disease, dementias including Alzheimer's disease, and multiple sclerosis. Psychiatric conditions, including schizophrenia and clinical depression, are thought to be associated with brain dysfunctions. The brain can also be the site of tumor, both benign and malignant; these mostly originate from other sites in the body.

The brainstem lies beneath the cerebrum and consists of the midbrain, pons and medulla. It lies in the back part of the skull, resting on the part of the base known as the clivus, and ends at the foramen magnum, a large opening in the occipital bone. The brainstem continues below this as the spinal cord, protected by the vertebral column. Ten of the twelves of cranial nerves emerge directly from the brainstem. the reticular formation, a network of nucieil of ill-define formation, is present within and along the length of the brainstem. Many nerves tracts, which transmit information to and from the cerebral cortex to the rest of the body, pass through the brainstem.

https://www.verywellmind.com/lesson-three-brain-and-behavior-2795291
The Psychology of The Brain and Behavior, by Kendra Cherry, and I quote; That play a role in how we think, feel, react and behave. Every year, millions of people are affected by disorder of the brain and nervous system including Alzheimer's, Parkinson's disease, stroke, and traumatic brain injuries. These illnesses and injuries highlight the importance of the biological base for our behavior.

The area of psychology that seeks to understand how the brain affects behavior is known as biopsychology, although you, may also hear this subject referred to as psychology or behavior neuroscience.

Neurons are the basic building blocks of life. These highly specialized cells are responsible for receiving and transmitting information from one part of the body to another. In this article, you'll learn more about how neurons function. Understanding the Neuron's in the Body.
In order to better understand how a neuron works to transmit information throughout the body, it is essential to know the different parts of a neuron. Learn about the structure of a neuron and how neural signals are transmitted in this overview of neuron anatomy.

Neurotransmitters
You've see how a cell is structured and how nerve impulses are propagated down the cell, but how does this information travel from one cell to the next? Learn more these chemical messages that transmit signals from one cell to the next in this overview of neurotransmitters.
Communication Systems
Neurons make up only a small part of the brain body's complex communication system. The nervous system is composed of two main parts: the central nervous system and the peripheral nervous system. Additionally, the endocrine system plays an important role in communication.

The brain
Technological advances in recent years have allowed scientists to study the human brain in ways that were not possible in the past; unquoted.

One would think. Well, maybe one would not! But to be classify one would think more wisely, and more intelligently toward what does it mean to be different. If only I had a Brain, the Tin Man said. But not everything is written in stone. Because no two people think alike. Lets talk about this word classification. First of all, what does it mean, and secondly, how does it relates to the word predator? Predators were being classify in some of the material and given justification as to why they did what they did. To do something wrong -you were classified. To speak out of tongue-you were classified. To dress a certain way-you were classified. To act differently (out of the norm) you were classified. Now I get the picture. Do you? It was based on a number of things even gender, and age of the victim. You can't call that white rice for nothing. Everything we do is a record of our past, present, and future. That determines a lot; our behavior, demeanor, our lifestyle, and how we feel and think to say the least. What stripes me the most is how this theory relates to classification, not just to classification but to the classification of predators. This society in which we live in language is important. How we say something. What we say. It brans up creating a social path within our society, community, and culture.

Generally speaking it dictates our norm. What we do. what we don't do. In reality, a stalker is a stalker. A predator is a predator. A kidnapper is a kidnapper. An abductor is an abductor. Classifying you differently doesn't who you are or what you are.

Society is not responsible for their sickness that is within them. The key word is society. The word that bridge the different is classification. The other word if you really th..nk about it is gender. Woman, man, He, and she. No two are the same. Our society consist of both sex, both have a brain. But what make them different? It's not so much as to who they are. But the true distinguish is in what they do. That bring us to the word sex. how so; emotions, feelings, desire, pleasure, lush, love, togetherness, and love. How can such a small little word cause problems within a society? Is that what a predator wants? How would you classify that? Here are some words to think about with regard to classification of women and men base on what they do to women, children, and others.

Chronophilia ….. Pedohebephilia ….. infantophilia …..Pedophilia……. Hebephilia ….. Ephebophilia….. Mesaphilia….. Gerontophilia…… Paldophiles…… These next group of words explain and dissect who we are. What we are as human beings. These are words of science. These are words asking questions and analyzing what we have become. These words therefore are not just words. They have a language. They have a purpose. They have a meaning and direction. Society, Ecosystem, Species, Mental Culdesac, Human Predator, Ominivores, Human Prey, Super Predator, Human bystander, Phenomenon, Predation, Social Stratification, Human behavior, Exploitative, Metalphor, relationship, Characterized, Patential Pitfall, Autorophs, Dominant, Multitudinous, Substitution, Social behavior, Domestication, Social Science, Traits, Social Norms, Matirath, Genetics, Climate, brain, mind, Ontology, Behaviorsm, Spirituality, Gender, Sexual identity, Sex-arbitrary, Genital, Morphology, Gonadal sex, Chronosomal sex, mental disorder, Mental illness, Psychiatric, Nervous illness, Continurim, Classification, Mood disorder, Psychopathology, Cognitive, Dissociative, Ephebopohtlia, Pseudonym, Introinerion, Ecological, Organ, Distress, Attraction, Fantasies, Abnormaltities, Offender,. Approbation, Newroticissm, Sexual gralification, Child Pornography, Tranomittability, Molesters, Sexual stimuli, Hypothalsmus, Ssimplification, Distinguishing, Virtuous, Extrafamilial, Pederosis, Serotomin.

https://www.sciencedirect.com/science/article/abs./pil/S000632070400254X
Human---predator-prey conflicts; ecological correlate, prey losses and patterns of management, and I quote; Conflicts between humans and predators are the product of socio-economic and political landscapes and are particularly controversial because concerned have economic value and the predators involved are high profile and often legally protected. We surveyed the current literature for information on ecological and social factors common to human—predator-prey conflicts.

We used this information to examine whether losses to predators and patterns of investment in husbandry could be linked to these factors. We found that livestock losses to predators were low and were negatively associated with net primary productivity and predator home range sizes, but were not affected by predator density, methods of husbandry or human population density.

While there was no effect of husbandry on losses, variation in husbandry was explained by net primary productivity, predator density and percentage of stock killed by predator. Inconsistent and sparse data across conflicts may have limited our ability to identify important factors and resolve patterns, and suggests that there is no reliable or consistent framework for assessing and managing human—predator conflicts that involve game and livestock species. Our approach highlights the type of data that could be very informative to management if collected across a rang of cases and habitats; unquoted.

Some of you undoubtedly will speak out of tongue as you gassy for breath wondering why such an introduction has been introduced narrating this article that follows. We sometime don't know what to think. We sometime don't know what to do. Does that make us different from the norm? has our skin color change it tong or is it the voice of yesterday that sets the stage for better tomorrow? I don't know. Hey, you tell me. So, I asked what brings up to this subject of the mind, mind vs. brain or is it just being human? So, I asked human behavior, human being, human structure, human voltanic, but to say the least human struggle. If I look at you differently. Would you say that I have a problem or open mindedly a jack ass? People see you and judge you as a first impression. However, the way that you presents yourself to others that's how they judge you. Are you a dog. Are you a cat? Are you a bitch? You're the best person to answer that question. Why? Because no one know you better than yourself.

Human behavior is how we per see others. To understand human behavior we need to know makes up human. Is it our skin? Is it our sex? Is it the way we dress? Is it the way we talk? is it what we do? Good question! Yes. So, I asked, what can we learn from these questions? To behave is to obey. To be human is to be alive. To be alive is to ask questions. To ask questions is to learn. To learn is to reason. To reason is to understand. To understand is to listen. To listen is to comprehend.

Behavior is not something that you were born with. Behavior is learn. Human behavior has the in and out of intent. You intent that you are human. But yet you presents yourself like an animal. Some people might call this and I quote, the color of grey. Since, I'm no expert you tell me. We live in a civilized society and therefore we are expected to behave a certain way. We are expected to know right wrong. Well, well, ain't that a mouth full. To put it in a different way, someone who say spare me the lecture. That's what makes up human.

Being human we will make mistakes. We will say and do the wrong things. We will speak out of tongue. Some will seek education. Some will not. Some will see occupation. Some will turn to crime. If that's true we all are in deep shit. So, how do we over come such human behavior? Should the human body be dissect? Butt, what does human behavior has to do with those who are predators? Does it give them and excuse, reasons, and or justification for preying dangerously on others? Should we think that way or should we just put them out of their misery? Would that not solve the human behavior problem? Do I proclaim to be right, no, of course not. But I would like to hear from you, the readers. The truth is; everybody has rights and so does predators. If you don't infringe on my right as a human being. I will not infringe on your right to do the same. It's almost like saying; "An Eye For An Eye". That's only true if you believe in yourself.

First of all, regardless of what (predators) problems are we live within a civilized society and in doing so there are boundary of protection governing what you can and cannot do. When you speaking of (predators) over step those boundaries there are consequence punching you for your crimes and wrong doing. Human behavior, well, I would think that says a lot. Because predators preys on the young and innocent, young children and teenagers, and the week. But from what I understand everyone is a potential pray. It all depends on the purpose of their abduction and kidnapping. Have I given you something to think about? Well, there is more. Predators mentally and physically hold you in chains, holding you holistic preying on you without your knowledge, observing you up close and personal, watching your every move, and where ever you may be waiting to abduct and kidnap you.

When that happens you will not know what to do. It's too late. You have been forced into a deadly spider well helplessly struggling to relieve yourself of capture but there is no way out. Because you are now at their mercy, the mercy of the predators, standing there looking down on you, and staring cold heartdedly at your binding legs and arms. Leaving you speakless with a gab coving your mouth. It wasn't something that you expected to happened. Therefore you were not prepare to act. Well, maybe now you will not hesitate to buy this book. And again, who really knows! Maybe the safety of your child is second nature has no value and has no important. What does it mean to act? To act is to do something, to do something is to be prepare, to be prepare is to have something in mind, to have something in mind, is to plan, to plan is to think, to think is to have a clear head. When you are abducted and kidnapped your brain take over controlling your actions, feelings, emotions, mind, and your behavior.

It's almost like your body is on "lock down". You can't think. You can't move. You are speechless. You, yourself cannot do nothing. Because of whatever happened your mind is in a dejected state of delirium, and therefore cannot accept what has happened. It's almost like your waking up from a long sleep. A nightmare being in the back of a strange vehicle, tied up, drug, and a sack over your head. Next knowing where you are, not knowing who they are, "suddenly" your body awaits causing your brain to take over. "Imagine that"! Scary, it shouldn't be. It has been said, and I quote, "a soft ass makes a hard head"! Meaning you fail to listen. You should had been there for the child. You should had been more prepare and on the alert. "aware of your surrounding". So, who are the blame? He, who, they, everybody? No, no, no, Yourself. To be more clear you need to take responsibility for yourself, for your actions versus no action. do it while you still have time to think about it. Because when the gun is no longer pointed at you but now at your child "you have waited too long".

https://www.resillience.org/stories/2018-07-30/human-predators-human-prey/
Society as Ecosystem in a Time of Collapse, Part 1, and I quote; A lion runs down a gazelle; a raiding band brandishing clubs, bows, and arrows descends on a tribal village; a loan shark confronts a delinquent borrower. In each of there three scenarios one party seeks to gain at the expense of the other. Without a moment's hesitation, we classify the first interaction, between the lion and gazelle, as a predator—prey relationship. Biologists and ecologists have studied such relationships in detail for many decades, codifying principles that help us understand and predict the behavior of entire ecosystems. Could we use predator—prey relationships among widely divergent species in nature as a metaphor to help in understanding the behavior in complex human societies, in which some people gain at the expense of others?

A complex or stratified human society can be thought of an ecosystem. Within it, humans (all a single species), because of their differing social classes, roles, and occupations, can act, in effect, as different species. To the extent that some exploit others, we could say that some act as "predators", others as "prey". There may even be human analogues to subcategories of predatory behavior such as parasitism and infection.

Within non-human species in nature, forms of competition or exploitation unquestionably exist. But the extent and variety of human ways of exploiting other humans defy comparison with the behavior of any other animal; hence the "predation" metaphor.

Human groups have "preyed" upon one another via two pathways---intragroup and intergroup---which have often intersected or run parallel. Members of a complex society can "prey" upon other members of the same society via slavery (including sex slavery and debt slavery), caste, class, taxes, rents, crime, and debt; on the other hand, one society can "prey" upon a different society through raid, invasion, plunder, conquest, colonization, or (again) debt. Seeing human social role in term of "predator-prey" relationships should be interpreted as assigning superiority. In nature, one can't say that any species is superior or inferior to another on the basic of its ecological function. Hares are as important to the web of life as foxes. Nevertheless, as we'll see in a later section of this essay, some "predator" humans have created belief systems, racism) based on the notion of superiority in order to support and maintain exploitative relationships.

These belief systems have no objective basis other than their functional usefulness to "predators". In fact, seeing these belief system for what they are---efforts to justify exploitation---is an essential way to reduce their power. As human bystanders, we may admire an animal predator (such as a wolf), and may sympathize with a prey animal (such as a deer), But, taking a larger and more dispassionate view (i.e., the view of a biologist), we understand that both wolf and deer are integral to the balanced working of the larger ecosystem. In human society, however, that neutral stance must inevitably confront morality. That's because "predator-prey" relationships among humans are, again, not biologically based; they are socially constructed. Therefore they are inevitably, and always have been, subject to negotiation, moral judgment, resistance, and rebellion.

Human society currently is so complex that it may be hard to know who is "predator" and who is "prey" in any given situation. In all likelihood, most people simultaneously serve both functions in different aspects of their lives. Rather than attempting to throw specific people, groups, or occupations into mental bins, it is more useful for our purposes here to identify general systemic means of exploitation"; unquoted.

WALKING AT NIGHTS

What are we talking about? What do we want? What does it matters whether your right or wrong just make sure you take your "ass" home. Because one day you will learn not to do certain things. Some people listen and some don't. The question is; which one are you? Many children and young adults have been found in places barely alive or dead. Parents have held meeting discussing the problem with local authorities.

They talked about abandon houses, buildings, and businesses although board up but still presents a problem for the city. What problems you asked? the homeless, gangs, and gangsters, hiding out in such a place. All up to no good. Why would you want to be there? They rape, rob, all of those things but not to say the least who could you blame. That is not all they do which is something you should know. They kill, abduct you and kidnap your sister to. What a foolish game you're playing walking the streets especially at nights. Why do you go out at nights? To hang out with friends? To hang out with your boy / girl friend? To party at night clubs? Whatever your reason is its not safe.

Surely your parents have told you don't go out at nights. But of course you didn't listen. You love and crave the streets making it your second home. Why should you be so bold and live such a life, don't you know the streets are not safe, so why do such a thing, to live or die you'll have yourself the blame so yield to the warning my child and listen well or you just might end up dead. You love being out there when things happen such as fights, and of course loud music. Does it not excite you? Lucky you. Lucky me. But what a fool you will be.

You're putting your life in danger walking the streets. Your walking the streets not thinking about safety at all. The bright lights shines down on you as you walk from streets to streets, holding your purse, talking and swinging your ass from side to side. Men watching every move you make but you don't know that because your mind is in the clouds. Your walking alone having a good time when all of a sudden your life has taken a turn of death, taking you and your friends away never to be heard from again. They drug you and pulled a sack over your

head. Tied you up, arms and feet, tape over your mouth keeping you quiet, and put you and your friends into a bed. When you and your friends awakened the next morning your head felt strange not knowing who or what to blame. You and your friends were tired and weak. I guess the ride to where ever you are caused all that. But it's not over don't you know? It's just the beginning of what's going to happen to you. Open your eyes bitch and let your arms hang low. Spread your legs and get ready for the show. We have a game to play and it has just begun "you're the main prize baby" don't you know? If you mess with me I'll kill you and rape you all. It doesn't matters to me if you live or die Its just a question when and how. Do what I say not what you want; because if you try to escape know this "first" we'll chase you down like a dog ending your pain fearlessly throwing your body to the hogs. They will eat you alive tear your body apart and you would wish that you were dead from the start. So don't mess with me if you know what's good for you. Because I will kill you leaving nothing behind that's why its called a crime. When you're dead no questions are ask; is that not true or do you know, if not call someone and open the door. All your questions will be answered one by one dead or not why should I lie? People go about their business like it was yesterday playing the roll like you and me, taking care of their family and having fun because a new life has just begun.

They say when it rains it pours; is that not true? What does it all mean? Will you feel dead or will you feel alive? Here we are at the point of no return. What does we do now? Have you thought about the walking dead? How would they feel in this situation? What would they do in this situation? How does it feels to be chain up and tied to something restricting you and your freedom? Wouldn't you rather be dead? Walking together or by yourself; you have now become fresh meat of prey, for that would – be – predator waiting to abduct and kidnap you. What would you do? What would you say? A predator is less then a mile away he / she is waiting for you. So keep walking my child he'll get you. Your mother told you don't go out at nights. But you said I'm not staying home. You can't make me stay. "You can't make me stay". I guess you were right. When your parents called for you the next morning; you were no where to be found. They called the police and looked around low and behold what did they see.

Not you, not anything, nothing that could turn things around. What matters now is getting you back not just back but alive. If you wasn't so stubbing and listen to your parents, you would be home safe sleeping in your bed. The police and your parents would not be looking for you. But your stubbiness gave them no choice. The kidnappers has taken you far, far, away. Now your parents must pray for your safe return. What does it matters to you? You got your wish. To stay out all night and kick it with your friends. Well, what more can I say? They must pay the captures to get you back or risk loosening you forever "is that not true? So, home sweet home once again but what have you learned from the wind? If the wind could talk what would it say? Stay home my child walk another day. Listen to your parents and don't go astray. This might sound foolish to you but think again the whole purpose of this event to help you keeping you safe is what I do.

Sex, you male, me female. Our biological make up as a human being. To distinguish between one must be male and the other must be female. Therefore you now have "man and woman". The word sex can mean different things to different people. Generally speaking sex is more than just a three letter word. Sex is what we do. It plays an important, a role specialty, in our life as human beings. But it lack the respect that it openly deserves. We tend to associate the word sex with sex or should I say sexual intercourse, sexual pleasure, love making, feelings and emotions. The touching of the heart. How so; is it not true that when you feel sexual your heart skips a beat announcing and acknowledging the sexual pleasure of another? The interacting sexually between two people. Therefore sex is what? But on the other hand; force sex is rape. Rape is criminal. In a civilizes world a society in which we live sex is commonly an exchange of our feelings and emotions. Some people would call it over active hormone. "A desire to please the other". Predators view sex as a taken of the flesh putting you in a state of fear for your life and safety. "An at will sex by force". Your being force against your will to give freely sex to please them. That's when sex become ugly, dirty, and unclean. if you prefer to express it differently, fine, that's ok with me. But it doesn't change the fact that you were force to surrender your body unto them. Being forced raped it become a sickness, shame, embarrassment, and criminally a crime of passion. They lived among us Facelessly preying on the young and the weak. Because predators can be anyone being safe from harm is not an option. Because they are a threat to you and others. They care nothing about you. What more frightening is that He / She can be standing right next to you. "A predator can be anyone. Predators are not just males but also women. Therefore let me ask you a question. Who can you trust? Answer: trust your heart.

Trust your guts. And, trust your parents. The key word here is society. to be a society there must be people. A society without people is only land. land itself is just something to look at. Something to be admire. The purpose of the land lives within us. therefore it must mean something. It must stand for something. Now that we know what a society is we need to associate it with the goodness of mankind. What a statement! But what does all this mean? Land is earth. Earth is the ground. Predators are the stink of the earth (The face behind the mask). Because you're not going to know who they are (He / She) until they strike. No mercy for them. Maybe grief. With regard to society let them burn in hail. let us send a message. "Enough Is Enough". It must stop. Lets do a word quiz of understanding; Society barriers no fault. What hangs in the wind is the truth. Trust, belief, and salvation. To be a society you must live as people and without fear or threat of being stalk, and hunted.

https://en.wilkipedia.org/wilki/Ephebophilia
Ephebophilia, and I quote; is the primary sexual interest in mid-to-late adolescents, generally ages 15 to 19. The term was originally used in the late 19th to mid 20th century. It is one of a number of sexual preferences across age groups subsumed under the technical term chronophilia. Ephebophilia strictly denotes the preference for mid-to-late adolescents sexual partners, not the more presence of some level of sexual attraction.

Characteristics; Mid-to-late adolescents usually have physical characteristics near or identical to that of legal adults. Because of this, scholars Skye Stephens and Michael C, Seto argue that ephebophilia contracts what a paraphilia entails since "older adolescents, as reflected in self-report, psychological, and pornography use studies. Psychiatrist and sexologist Fred Berlin states that most men can find person in this age group sexually attractive, but that "of course, that doesn't mean they're going to act on it. Some men who become involved with teenagers may not have a particular disorder. Opportunity and other factors may have contributed to their behaving in the way they do". According to psychologist and sexologist James Cantor, it is "very common for regular men to be attracted to 18-year-olds or 20-year-olds. It's not unusual for a typical 16-year-old to be attractive to many men and the younger we go the fewer and fewer men ae attracted to that age group; unquoted.

WALKING IN THE WOODS

Walking in the woods is usually something entertaining, healthy, and a walk in the park. But maybe not in this case as far as we know thus far. Although that could change at anytime don't you know? Don't wait for me to show you the ropes. I'm not your guide nor your map of information, and surely its too late to turn around just don't get lost because it will be my behind. If he don't know, I don't know, who should you turn to next, maybe your mother pat her on the back surely she will lead you right. Hail, what does it matters as long as you go a walk in the wood should be safe liking baking doe. Laugh if you want I have nothing more to say go home and come back take the trails another day. I will walk with you and tell you no lie that is why we travel so far. Remember it's not uncommon to walk in the woods especially on a nice day. Something people do even when they play. The woods does attract the attention of many of us that's why people come and hang out with us.

You feel totally relax, brave the less, and as peaceful as can be its no wonder your standing against the tree. Although nothing is wrong with that what am I suppose to say maybe its you so please don't go away. Nature is where the heart is nothing more should I know when we walk in the park a voice speaks to me go west my friend and leave the rest up to me. There is nothing to be afraid of so walk on walk on but whatever you do go home go home. Walking in the woods what does it do for you? It's a way of escaping the city, and life within the mind of others. Your not looking for anything special but something usually pops up unexpected. It could be anything such as a wrong trail, a man with a gun, and an accident, to include a kidnapping or someone being abducted, killed and taken capture.
That would definitely spoil the walk in the park. Thank God for small favors. Now you wish that you would had listen to that little voice inside of you. Remember, your body give off warning signs. The problem is; we hesitate to listen to them. A walk in the woods my ass; look what has become of you. A head in the clouds bares unwanted action by others. You my man what have you to say enjoy your walk and return another day. Hey, I should send you home to think about the end because as you know we will never win. Although we try hard but that's not enough mother nature answered sending you this way telling you my child that nature is here to stay.

It's not a war that you should fight. Because walking in the woods "is that not right"! What is going to happen to us; well, no one knows. Things happens, things happens but not always in your favor. The question is; what are you going to do? Because your walk in the woods is now over. a far away house awaits you with no means of escaping. How in the hail do you plan on making it? Tears can't help you not even a scream the best thing that you can do is sleep and dream. That will help you to deal with what's going to happen next putting your heart at rest nevertheless. It's the best thing you can do for the moment right now because they will kill you and that's no lie. Don't look at me like that and please don't cry so whatever you do keep walking the trail and maybe they will fall on a nail. Should we be so lucky so you ask; just make sure you don't fall on your ass. There are natural weapons in the woods. It could be anything such as a stick, tree, hole in the ground, a poison plant, snakes, bobcats, and lot, lots more. You just has to uncloudy your mind and your head. Think like an out doorman. Think like a hunter. Pretend that you're on a survival training and kick ass. Just don't give us. The ship has not sink. Hey, who am I? It doesn't take much to spoil a day in the woods.

The kidnappers whoever they are they are out for blood. What does you expect me to do? I'm in the woods just like you. What can I do to help you? It's not a pretty picture is that not true? I can only do what I can do. These people are for real can't you see? The kidnappers don't know what's in your head. But you can help the situation and hopefully change their mind. But whatever you do don't undermine their skill because it could get you killed. Think before you act, move or fight. There is no reason to die even if its right. The kidnappers doesn't care they will rather see you die. The kidnappers doesn't care so why should I? What have you learn? What can you say? Live and let live come back another day. Let mother nature take you away but whatever you do don't let kidnappers get in your way. Be smarter than them and stay calm figure your way out even if it means using a gun. If a gun can save your life use it at will but whatever you do just don't stand still. Use whatever mother nature provides to say your life remember there is a weapon all, all around. Clear your head and fear no man it could save your life like "quick-sand. That's why we called him the sand man, well, that's not true but if you get my point it will keep you from turning blue. Again, what have you learn? What can I say? But at least you lived

to see another day. Be smart my child. Do not run and do not cry the kidnappers will shoot you in the eye. They have no sympathy not for you or for me they will put your body in the sea. You will never be heard of or ever be seem again. Your parents would be worry about you until the day ends. But nevertheless it is what it is and there is nothing you can do to change their mind your going to die its just a matter of time. What goes through your mind when you're abducted and kidnapped in the woods? Most people asked; what are you going to do? Why are you doing this to me? What do you want from me? Where are you taking me? Some few fundamental gone unanswered.

Everyone knows how it feels to go walking in the woods. You can have cook outs, fish, and hake all about trailing in all directions to entertain our ego as you look in around at the trees, plants, flowers, and most importantly the mountains so far away. The fresh air can just take your breath away. a swim in the lake, the river enjoying the breathless cool water of the sea. What a beautiful it all means to me. But there is danger all around you a wrong turn perhaps could end your day. Because those woods your in has many trails therefore whatever happens can happen to anyone. Hey, I don't have all the answers but one thing for sure someone does. Make no misstate about it anyone can get abducted and kidnap in the woods. You will not know what to do. You will not know what to think. You'll be too afraid and confuse to move. Your not going to know what to expect. Your entire surrounding will be unfamiliar and strange. So now you asked; what's next? Answer; that depends on you.

https://en.wilkipedial.org/wilki/Mental_disorder
Mental Disorder, and I quote; also called a mental illness or psychiatric disorder, is a behavior or mental pattern that causes significant distress or impairment of personal functioning. Such features may be persistent, relapsing and remitting, or occur as a single episode. Many disorders have been described, with signs and symptoms that vary widely between specific disorders. Such as may be diagnosed by a mental health professional. The causes of mental disorders are often unclear. Theories may incorporate findings from a range of fields. Mental disorders are usually defined by a combination of how a person behaves, feels, perceives, or thinks. This may be associated with particular regions or functions of the brain, often in a social context. A mental disorder is one aspect of mental health. Cultural and religious beliefs, as well as social norms, should be taken into account when making a diagnosis. Treatment are provided by various mental health professionals. Psychotherapy and psychiatric medication are two major treatment options. Other treatments include lifestyle changes, social interventions, peer support, and self-help.

According to DSM-IV, a mental disorder is a psychological syndrome or pattern which is associated with distress (e.g. via a painful symptom), disability (impairment in one or more important areas of functioning), increased risk of death, or causes a significant loss of autonomy; however it excludes normal responses such as grief from loss of loved one, and also excludes deviant behavior for political, religious, or social reasons not arising from a dysfunction in the individual.

The terms "mental breakdown" or nervous breakdown" may be used by the general population to mean a mental disorder. The terms "nervous breakdown" and "mental breakdown" have not been formally defined through a medical diagnostic system such as the DSM-5 or ICD-10, and are nearly absent from scientific literature regarding mental illness. Although "nervous breakdown" is not rigorously defined, surveys of laypersons suggest that the term refers to a specific acute time-limited reactive disorder, involving symptoms such as anxiety or depression, usually precipitated by extended stressors. Illness

About half of them are depressed. Or at least that is the diagnosis that they got when they were put on antidepressants ….. They go to work but they are unhappy and uncomfortable; They are somewhat anxious; they are tired; they have physical pains—and they tend to obsess about the whole business. They have various physical pains—and they tend to obsess abut the whole business. There is a term for what they have, and it is a good old-fashioned term that has gone out of use. They have nerves or a nervous illness. It is an illness not just of the mind or brain, but a disorder of the entire body; unquoted.

Interview with "you" the people
First of all; I am not trying to be politically correct posting articles of interest and vending my personal point of view. But it is what it is. You and no other can change that. You don't has to like what I say. Hopefully you will draw your own conclusion. Since no one make up is the same the structure of your body, sole, and mind will answer the call. Too long have we waited to do the right thing with regard to protecting our love ones (our child). Too long have we stood there and done nothing. Too have we look around and said nothing is going on. Too long have we said that my child can take care of him/herself and were wrong. Too long have we closed our eyes and look the other way. We as parents need to wake up. We need to focus on the health, safety, and protection of our children. This is why I am speaking to you today as you read my book. Open your eyes and listen! I am pouring out my heart to you. I published this book for you. We could call it a brainstorm, and material of interest.

Once you start reading this book and various subject matters you should hopefully understand the nature, and content of what has been written. But most importantly the material should cause you to ask questions. I felt that you the reader should open up and enlighten your mind of understanding broaden your need for logic with regard to the society in which we live as human beings. We as human beings tend to take life for granted. We tend to take each other for granted. We see the world as an empty planted, and therefore thinks negative when it come to things that we should had already known
Such as being aware of your surroundings, how to identify a potential predator, signs to watch out for, where not to go, what not to wear, how late to stay out, when not to hitch hike, who not to ride with, who not to talk to, how to approach strangers, when to say no /stop, whose a friend and whose not, when not to open your door, and why you should not walk along.

As parents, you have many questions such as; Is my child safe, can I trust my myself to leave my child home alone, Can I trust my child to do the right thing, will my child be next to be abducted / kidnap, will my child know what to do if they are abducted / kidnap, Is my child smart enough to escape from the abductors / kidnappers, Will I ever see my child again, Will the abductors / kidnappers demand a ramson. Why did I wait now to care about the safety of my child, how serious does the police take abduction / kidnapping, (a question that all parents should ask themselves), will the police give up hope of finding my child, will I have to hire a private investigator to find my child, will my child be find alive and safe, (only time will determine that), how do I know that my child will not be dead, should I stop my child from using the computer and social media, what can I do to make my child understand that danger awaits them and that anyone can be a predator,

Most importantly as parents you should give them an opportunity to be heard, and to ask questions. By them asking questions; they will understand more clearly what you're trying to say to them. "call it breaking the ice"

https://en.wilkipedia.org/wilki/John_Money
John Money, and I quote; was a New Zealand American psychologist, sexologist and author specializing in research into sexual identity and biology of gender. He was one of the first researchers to publish theories on

the influence of societal construct of "gender" on individual formation of gender identity. Money introduced the terms gender identity, gender role and sexual orientation and popularized the term paraphilia. Recent academic studies have criticized Money's work in many respects, particularly in regard to his involvement with the involvement sex-reassignment of the child David Reimer, his forcing this child and his brother to simulate sex acts which Money photographed and the adult suicides of both brothers.

Money proposed and developed several theories and related terminology, including gender identity, gender role, gender-identity / role and lovemap. He popularized the term paraphilia (appearing in the DSM-III, which would later replace perversions) and introduced the term sexual orientation in place of sexual preference, arguing that attraction is not necessarily a matter of free choice. Money's definition of gender is based on his understanding of sex differences among human beings. According to Money, the fact that one sex produces ova and the other sex produces sperm is the irreducible criterion of sex difference. However, there are other sex-derivative differences that follows in the wake of this primary dichotomy. These differences involves the way urine is expelled from the human body and other questions of sexual dimorphism. According to Money's theory, sex-adjunctive differences are typified by the smaller size of females and their problems in moving around while nursing infants.

How can one argue this point when the structure of the female body is in fact different from that of the male body. However each having its own purpose and function with respect to the other. If you think about it that's what makes us who we are without drawing attention to the obvious. Our brain for instance speaks for itself; we do not feel and or think alike. We do not see things the same way. We do not dress alike. We do not have the same sex organs. Hey, I could say more but I'm sure that you get the picture. Women, generally speaking are thought to be smarter than men. As for age is concern more intelligent. "Go Figure"! This then makes it more likely that the males do the roaming and hunting. Sex-arbitrary differences are those that are purely conventional: for example, color selection (baby blue for boys, pink for girls).

Finally, Money created the now-common term gender role which he differentiated from the concept of the more traditional terminology sex role. This grew out of his studies of hermaphrodites. According to Money, the genitalia and erotic sexual role were now, by his definition, to be included under the more general term "gender role" including all the non-gender and non-erotic activities that are defined by the conventions of society to apply to males and females; unquoted.

WHEN A WOMAN GOES OUT LOOKING FOR A MAN
(I look forward to)

When a woman goes out looking for a man; she calls Jake and she calls Sam. She dress her best as sexy as can be showing her ass to you and to me. She put on high – hill shoes, showing her long legs and stockings, and her ass to boot. Showing her ass to all like animals in the zoo. She is a tall woman with panty-hoses on "alligator style" wearing a very sexy dress causing everyone to smile. When she walks, she shake and bake twisting her ass from side to side showing her long legs. Men are watching near and far as she walks to her car. She takes out her keys. They drops to the ground. She bends over to pick them up showing her behind. The wind started to blow capturing her keys blowing them under her car, and across the streets. She saw a guy going after her keys picking them up while eating cheese. He walked up to her looking her up and down. Before she could say anything he's touching her behind. She stood there in shock staring at him. She grabbed his cock squeezing it hard. The pain, the pain; he's yelled out loud. Please let go my penis I'll bother you no more.

Here are your keys take them and go. Get your bloody hands off my stroke. Pretty girl, got back her keys. She opened her door, again, her keys falls down. But this time they falls down inside the car. She bends over inside the car looking for them wearing only panty-hoses sticking out into the wind. Lucky for her a man came along someone she knew long time ago. He found her keys and gave them to her. She kissed him, squeezing his cock, and invited him over at eight O' clock. Eight O' clock comes and there is a knock on the door. She's in the shower bathing herself. He rings the door bell but no one comes. She goes to the door naked with everything hanging out. Her breath bouncing and in an attention like a stick. Her ass is round free as a kite. He stares down at her with delight. She walks closely up on him dropping all that matters the most. Hands hanging down low as she stares sexually into his deep blue eyes. Her heart is beating fast as her legs trimable. Forcing her emotions to run wildly as her hands pulls him very closely touching her booty squeezing her tightly spreading the love between them.

you can't handle the heat get out of the kitchen. Well, that might whole true in this case. She is starting to let go. She is starting to giver in. She has let her hair down but only for him. They have evade the predator thinking not about him. They have out smart the predator by keeping a low profile. She and her man sworn not to die. They know what to expect. They know what to do. So, if I can say this; and of course I will. The predator, the predator is no threat to them. It's not who you talk to. It's not what you say. It's who you know; and knows you the best. The bottom line you must be safe. Monkey see. Monkey do. Hey Mr. Predator where are you? Hey Mr. Predator what have you to say? Don't you think this is a beautiful day? Look how green the grass is and flowers growing. They looked so beautiful in the sun. This is a day that God has made. He don't need you to get in the way. We should bless this day even predators to because we don't live in a zoo. Roses are red and violets are blue. Our life Mr. Predator how precious it is. It means a lot to me even if not to you.

I have a life to live whether you like it or not. I have a life to live and children to grow. I have a life to live and school to look forward to. I look forward to marriage and traveling the world. I look forward to doing all these things and more. I look forward to marrying the man of my dream so please Mr. Predator don't take that away from me. This man in my life stands tall and strong. Hey Mr Predator, what can go wrong? Hey, Mr. Predator, there is so much I still need to do. I love my family; what more should I say? It cleanse my heart to live another. life Mr. Predator you have no respect for. That explains everything about you. You fail Mr. Predator to see the truth. That's why your going down Mr. Predator is that not the truth? This world Mr. Predator is not only about you. Maybe you should back off while you can. Young people today wants nothing to do with you. Your not going to make our children feel blue. Whether or not that's true only time will tell get out of my life Mr. Predator and go to hell.

https://www.ncbi.nlm.nih.gov/pmc/articles/PMC2763392/
The Future of Psychology: Connecting Mind to Brain, by Lisa Feldman Barrett, and I quote; Psychological states as thoughts and feelings are real. Brain states are real. The problem is that the two are not real in the same way, creating the mind-brain correspondence problem. In this article, I present a possible solution to this problem that involves two suggestions. First, complex psychological states such as emotion and cognition an be thought of as constructed events that can be causally reduced to a set of more basic, psychologically primitive ingredients that are more clearly respected by the brain. Second, complex psychological categories like emotion and cognition are the phenomena that require explanation in psychology, and, therefore, they cannot be abandoned by science.

The difficulty in linking the human mind and behavior on the one hand and the brain on the other is rooted, ironically enough, in the way the human brain itself works. Human brains categorize continuously, effortlessly, and relentlessly. Categorization plays a fundamental role in every human activity, including science. Categorizing functions like a chisel, dividing up the sensory world into figure and ground, lending us to attend to certain features and to ignore others. Via the process of categorization, the brain transforms only some sensory stimulation into information. To categorize something is to render it meaningful. it then becomes possible to make reasonable inferences about that thing, to predict what to do with it, and to communicate our experience of it to other.

The brain's compulsion to categorize presents certain unavoidable challenges to what can be learned about the natural world from human observation. Psychologists know that people don't contribute to their perceptions of the world in a natural way. Human brains do not dispassionately look on the world and carve nature at its joints. Even the most basic categories in psychology appear to be observer dependent. Take, for example, behaviors (which are intentional, bounded events) and actions (which are descriptions of physical movements). We easily and effortlessly see behaviors in people and in nonhuman animals. We typically believe that behaviors exist and are there to be detected, but not created, by the human brain. Behaviors are actions with a meaning that is inferred by an observer. Social psychology has accumulated a large and nuanced body of research on how people come to see the physical actions of others as meaningful behaviors by referring the causes for those actions (usually by imputing an intentions to the actor; for a review. Let me be clear about what I am saying here---it is a brute fact that the brain contains neurons that fire to create mental states or cause behavior and this occurs independent of human experience and measurement. In real life, however, there are no independent variables. Our brains (not an experimenter) help to determine what is a stimulus and what is not, in part by predicting what will be important in the future; unquoted.

https://en.wikipedia.org/wiki/Human_behavio#-text=Human behavior is the potential, stimuli throughout their life.

Human Behavior, and I quote; is the potential and expressed capacity (mentally, physically, and socially) of human individual or groups to one's personality, temperament, and genetics may be more consistent, other behaviors will change as one moves along different stages of their life, i. e, from birth through adolescence, adulthood, and, for example, parenthood and retirement. Behavior is also driven, in part, by thoughts and feelings, which provide insight into individual psyche, revealing such things as attitude and values. Human behavior is shaped by psychological traits, as personality type vary from person to person, producing different actions and behavior. Extraverted people, for instance, are more likely than introverted people to participate in social activities like parties. The behavior of humans (just as of other organisms) falls upon a spectrum, whereby some behaviors are common while others unusual, and some are acceptable while others beyond acceptable limits. The acceptability of behavior depends heavily upon social norms and is regulated by various means of social control, partly due to the inherently conformist nature of human society in general. Thus, social norms also condition behavior, whereby humans are presented into following certain rules and displaying certain behaviors that are deemed acceptable or unacceptable depending on the given society or culture.

Human behavior is studied by the social sciences, which include psychology, sociology, economics, and anthropology. In sociology, behavior may broadly refer to all basic human actions, including those which possess no meaning; actions directed at no person. Behavior in this general sense should not be mistaken with social behavior.

Religion and Spirituality

Another important aspect of human behavior is religion and spirituality. According to a Pew Research Center report, 54% of adults around the world state that religion is very important in their lives. Religion plays a large role in the lives of many people around the world, and it affects their behavior toward others.

Weather and Climate

The weather and climate have a significant influence on human behavior. The average temperature of a country affects its traditions and people's everyday routines. For example, Spain used to be a primarily agrarian country, with much of its labour force working in the fields. Spaniards developed the tradition of the siesta, an after-lunch nap, to cope with the intense midday heat. The siesta persists despite the increased use of air conditioning and the move from farming to office jobs. However, it is less common today than in the past; unquoted.

https://www.aetv.com/real-crime/why-do-some-people-kidnap-kids

REAL CRIME; What Drives Some People to Kidnap Children, by C.M. Frankie, and I quote; "I want to be somewhere else, but I am here and I must not panic". Jaycee Dugard wrote in her memoir, which described 18 years of pain and brutality at the hands of kidnapper Philip Garrido.

The sex-crime parolee abducted the sunny 11 year old in 1991 while she walked to her school bus stop in northern California.

"it hurts more when I try to struggle, so I try not to get away from him. Everything will be okay. I tell myself. He will be the nice person soon, "Dugard recounts in A Stolen Life.

The specter of menacing stranger seizing a child like Dugard—or snatching fifth grader Jeanine from her Chicago-area home in 1983----haunts many parents.

The trigger to an abduction "can be as simple as a custody battle, "says Geoffrey Greif, a professor at the University of Maryland School of Social Work.

The U.S. Department of Justice in 2002 studied family abductions involving 203,900 children and found the majority 53 percent-involved biological fathers taking their children. Biological mother's kidnapped their children in 25 percent of the cases. When marriages sour, the parent without custody may seek revenge on his or her ex.

Tips to the Jacksonville sheriff's office led to the eventual arrest of Williams in 2017. Manigo has defended the woman she thought was her mother. "She took care of everything I ever needed. "Manigo said.

Three of the five victims of stereotypical child kidnappings in 2011 were sexually abused, assaulted or exploited, the OJJD report states.

Psychosis and happenstance put serial killer Brian Dugan in Jeanine Nicarico's path in February 1983.

The bubby 10-year-old had the flu, and her parents kept her home for the day while they worked.

Dugan, out on parole for arson and burglary, was looking for an easy burglary when he cruised by the Nicaricos' house in Naperville, a Chicago suburb He realized Jeanine was alone and kicked the door in. Dragging the girl to his car, he later assaulted and beat her to death with a tire iron on a hiking trail.

When tips led investigators to Garrido, she likened the experience to "breaking an evil spell".

"I know that I am not the only child to be hurt by a crazy adult. "she writes. "My goal is to inspire people to speak out when they see that something is not quite right around them".

But children face an even more prevalent danger; sexual abuse by adults. The National Center for Victims of Crime finds that one in five girls and in 20 boys is a victim of child sexual abuse.

That's why experts urge parent to go beyond conventional warnings like "don't talk to strangers".
If you want to protect your kids from abuse". Finkelhor says, you need to talk to them about touching rules and explain—if someone wants to touch you in certain parts of your body—that's wrong".

Say you're marrying a man, and I don't like him". Greif says. "Our daughter comes to me and says "that man comes into my bedroom at night and I don't want him to. "If legal recourse offers no protection, he adds. "at what point, does a parent decide to break the law?

In 70 percent of family abductions, children were returned in a month or less. But in 6 percent of all cases, the child was found but not returned; and in 3 percent the child was never located.

Among those children still missing is Timmothy Pitzen, a 6 year old from Aurora, Illinois, whose mother Amy Fry-Pitzen signed her son out of school May 11, 2011, citing a family emergency.

Mother and son went on a mini-vacation, visiting the zoo and a water park. On May 14, 2011, a maid found Fry-Pitzen dead in a motel room in Rockford, Illinois. Timmothy had vanished—and his mother had left a disquieting note.

"Tim is somewhere safe with people who love him and will take care of him. You will never find him", she wrote.

The little boy's blood was found in Fry-Pitzen's car, but relatives haven't given up hope.

Mental illness factors into 9 percent of "stereotypical abductions", where children are taken by a slight acquaintance or a stranger, according to a U.S. Office of Juvenile Justice and Delinquency Prevention report. Sometime abduction can result from acute emotional distress. For Gloria Williams, who masqueraded as a nurse at a Jacksonville, Florida, hospital and walked off with newborn Kamiyah Mobley in July 1998, the crime was an impromptu act. It occurred, Williams testified, on the heels of a miscarriage, abuse by her boyfriend and the loss of her two sons in a custody fight.
Sex trafficking is big business. Globally, it generates ten of billions of dollars in profit every year. Here in the United States, it ensnares hundreds of thousands of victims. And while the stereotypical image of a trafficking victim is a foreign national, many of the exploited are underage American girls.

"if you're a victim of a sex crime, it makes you VULNERABLE", says Lewis. "In some scenarios, that's what they know. That's how they know to survive, and how to keep someone from threatening or harming them".

"The trafficker is thinking of this as a way to make money,' Williamson tells A&E Real Crime. They want to take that child and start making money as quickly as possible. So if they can get a kid who already know what's expected of them, it's going to be faster—as opposed to a kid who has never had sex or never been victimized before.

One particular treacherous place, says Williamson, is social media. There are two major reasons the internet is such a rich trolling ground for sex traffickers, she says.

The first is the willingness of the young to share their vulnerabilities with the online world, unwittingly allowing predators to recognize them as potential targets.

"Online, you can scroll through profiles and you can oftentimes figure out who is in child welfare, who has a foster parent, who has been involved in juvenile justice or recently out of the hospital for suicidal ", ideation, she says.

Sex traffickers will pose online as young attractive men to better improve chances of making an online connection, Williamson says, and then will linger for an extended stretch of time; liking photographs, commending on posts, making themselves feel familiar to their target. "to get you used to it and to desensitize you.

A commonly held (and sensational) idea about sex trafficking is that it starts with a kidnapping; a young girl forced into a windowless van, then driven across state borders, where she's fed drugs and kept locked up in a brothel. And while cases like that do exist, they're more an exception rather than the rule. says Lewis.

Traffickers "can be anything from a girlfriend, a boyfriend, to a family member—they can be someone who recruits their victims through online gaming, "says Lewis.

"Typically there's a moment at which things change ", Williamson says. "We've had kids….who literally vanish across state lines. They might end up in a hotel, where (the perpetrator) might rape her—they might immediately put them out (on the streets)…sometime it's gang rape.

But the coercion can take many forms; a foster parent telling youth they have to contribute toward rent, or a threat to target a young person's sister if they refuse to do as told; unquoted.

The brain versus the mind, is there a different? Even so, what different does it make? What different does anything make since we tend to take things for granted? Nothing bothers us until something happens. Then suddenly you now have something to say. Your mouth opens up. Your eyes looks out into open space. The tone of your voice sounds like a barking dog. Your hands turns into claws. Everything now about you has changed. Your listening to the radio and hears an amber alert someone gone missing. Your heart skip a beat. Your mouth closes tightly. Your body freezes can't move. Out of the blue someone shakes you asking what's wrong. You wake up staring into space as if you were hit by a train. Your not sure what happened. But without a doubt something is wrong. In one word and abduction and a kidnapping took place.

What a shock! We feel safe within the walls of our resident. We feel safe when others are around. We feel safe when our parents are home. My question is, how safe are you? Are you really safe at anytime? Are you safe in groups? Are you safe inside a vehicle? Are you safe within the walls of your resident? First of all, to be safe is to feel safe. House is a dwelling. A dwelling is a place to stay. For you to be abducted and kidnapped you must be a person of interest. You must be someone they want. They therefore have a purpose in mind. You became their target. You became their pray. To abduct and kidnap is to take without consent, without permission, and without knowledge of the other. To abduct you means to take you. To kidnap means to take you. To take you where is not important. The whole ideal is to take you from where you are to an unknown place of familiarization. No matter how you got there it doesn't change the fact that you were taken against your will.

You may feel that you did the right thing but deep down your wrong. Because you have just created a serious problem with the other person. Your now running, driving off with the child, and thinking that you're going to get away. What make you think that you are? Your trait is not without fault because your trail is fresh. Evidence of the crime has been left behind. It's just a matter of time, days, when the law lash on and catch up with you. So, let me ask you one question. Was it worse it? What do you expect to gain? How far do you think that your going to get? Have you heard of Amber Alert? Have you heard of the TV? Have you heard of the Radio? Here is a question for you. Why did you do it? When a person abduct and kidnap a child their not thinking about the consequences or the big hands of the law. Only getting the child. How far they can get away. Their not worry too much about anything else. Because they feel that they are home free once you the victim is in their hands of control. You have now became their borrowing chip. Your now their ticket from hell cross country piece of mind. Why? Because their not being chase by the law. No one know where they are. No one know who they are. they plan on keeping it that way.

A little information that you may want to know; never if abducted and or kidnapped look at their face. If they catch you looking at their face. You will surely unless there is a guardian angel somewhere you will be killed. If they do catch you looking at their face; cry like a baby and beg for mercy. If blinders are covering your face or just your eyes. No, no, no, do not take them off. If they ask if you can see them say No. Even if they call you a liar continue to say No. You need to be very convening. REMEMBER THIS; Being abducted and kidnapped is like playing Hide and Seek. Think of something, anything that might help you to get word to your parents, friend, and the law Enforcement Authorities. Think of it like a game. Playing such a game. What are we looking for? Clues. A clue can be anything; such as the ground, marking on the ground, sticks, rocks, small trees, bushes, dead animal, cave, old abandoned house, river, boat, something that belongs to a man or a woman, noise, smoke, trail, color of something, particular smell, anything that you can think of will help. Since you cannot out run them maybe not even be able to get free then REMEMBER THIS: YOU WILL NEED TO OUT SMART THEM. It's almost like the saying; if you can't be them join them. But in this case you will need to out smart them. Doing so might just save your life. Remember; time is of the essence.

Why Men Might Kidnap and Abduct Children

1. He has a problem with the mother
2. Something happened so now they can't see eye to eye.
3. Fights, Arguments
4. Betrayal, cheating, gambling problem
5. Falling out of love and affection for each other
6. One wants to get marry and the other does not
7. Girl friend, wife lack of attention
8. She wants a divorce

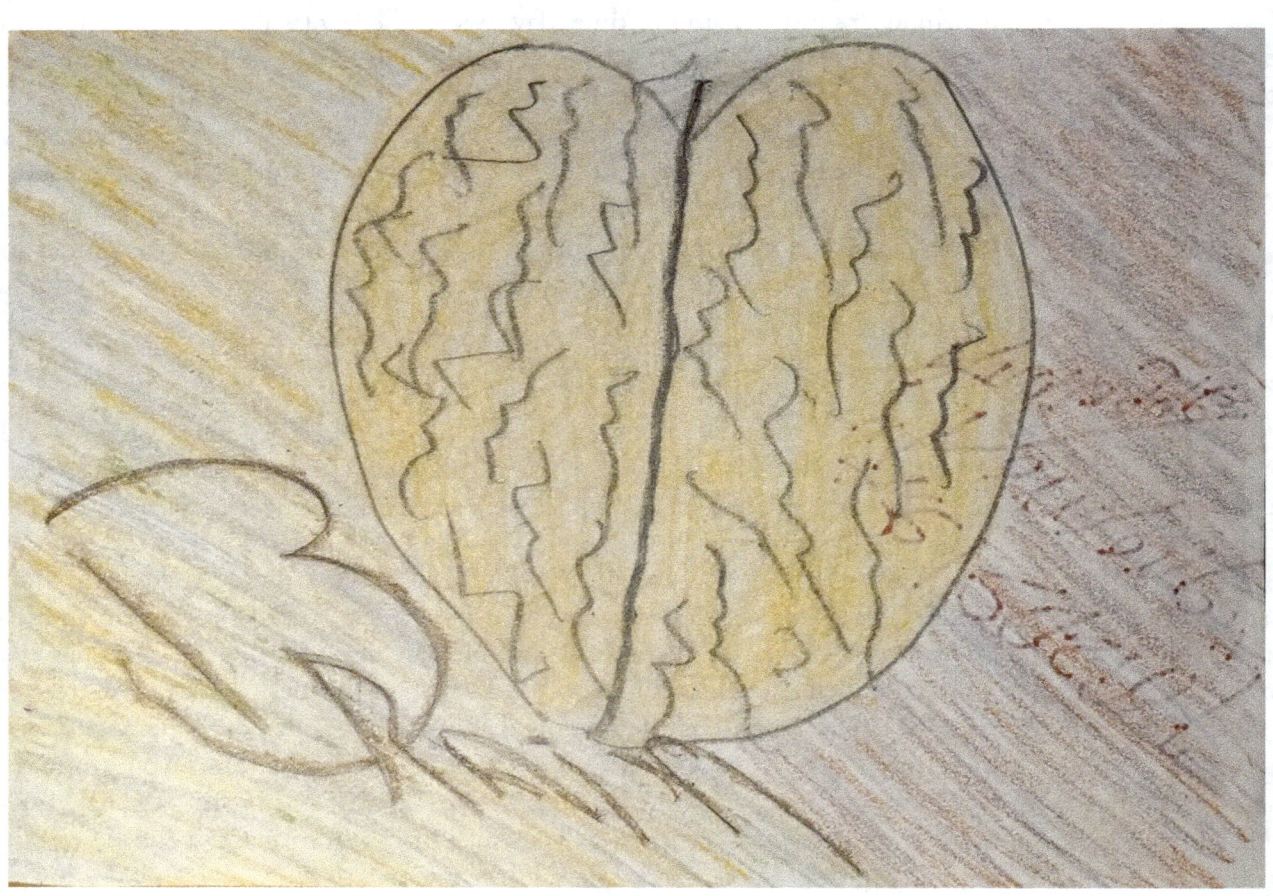

9. She wants full custody of the child / children
10. He sees her as a non-fit mom, and financially not able to care for the child / children
11. She is an alcoholic and smokes too much
12. She is a drug user.
13. When she get drunk she turns violent
14. She is abusive toward the child / children
15. She uses profanity when talking to the child / children
16. She is suicidal
17. She can't cook
18. She let her Boy Friend molest the child / children
19. She is violent
20. She gets angry a lot
21. She pays no attention to the child / children
22. She is a poor housekeeper
23. The kitchen sink is always full of dishes (unless I wash them)
24. She refuse to work (very lazy)
25. She's asking for too much money for child support
26. She will not let me visit the child / children
27. She will not let them talk to me
28. She is always calling me a dead-beat dad
29. She's a whore and a prostitute
30. She will not agree to anything

Why Women Might Kidnap and Abduct Children

1. He malediction me -want to control me
2. He tries to make a fool out of me
3. He tries to make people think that's something wrong with me
4. He is hard up for sex (wants it all the time)
5. H tries to make people think that I am not a good mother
6. Always complaining to my friends
7. Calling my parents too much
8. Cries like a baby when he can't get his way
9. Wants to have sex with me without protection
10. Tell other men to have sex with me (meretricious)
11. He's always late picking up the child / children
12. He sometime do not show at all
13. When we go out with the child / children I must pay
14. He's always short of money
15. He's physically abusive, violent, and hits me
16. He has no patient with the child / children (yells at them)
17. Wants to have sex with me (where doesn't make a different) even in the present of the child /children
18. When I say No / Stop. He gets very angry and pulls the covers off me
19. He has bad habits – smokes at the table. Eats with his mouth open. Must have a beer at every meal. He slammed doors when upset. He disrespect me a lot calling me stupid, stinky breath, shit face.

When two people married or perhaps Single, has a child / children and can't get along it's time to seek help from family, friends, professional such as clergy, marriage counselor, and may even a stranger. It really doesn't matters "who" as long as you seek help. Because other lives are involved, and their health, and welfare should come first. When you raise war on each other (battle station) you literally does the same on your child / children (they are one outside looking in observing the two of you) A smart man once said; "It's not over until its over". Why is that? Because when the dust clears the child / children usually ends up getting hurt. You have now put them in an awkward spot to choose between the two of you. "That's not a good thing". Resentment has now has set in causing the child / children to re-act to whatever has transpire between the two of you in court. "Now the clock is ticking".

How to protect a child from predators

To protect a child from predators you need to think like a child -to think like a child -you need to do childness things – to do childness things – need to act like a child -to act like a child -need to imagine yourself as a child. Walk in their shoes. Do what they would do. Go where they would go. Create a mirror of protection. Than ask yourself this one question. What would I do to protect my child / children from the hands of predators and danger?

Child abduction or child theft is the unauthorized removal of a minor (a child under the age of legal adulthood) from the custody of the child's natural or legally appointed guardians. The term child abduction includes two legal and social categories which differ by their perpetrating contexts: abduction by members of the child's family or abduction by strangers:

- Parental child abduction is the unauthorized custody of a child by a family relative (usually one or both parents) without parental agreement and contrary to family law ruling, which may have removed the child from the care, access and contact of the other parent and family side. Occurring around parental separation or divorce, such parental or familial child abduction may include parental alienation, a form of child abuse seeking to disconnect a child from targeted parent and denigrated side of family. This is by far, the most common form of child abduction.
- Abduction or kidnapping by strangers (by people unknown to the child and outside the child's family) is rare. Some of the reasons why a stranger might kidnap and unknown child include:
- Extortion to elicit a ransom from the parents for the child's return
- Illegal adoption, a stranger steals a child with the intent to rear the child as their own or to sell to a prospective adoptive parent.
- Human trafficking, stealing a child with the intent to exploit the child themselves or through trade to someone who will abuse the child through slavery, forced labor, or sexual abuse.

By far the most common kind of child abduction is parental child abduction (200,000 in 2010 alone). It often occurs when the parents separate or begin divorce proceedings. A parent may remove or retain the child from the other seeking to gain an advantage in expected or pending child – custody proceedings or because that parent fears losing the child in those expected or pending child – custody proceedings; a parent may refuse to return a child at the end of an access visit or may flee with the child to prevent an access visit or fear of domestic violence and abuse. Parental child abductions may result in the child be kept within the same city, within the state or region, within the same country, or sometimes may result in the child being taken to a different country.

Most parental abductions are resolved fairly quickly. Studies performed for the U.S. Department of Justice's Office of Juvenile Justice and Delinquency Prevention reported that in 1999, 53% percent of family abducted children were gone less than one week, and 21% were one month or more. Parental abduction has been characterized as child abuse, when seen from the perspective of the kidnapped child.

International child abduction occurs when a parent, relative or acquaintance of a child leaves the country with the child in violation of a custody decree or visitation order. Another related situation is retention where children are taken on an alleged vacation to a foreign county and are not returned. While the number of cases which is over 600, 000 a year consists of international child abduction is small in comparison to domestic cases, they are often the most difficult to resolve due to the involvement of conflicting international jurisdictions. Two-thirds of international parental abduction cases involves mothers who often allege domestic violence. Even when there is a treaty agreement for the return of a child, the court may be reluctant to return the child if the return could result in the permanent separation of the child from their primary caregiver.

This could occur if the abducting parent faced criminal prosecution or deportation by returning the child to child's home country. The Hague Convention on the Civil Aspects of International Child Abduction is an International human rights treaty and legal mechanism to recover children abducted to another country. The Hague Convention does not provide relief in many cases, resulting in some parents hiring private parties to recover their children. Covert recovery was first made public when Don Feeney, a former Delta Commando, responded to a desperate mother's plea to locate and recover her daughter from Jordan in the 1980's. Feeney successfully located and returned the child. A movies and book about Feeney's exploits lead to other desperate parents seeking him out for recovery services.

By 2007, both the United States, European authorities, and NGO's had begun serious interest in the use of mediation as a mean by which some international child abduction cases may be resolved. The primary focus was on Hague Cases. Development of mediation in Hague cases, suitable for such an approach, had been tested and reported by REUNITE, a London Based NGO which provides support in international child abduction cases, as successful. Their reported success lead to the first international training for cross-border mediation in 2008, sponsored by NCMEC, HELD at the University of Miami School of Law, Lawyers, Judges, and certified mediators interested in international child abduction cases, attended.

BY STRANGER TO RAISE

A very small number of abductions result from – in most cases – women who kidnap babies (or other young children)to bring up as their own. These women are often unable to have children of their own, or have miscarried, and seek to satisfy their unmet psychological need by abducting a child rather than by adopting. The crime is often premeditated, with the woman often simulating pregnancy to reduce suspicious when a baby suddenly appears in the household.

Historically, a few states have practiced child abduction for indoctrination, as a form of punishment for political opponents, or for profit. Notable cases include the kidnapping of children Nazi Germany (400,000 children kidnapped for possible Germanization), the lost children of Francoism, during which an estimated 300,000 children were abducted from their parents. Some other abductions have been to make children available by child – selling for adoption by other people, without adopting parents necessarily being aware of how children were actually made available for adoption.

ABDUCTION BEFORE BIRTH

Neonatal infant abduction and parental fatal abduction are the earliest ages of abduction, when child is expansively defined as a viable baby before birth (through the age of majority (the age at which a is as).

CHRONOPHILIA

The term chronophilia was used by John Money to describe a form of paraphilia in which an individual experiences sexual attraction limited to individuals age ranges. The term has not been widely adopted by sexologists, who instead use terms that refer to the specific age range in question. An arguable historical precursor was Richard von Krafft-Ebing's concept of "age fetishiam.

Pedohebephilia refers to an expansion and reclassification of pedophilia and hebephilia with subgroups, proposed during the development of the DSM-5, it refers more broadly to sexual attractions. Under the proposed revisions, people who are dysfunctional as a result of it would be diagnosed with pedohebephilic disorder. People would be broken down into types based on the idea of being attracted to one, the other or both of the subgroups. Infantophilia (sometimes called nepiophilia) is a subtype of pedophilia describing a sexual preference for children less than 5 years old (including toddlers and infants).

Pedophilia is a psychological disorder in which an adult or older adolescent experiences a sexual preference for prepubescent children. According to the fifth edition of the Diagnostic and Statistical Manuel of Mental Disorders (DSM-5), pedopohilia is a paraphilia in which a person has intense sexual urges toward children, and experiences recurrent sexual urges toward and fantasies about children. Pedophilic disorder is further defined as psychological disorder in which a person meets the criterial for pedophilia above, and also either acts upon those urges, or else experiences distress or interpersonal difficulty as a consequence. The diagnosis can be made under the DSM or ICD criteria for persons age 16 and older. Not all pedophilies commit child sexual abuse, and not all child molesters are pedophiles.

https;//en.wilkipedia.org/wiki/Pedophilia#Definitions
Pedophilia emerges before or during puberty, and stable over time. It is self-discovered, not chosen. For these reasons, pedophilia has been described as a disorder of sexual preference, phenomenologically similar to a heterosexual or homosexual orientation. These observations, however, do not exclude pedophilia from the group of mental disorders because pedophilic acts cause harm, and mental health professionals can sometime help pedophiles to refrain from harming children. I think without the need of this word Pedophilia, we all have a sexual preference male prefer female, female prefer male. But now that we must use the word "Other" that may have changed. I could put it differently but what sense would it make? Because you are what you are. You are who you are. Enough has been said. You keep your dress on. I'll keep my pant on. Because you can't wear both at the same time. In response to misinterpretations that the American Psychiatric Association considers pedophilia a sexual orientation because of wording in the printed DSM-5, manual, which distinguishes between paraphilia and what it calls "paraphilic disorder" subsequently forming a division of pedophilia" and pedophilic disorder", the association commented; Sexual orientation is not a term used in the diagnostic criteria for pedophilic disorder and its use in the DSM-5 text discussion is an error and should read 'sexual interest.' They added, in fact, APA considers pedophilic disorder a 'paraphilia, not a sexual orientation. This error will be corrected in the electronic version of DSM-5 and the next printing of the manual. They said they strongly support efforts to criminally prosecute those who sexually abuse and exploit children and adolescents, and "also support continued efforts to develop treatment for those with pedophilic disorder with the goal of preventing future acts of abuse.

COMORBIDITY AND PERSONALITY TRAITS

Studies of pedophilia in child sex offenders often report that it co-occurs with other psychopathologies, such as low self-esteem, depression, anxiety, and personality problems. It is not clear whether these are features of the disorder itself, artifacts of sampling bias, or consequences of being identified as a sex offender. One review of the literature concluded that research on personality correlates and psychopathology in pedophiles is rarely methodologically correct, in part owing to confusion between pedophiles and child sex offenders, as well as the difficulty of obtaining a representative, community sample of pedophiles. Seto (2004) Points out that pedophiles who are available from as clinical setting are likely there because of distress over their sexual preference or pressure from others. This increase the likelihood that they will show psychological problems. Similarly, pedophiles recruited from a correctional setting have been convicted of a crime, making it more likely that they will show anti-social characteristics.

Impaired self-concept and interpersonal functioning were reported in a sample of child sex offenders who met the diagnostic criteria for pedophilic by Cohen et al. (2002), which the authors suggested could contribute to motivation for pedophilic acts. The pedophilic offenders in the study had elevated psychopathy and cognitive distortions compared to healthy community controls. This was interpreted as underlying their failure to inhibit their criminal behavior. Studies in 2009 and 2012 found that non-pedophilic child sex offenders exhibited psychopathy, but pedophiles did not. Wilson and Cox (1983) studied the characteristics of a group of pedophile club members. The most marked different between pedophiles and controls were on the introversion scale, with pedophiles showing elevated shyness, sensitivity and depression. "The pedophiles scored higher on neuroticism and psychoticism, but not enough to be considered pathological as a group. The authors caution that "there is a difficulty in untangling cause and effect.

We cannot tell whether paedophile gravitate toward children because, being highly introverted, they find the company of children less threatening than that of adults, or whether the social withdrawal implied by their introversion Is a result of the isolation engendered by their preference ie. Awareness of the social disapprobation and hostility that it evokes". In a non-clinical survey, 46% of pedophiles reported that they had seriously considered suicide for reasons related to their sexual interest, 32% planned to carry it out, and 13% had already attempted it. A review of qualitative research studies published between 1982 and 2001 concluded that child sexual abusers use cognitive distortions to meet personal needs, justifying abuse by making excuses, redefining their actions as love and mutuality, and exploiting, the power imbalance inherent in all adult—child relationships. Other cognitive distortions include the idea of "children as sexual entitlement-bias.

Pedophile views of child pornography are often obsessive about collecting, organizing, categorizing, and labeling their child pornography collection according to age, gender, sex act and fantasy. According to FBI agent Ken Lanning, "collecting" pornography does not mean that they merely view pornography, but that they save it, "it comes to define, fuel, and validate their most cherished sexual fantasies. Lanning states that the collection is the single best indicator of what the offender wants to do, but not necessarily of what has or will be done. Researchers Taylor and Quayle reported that pedophilic collectors of child pornography are often involved in anonymous interest communities dedicated to extending their collections.

CAUSES

Although what causes pedophilia is not yet known, researchers began reporting, a series of findings linking pedophilia with brain structure and function, beginning, in 2002. Testing individuals from a variety of referral sources inside and outside the criminal justice system as well as controls, these studies found associations between pedophilia and lower IQ, poorer scores on memory test, greater rates of non-right-handedness, greater rates of school grade failure over and above the IQ differences, lesser physical height, greater probability of having suffered childhood head injuries resulting in unconsciousness, and several differences in MRI-detected brain structures.

Such studies suggest that there are one or more neurological characteristics present at birth that cause or increase the likelihood of being pedophilic. Some studies have found that pedophiles are less cognitively impaired than non-pedophilic child molesters. A 2011 study reported that pedophilic child molesters had deficits in response inhibition, but no deficits in memory or cognitive flexibility. Evidence of familial transmittability: "suggests, but does not prove that genetic factors are responsible" for the development of pedophilia.

Inpatients" may be altered by disturbance in the prefrontal networks, which "may be associated with stimulus-controlled behaviors, such as sexual compulsive behaviours". The findings may also" a at of.

The ICK-10 defines pedophilia as "a sexual preference for children, boys or girls or both, usually of prepubertal or early pubertal age. Like the DSM, this system's criteria require that the person be at least 16 years of age or older before being diagnosed as a pedophile. the person must also have a persistent or predominant sexual preference for prepubescent children at least five years younger than them. The ICK-11 defines pedophilic disorder as "sustained, focused, and intense pattern of sexual arousal—as manifested by persistent sexual thoughts, fantasies, urges, or behaviours—involving, prepubertal children. It also states that for a diagnosis of pedophilic disorder, "the individual must have acted on these thought, fantasies or urges or be markedly distressed by them. This diagnosis does not apply to sexual behaviours among pre-or post -pubertal children with peers who are close in age.

Neither the DSM nor the ICD-11 diagnostic criteria require actual sexual activity with a prepubescent youth. The diagnosis can therefore be made based on the presence of fantasies or sexual urges even if they have been acted upon. on the other hand, a person who acts upon these urges yet experiences no distress about their fantasies or urges can also qualify for the diagnosis. Acting on sexual urges is not limited to overt sex acts for purposes of this diagnosis, and can sometimes include indecent exposure, voyeuristic or frotteuristic behaviors, or masturbating to child pornography. Often, these behaviors need to be considered in-context with an element of clinical judgment before a diagnosis is made. Likewise, when the patient is in late adolescence, the age difference is not specified in hard numbers and instead requires careful consideration of the situation.

BEHAVIORAL INTERVENTIONS

Behavioral treatments target sexual arousal to children, using satiation and aversion techniques to suppress sexual arousal to children and convert sensitization (or masturbatory reconditioning) to increase sexual arousal to adults. Behavioral treatments appear to have an effect on sexual arousal interests during phallometric testing, but it is not known whether the effect represents changes in sexual interests or changes in the ability to control genital disabilities, applied behavior analysis has been used. Pharmacological interventions are used to lower

the sex drive in general, which can erase the management of pedophilic feelings, but does not change sexual preference. Antiandrogens work by interfering with the activity of testosterone. Cyproterone acetate (Androcur) and medroxprogesterone but few high-quality studies exist. Cyproterone acetate has the strongest evidence for reducing sexual arousal, while findings on medroxyprogesterone acetate have been mixed. Ok; everyone of us male and female alike become sexual arouse. Therefore at some point we are sexual attracted to the other. But, the question is; who are we attracted to children or adults? Hear a question that rings a bell; who do they say that I am? To be more clear; who am I, and what am I? In today's society; it's sometime very difficult to distinguish males from females. Why; because we have cross dressers. For instance, we have Vertebrates, Homosexuality, and Hermaphroditism.

Gonadotropin-releasing hormone analogues such as leuprorelin (Lupron), which last longer and have fewer side-effects, are also used to reduce libido, as are selective serotonin reuptake inhibitors. The evidence for these alternatives is more limited and mostly based on open trials and case studies. All of these treatments, commonly referred to as "chemical castration", are often used in conjunction with cognitive behavioral therapy. According to the Association for the "Treatment of Sexual Abusers, and counseling within a comprehensive treatment plan.

Pedophilia and Child Molestation

The prevalence of pedophilia in the general population is not known, but is estimated to be lower than 5% among adult men. less is known about the prevalence of pedophilia in women, but there are case reported of women with strong sexual fantasies and urges toward children. Most sexual offenders against children are male. Females may account for 0.4% to 4% of convicted sexual offenders, and one study estimate a 10 to 1 ratio of male-to-female child molesters. The true number of female child molesters may be underrepresented by available estimates, for reasons including, a societal tendency to dismiss the negative impact of sexual relationships between young boys and girls and adult women, as well as women's greater access to very young children who cannot report their abuse", among other explanations. In Psychopathia Sexualis, the term appears in a section titled "Violation of Individuals Under the age of Fourteen", which focuses on the forensic psychiatry aspect of child sexual offenders in general. Krafft-Ebing describes several typologies of offender, dividing them into psychopathological and non-psychopathological origins, and hypothesizes several apparent causal factors that may lead to the sexual abuse of children.

Krafft-Ebing mentioned paedophilia erotica in a typology of "psycho-sexual perversion". He wrote that he had only encountered it four times in his career and gave brief descriptions of each case, listing three common traits:

1. The individual is tainted (by heredity) heredital belastete.
2. The subject's primary attraction is to children, rather than adults.
3. The acts committed by the subject are typically not intercourse, but rather involve inappropriate touching or manipulating the child into performing an act on the subject.

Further clarifying this point, he indicated that cases of adult men who have some medical or neurological disorder and abuse a male child are not true pedophilia and that, in his observation, victims of such men tended to be older and pubescent. He also lists pseudopaedophilia as a subsequently turns to children for the gratification of their sexual appetite" and claimed this is much more common.

Law and Forensic Psychology

Pedophilia is not a legal term, and having a sexual attraction to children is not illegal. In law enforcement circles, the term pedophile is sometimes used informally to refer to any person who commits one or more sexual-based crimes that relates to legally underage victims. These crimes may include child sexual abuse, statutory rape, offenses involving child pornography, child grooming, stalking, and indecent exposure. One unit of the United Kingdom's Child Abuse Investigation Command is known as the "Paedophile Unit" and specializes in online investigations and enforcement works. Some forensic science texts, such as Holmes (2008), use the term to refer to offenders who target child victims, even when such children are not the primary sexual interest of the offender. FBI agent Kenneth Lanning, however, makes a point of distinguishing between pedophiles and child molesters.

Civil and Legal Commitment

In the United States, following Kansas v. Hendricks, sex offenders who have certain mental disorders, including pedophilia, can be subject to indefinite civil commitment under various state laws (generically) called SVP laws and the federal Adam Walsh Child Protection and Safety Act of 2006.

In Kansas v. Hendricks, the US Supreme Court upheld as constitutional a Kansas law, the Sexually Violent Predator Act, under which Hendricks, a pedophile, was found to have a "mental abnormality defined as a "congenital or acquired condition affecting the emotional or volitional capacity which predisposes the person to commit sexually violent offenses to the degree that such person is a menace to the health and safety of others", which allowed the State to confine Hendricks indefinitely irrespective of whether the State provided any treatment to him.

In United State v. Comstock, this type of indefinite confinement was upheld for someone previously convicted on child pornography charges; this time a federal law was involved— the Adam Walsh Child Protection and Safety Act. The Walsh Act does not require a conviction on a sex offense charge, but only that the person be a federal prisoner, and one who "has engaged or attempted to engage in sexually violent conduct or child molestation and who is sexually dangerous to others", and who "would have serious difficulty in refraining from sexually violent conduct or child molestation if released. In the US, offenders with pedophilia are more likely to be recommended for civil commitment than non-pedophilic offenders. About half of committed offenders have a diagnosis of pedophilia. Psychiatrist Michael First writes that, since not all people with a paraphilia have difficulty controlling their behavior, the evaluating clinician must present additional evidence of volitional impairment instead of recommending commitment based on pedophilia alone. Society and Culture Social attitudes toward child sexual abuse are extremely negative, with some surveys ranking it as morally worse than murder. Early research showed that there are a great deal of misunderstanding and unrealistic perceptions in the general public about child sexual abuse and pedophiles; unquoted.

With respect to credit and recognition of this material I acknowledged the content and nature of THE ENCYCLOPEDIA OF (SEXUAL BEHAVIOR), Copyright in 9161 by Hawborn Books, Inc, Copyright under International and Pan-American Copyright Conventions.

Pornography and Art

Pornography, and I quote, is a term that was originally used to describe prostitutes and their trade but has in recent years been employed to describe literature or art that has been created with the deliberate intention of arousing sexual desire. It is often confused with erotic realism. Thus, some of the descriptions in James Joyce's

Ulyssed or some of the vitally alive nudes of Renoir or Pascin may arouse the most lascivious thoughts in certain readers or viewers; but this does not seem to have been the conscious intent of the creators of these descriptions or portrayals. As Forel (1922) points out, Greek art was enormously concerned with the nude female figure; but most of this art was far from being pornographic or "obscene", since the intention of the artist was to idealize the female form rather than to arouse sexual thoughts and fancies. The field of art and sex is usually complicated because the word sex has multiple meanings when used in relation to art.

1. Sex-depicting but noneroitic art. A considerable number of works of painting and sculpture depict or involve sexual content but do so in a nondynamic or nonarousing way. The majority of the better known examples of Greek nudes, for example, are sexual, in that they depict the feminine form, but they are not erotic, in that they do not arouse the sex impulses of the average viewers. The kiss, is sex-depicting (because it deals with sex-love processes) but not particularly, to most viewers, erotic or sex-arousing (because it is relatively objectively descriptive or self-contained rather than dynamically excitative). The kiss may also be deemed to be on the borderline of the two categories of sex depiction and sex arousal because (a) size-able minority of viewers may become sexually aroused by it and (b) an ever larger number of viewers may become amatively or emotionally (rather then sexually) aroused bi its GLORIFICATION OF YOUNG LOVE.

2. Sex-arousing or erotic but nonpornograhic art. A great many works of art not only depict sexual content but do so in a dynamic or arousing manner. Thus, Manet's Dejeuner sur l'herbe shows a nude in the company of several young Frenchmen and depicts the girl and her companions so that the average viewer's phantasies tends to move out from the time and place of the painting and to use it as a jumping-off point for his personal sex imaginings. The "peep-show" aspect of semi-nudity is drotic because it expresses the dynamism of undressing rather than the state of nudity.

3. Sex-arousing art or erotic and pornographic art. Sex-arousing art may be created by an artist who has little ideal of the potential arouseability of his work or who wishes to stimulate his viewers esthetically or emotionally and who employs deliberately sex-arousing themes to effect this end. Thus, if Rodin's male in The Kiss had his hands on the female's buttocks or genitals his status would be violently erotic but not necessarily pornographic; while if the female had been having active intercourse with the male or had been with another male the status would be pornographic. So, I say to you. Watch out for your children.

4. Know where they are at all times. Teach them protective skills and to be on the lookout for potential abductors and kidnappers. Because children are sometime snatch from under your wings and forced into prostitution. Say what you want but its true. TO DO NOTHING MEANS YOU DON'T CARE. BUT YOU WILL CARE WHEN IT HAPPENS TO YOUR CHILD. THAT PERSON COULD BE RIGHT UDNER YOUR NOSE THE PERSON YOU'RE TALKING TO! DON'T BE FOOL BY A SMILE. DON'T BE MISLEAD BY A FRIENDLY FACE; unquoted.

Child Sexuality, and I quote,
Freud held that the period of childhood personality development is divided into three stages, each of which is dominated by sexual tendencies. These sexual proclivities are in the nature of instinctual, unlearned urges and the goal of each is the hedonistic one of pleasure. Each tendency seeks its inevitable end in its culminating goal, or aim, of sensual gratification. Sexual Parts and Sexual Play, and I quote, Most frequently the sexual play of children appears to be with companions of approximately the same age (whether of the same or opposite sex), For the boys there is a steady increase in the total incicence of childhood sex play until adolescence. For girls there is a trend to be come more reticent in such play in the later years of childhood. For most of the girls

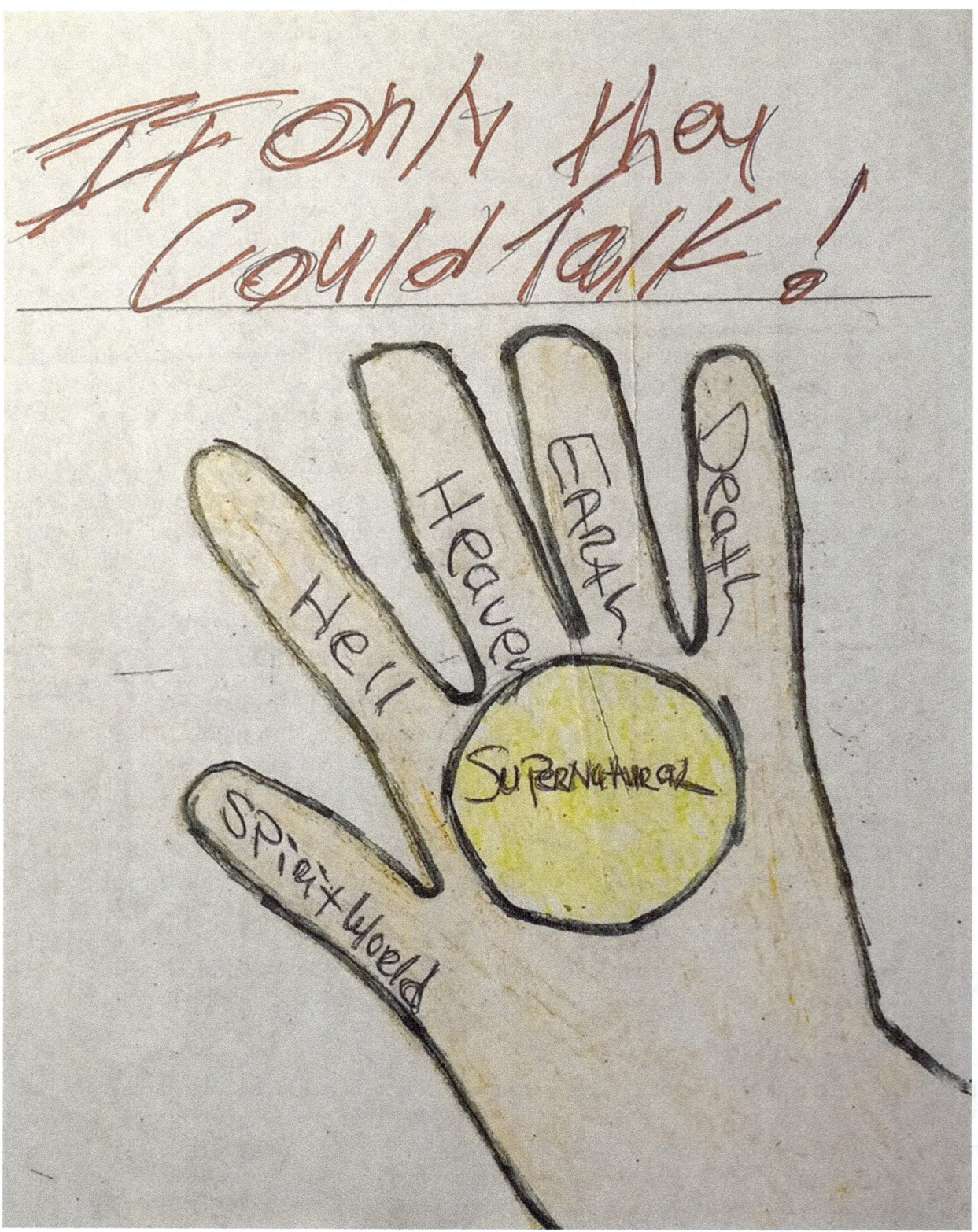

who are involved in heterosexual play such contacts of all types are confined to a time span of one year or less. Homosexual Play in the female sex is reported for very few children before 3 years if age but there is a steady increase from about 6 per cent at the age of 5 to 33 per cent at adolescence. For both sexes, manual manipulation is the sort of homosexual play next in order of incidence and in the records of children with homosexual play, 62 per cent of the girls and 67.4 per cent of the boys reported having had some such activity. For the girls just as in the case of heterosexual play, the homosexual play is in the great majority of case confined to one year of life and often to one or two such experiences; unquoted.

https://en.wikipedia.org/wiki/Intersex

Intersex, and I quote, people are individuals born with any of several variations in sex characteristics including chromosomes, gonads, sex hormones or genitals that, according to the UN Office of the High Commissioner for Human Rights, "do not fit the typical definitions for male or female bodies". This range of atypical variation may be physically obvious from birth – babies may have ambiguous reproductive organs, or at the other extreme range it is not obvious and may remain unknown to people all their lives. Intersex people were previously referred to as hermaphrodites or "congenital eunuchs". In the 19th and 20th centuries, some medical experts devised new nomenclature in an attempt to classify the characteristic that they had observed. It was the first attempt at creating a taxonomic classification syst4m of intersex conditions. Intersex people were categorized as either having true hermaphroditism, female pseudohermaphroditism, or male pseudohermaphroditism. These terms were no longer used: terms including the word "hermaphrodite" are considered to be misleading, stigmatizing, and scientifically specious in reference to humans. A hermaphrodite is now defined as "an animal or plant having both male and female reproductive organs". In 1917, Richard Goldschmidt created the term intersexuality to refer to a variety of physical sex ambiguities. In clinical settings, the term "disorders of sex development" (DSD) has been used since 2006.

Intersex people face stigmatization and discrimination from birth, or from discovery of an intersex trait, such as from puberty. This may include infanticide, abandonment and the stigmatization of families. Globally, some intersex infants and children, such as those with ambiguous outer genitalia, are surgically or hormonally altered to create more socially acceptable sex characteristics. However, this is considered controversial, with no firm evidence of favorable outcomes. Such treatments may involve sterilization. Adults, including elite female athletes, have also been subjects of such treatment. Increasingly, these issues are considered human rights abuses, with statements from international, and national human rights and ethics institutions (see intersex human rights). Intersex organizations have also issued statements about human rights violations, including the 2013 Malta declaration of the third International Intersex Forum. Some intersex persons may be assigned and raised as a girl or boy but then identify with another gender later in life, while most continue to identify with their assigned sex. In 2011, Christiane Volling became the first intersex person known to have successfully sued for damages in a case brought for non-consensual surgical interventions. In April 2015, Malta became the first country to outlaw |non-consenual medical interventions to modify sex anatomy, including that of intersex people.

Intersex people are born with sex characteristics (including, genitals, gonads and chromosome patterns) that do not fit typical binary notions of male or female bodies. Intersex is an umbrella term used to describe a wide range of natural bodily variations. In some cases, intersex traits are visible at birth while in others, they are not apparent until puberty. Some chromosomal intersex variations may not be physically apparent at all. According to World Health Organization: Intersex is defined as a congenital anomaly of the reproductive and sexual system. An estimate about the birth prevalence of intersex is difficult to make because there are no concrete parameters to the definition of intersex. People whose characteristics are not either all typically male or all females at birth are intersex. Some intersex traits are not always visible at birth; some babies may be born with ambiguous genitals, while others may have ambiguous internal organs (testes and ovaries). Others will not become aware that they are intersex unless they receive genetic testing, because it does not manifest in their phenotype.

LGBT and LGBT1

Intersex can be contrasted with Transgender), which is the condition in which one's gender identity does not match one's assigned sex. Some people are both intersex and Transgender. In an analysis of the use of preimplantation genetic diagnosis to eliminate intersex traits, Behrmann and Ravitsky state: "Parental choice against intersex may…..conceal biases against same-sex attractedness and gender nonconformity. The relationship of intersex to lesbian, gay, bisexual and queer communities is complex, but intersex people are often added to LGBT1 community. Organization Intersex International Australia states that some intersex individuals are same sex attracted, and some are heterosexual, but "LGBT1 activism has fought for the rights of people who fall outside of expected binary sex and gender norms.

SIGNS

There are a variety of symptoms that can occur. Ambiguous genitalia being the most common sign, there can be micropenis, clitoromegaly, partial Labial fusion, electrolyte abnormalities, delayed or absent puberty, unexpected changes at puberty, hypospadias, Labial or inguinal (groin) masses (which may turn out to be testes) in girls and undescended testes (which may turn out to be ovaries) in boys.

OTHER SIGNS

XX Intersex

This condition used to be called "female pseudohroditism", Person with this condition have female internal genitalia and karyotype (XX) and various degree of external genitalia virilization.

XY Intersex

This condition used to be called "male pseudohermaphroditism"', This is defined as incomplete masculinization of the external genitalia. Thus the person has the chromosomes of a man, but the external genitals are incompletely formed, ambiguous, or clearly female.

True gonadal intersex

This condition used to be called "true hermaphroditism". This is defined as having asymmetrical gonads with ovarian and testicular differentiation on either sides separately or combined as ovotestis.

Complex or undetermined or undetermined intersex

This is the condition of having any chromosome configurations rather than 46, XX or 46, XY intersex. This condition does not result in any imbalance between internal and external genitalia; unquoted.

This article that follows structed an urging nerve within me causing my heart to skip a beat lighting a fire storm of feelings as the ashes of the fallout drops to the ground attaching themselves the unborn wondering of the world to come. It's a strange feeling no doubt but what can one say when the devil walks the land by day and by night living a life fully out of sight not wanting others to know what they really are keeping it a secret from other family members and friends. A culture one would say base on whatever, religions, and or the family history from which it was birth bringing forth a new way of life, a life of secrecy and shame. Heart skip a beat, well. that don't usually happen. But what can I say? We chose to be this way. I don't know sometime what my heart directs me to write. But when I come across something of interest there is no stopping me from doing the right thing even if it hurts, even if it hurts the pain will soon go away. But it's always something that you should know. Who other then me should let you know? There is so much that we as parents, and as human beings does not know or have knowledge of until someone like myself reveals it to you. You as a writer or should I say me, will never know the ideology of such material until research is accomplished. Some in fact can cause you to bite your tongue grinding your teeth to the guns due to the nature of the content of the material as in this case. What am I talking about; to make it clear (1) incest, (2) taboo, and (3) intersex. God in question has his version of right vs wrong. To be told and to be inform. Whether or not you have the stomach for such material is irreverent. It could be something that you already know about but prefer not to talk about. Each of us live our life according to morals vs immoral, to include family history, culture, the Bible, religion, and strong belief. This material if nothing more should open your awareness, your eyes, to what might be happening around you. Because from darkness comes light. It's true; there are a lot of things that you don't know. It's even whole true with me writing this story, and at the same time opening your eyes. For the record; I do not condemn what others do. But two wrongs don't make a right. But you should know what's going on within your community, neighborhood, and most importantly within your family. I am not the enemy nor your whipping stick causing pain. The two articles that follows are some what related. God has something to say (let God be heard).

https://www.bibletools.org/index.cfm/useaction/topical.show/RTD/cgg/ID/2013/Satan-as-Predator.htm
What the Bible says about Satan as Predator
(From Forerunner Commentary)

Proverbs 6:30-21

This begins a long section of instruction regarding adultery, and harlotry. The first warning is to protect one's heart---not one's body-----from her because the body follows that heart's lusts. Since Babylon, the Great Whore, is our spiritual temptation, this is a veiled admoniton to steer clear of Babylon. Verse 26 reveals her predatory nature; she preys upon the precious lives of her victims like a cat preys on birds. Satan, the father of Babylon and its ways, "walks about like a roaring lion, seeking whom he may devour".

John W. Ritenbaugh
The Beast and Babylon (Part Nine): Babylon the Great

1 Peter 5:8

The great deceiver, more often than not, works under cover of darkness. As a skilled and experienced hunter, he patiently stalks his prey, invisible to them d(invisible is about as camouflaged as one can get). His night vision is acute, his senses much sharper than ours. He sees us when we do not even know he is there.

Even now, he is stalking su.

Lifted up in their pride, he and his demons had the gall to hunt God's throne, but they were soundly routed (Isaiah 14:12-15; Ezekiel 28:16-17; Luke 10:18). Now, as our adversaries, they hut God's people, trying to pick off the weak, the ailing, and those who have grown weary and dropped back from the herd. He is always looking for a way to maneuver us into a position by ourselves where he leap out of nowhere to maul us. Once he attacks,

he causes great pain---but he does not go immediately for the kill. He pins us down and wounds us first. Even while in his grasp, though, we can call out for help. "The LORD is near to all who call upon him, …He also hears their cry, and saves them".

Mike Ford
Stalked by Satan

Christ is also symbolized as a lion, but not as a lion seeking to devour. Lion for Christ is used in the sense of "controlled, majestic power", but for Satan it is the symbol for one who is ruthless, stealthy, powerfully aggressive, bent on defending its turf, and destruction, often working from ambush. There are many similarities with the attributes of the "serpent".

A pride of lions will stalk and attack animals that are larger than they are---including wildebeest and water buffalo weighing thousands of pounds. it is a beautiful, deadly sight to watch lions working together as a team to bring a water buffalo down.

When lions attacks, they do so through multiple attacks from every side. Eventually, one lion gets a grip on the throat of the water buffalo and kills it by strangulation. |It is a slow and painful death.

John W. Ritenbaugh
The Spiritual Mark of the Beast

This rebellion at the end of the Millennium is often overlooked in the joy of considering Christ's wonderful rule. Satan's influence is so powerful he can influence millions of people to follow him seemingly overnight. Having drawn away a third of the angels from God (Revelation 12:4; Isaiah 14:12-14) and overcome Adam and Eve, he has wielded almost total control over man.

His present power will be greatly magnified very shortly when he is cast down to earth to begin the Great Tribulation. He would deceive the very elect if it were possible (Matthew 24:24). It is no wonder Peter instructs us to be sober, to be vigilant, to resist Satan in faith that Christ might establish us in the end!

1 Peter 5:8-9

This verse indicates that there is little room for carelessness. We are being called upon to be thoroughly self—controlled and to be alert. Why? Because Satan aims to undermine our confidence, to sow discord, and to get us to stop believing and revert to carnality. These are the directions in which he will try to push us.

Notice Peter writes, "Whom he may devour. "May" indicates permission is given. He has the ability to devour us spiritually, but it does not have to happen. Putting the advice in verse 8 into more common language, instead of saying. "Be sober ", we might say, "Keep cool", Keep your head screwed on right", "Don't lose your presence of mind", "Try to keep calm about this", Don't be fearful", or "Don't lose your temper".

He also says to "Be vigilant ", which means "to watch". This same phraseology is used in reference to prayer. It is part of our responsibility to pray that we are not enter into temptation.

All of these things—the roaring lion, the resisting, the afflictions, suffering, persecution, perfection, and strength—are related as parts of operations that fulfill God's purpose for us. We have to begin by understanding that Satan—despite his incredible intelligence, cleverness, and power—is still yet an unwitting dupe in God's hands to bring about His purpose. God is far more powerful than Satan.

1 Peter 5:8-9

Satan is a formidable enemy, to be sure, but in a personal sense, he is not as directly dangerous to us as the world or our own human nature. The chance of his confronting us individually are small in comparison to the influence of our ever-present hearts and the world in which we conduct our lives. Certainly, as our Adversary, he "walks about like a roaring lion, seeking whom he may devour" (1 Peter 5:8). but unlike God. he is not omniscient. While he can be only at one place at one time, he has many assistants.

We are far more likely to be confronted by one of his demons assistants than the Adversary himself, which is bad enough. However, he and his demons have constructed attitudes, institutions, systems, and entertainments into the course of this world, which they effectively use against us, even when they are absent from the scene. Most of their evil influence comes from the system.

We need to remember, though, that God has put a wall of protection around us, so demons can go only so far in their attempts to corrupt us and destroy our loyalty to God and His truth (Job 1:6-10). Their major responsibility before God at this time appears to be to provide tests for us to meet and overcome, in the same way God used Satan to test Job and to tempt Christ (Matthew 4; Luke 4). In this respect, they play a large role in helping us to recognize evil.

God gives us advice regarding them in 1Peter 5:8-9: "Be sober, be vigilant; because your adversary the devil walks like a roaring lion, seeking whom he may devour. Resist him, steadfast in that faith, knowing that the same sufferings are experienced by your brotherhood in the world". In essence, His advice is, "Be self-controlled, be alert, and resist him" Peter's first term, "be sober", urges us not to let fear of him fluster us to the point that we cannot think clearly. The second term, "be vigilant ", charges us to be fully awake, to set ourselves in a state of watchfulness and readiness. The third term, "resist him", is a command not to turn and run but to stand firm.

James 4:7 adds additional advice: "Therefore submit to God. Resist the devil and he will flee from you. "Again, the charge is to resist, but it is directly coupled with submission to God. Submission is the voluntarily act of placing oneself under the authority of another to show respect and give obedience. if we submit to God, Satan will flee.

Ephesians 6:11 parallels the other two instructions. "Put on the whole armor of God, that you may be able to stand against the wiles of the devil. "Stand against" is yet another way of saying "resist him". "Stand" in the Greek indicates that one must hold fast a critical position as an army must do in warfare. However, it is not a passive term, describing something like an unmoving brick wall, but an aggressive, attacking term.

We have the God-backed promise that Satan will flee! Who can resist God's will? The key words here are "standing firm" and "faith" or "solid" is used in the sense of "unmovable" When linked with faith in practical terms, it means we are absolutely sure or immovably convicted in the face of a strong test; unquoted.

https://www.bibletools.org/index.cfm/fuseaction/Topical.show/RTD/ID/4219/Communication-from-Evil-influences.htm

Genesis 1:26-31

In the beginning, Adam and Eve were not created with the evil nature we see displayed in all of mankind. At the end of the sixth day of creation, God took pleasure in all the hand made and pronounced it "very good", including Adam and Eve and the nature or the heart He placed in them. An evil heart cannot possibly be termed "very good". They were a blank slate, one might say, with a slight pull toward the self, but not with the strong, self-centered, touchy, and offensive heart that is communicated through contact with the world following birth.

Comparing our contact with Stan to Adam and Eve's a sobering aspect is that God shows they were fully aware of Satan when he communicated with them. However, we realize that a spirit being can communicate with a human by transferring thoughts, and the person might never know it!

Following their encounter with the evil one, "the eyes of both of them were opened, and they knew that they were naked". Genesis 3: 7). This indicates an immediate change in their attitudes and perspectives. It also implies a change of character from the way God had created them, as hey had indeed willingly sinned, thus reinforcing the whole, degenerative process.

Six thousand years of human history exhibit that we very quickly absorb the course of the world around us and lose our innocence, becoming self—centered and deceived like everybody else (Revelation 12: 9). The vast majority in this world utterly unaware that they are in bondage to Satan – so unaware that most would scoff if told so.

https://www.bibletools.org/index.cfm/fuseaction/Topical.show/RTD/CGG/ID/3513/Garden-of-Eden.htm
What the Bible says about Garden of Eden

The word Eden in Hebrew means "delight" or" enjoyment"---t was a garden of delight or enjoyment. When the Septuagint Version was produced, its translators used the Greek word for "parkland" for Eden, from which came the word "paradise". In the Old Testament, Eden is often a symbol of great fertility, a place where things would grow. In other words, its environment was not only beautiful but also useful for producing things. In this case, God had in mind not merely an environment for vegetation, but for a relationship through fellowship—between God and Adam and Eve, who represented all of mankind. Spiritually, Eden symbolizes a rich and fertile place of unbroken fellowship.

Genesis 2:15

The Garden of Eden was the environment that God created for a relationship with him to take place. Adam and Eve's responsibility was to dress and keep it. They were put there, not to do nothing, not just to pluck fruit off a tree, not even merely to receive life, but to take care of the Garden.

Dress means "to embellish. "This may seen a little strange, but Adam and Eve were to take care of it so well that it would become better than it was when God gave it to them. We like to think of the Garden as being a place of absolute and perfect beauty. Instead, since God told them to "dress and keep it," it seems that it was not

complete. It had only been started. What he had done was certainly beautiful, not He wanted them to carry on and finish it.

Sexual Contacts with Adults, and I quote, Most of the literature given information about the incidence and frequency of sexual approaches of adults to children concentrates on the female sex. In all probability this reflects the Western cultural concern with the taboo of virginity as it relates to the female and is also indirectly an expression of the double standard of sexuality. Although there is no rational or factual reason for an increasing concern about this matter of sexual contacts of adults with children, there is still a widely held belief that all such contacts with the child are universally damaging to personality, character, future sexual adjustment, and future marital adjustment. The most frequent type of contact made by the male was that of showing his genitals organs, which occurred in 52 per cent of the cases that report contact with adults; unquoted. I wasn't quite sure of how to introduce these articles due to the nature of the material. Some people would call you a nut. And, would ask are you mad or out of your head? It stands to reason taking into consideration everything that has already been said. Therefore, why shouldn't I reveal the sin of human kindness when it goes beyond the boundaries of the norms.

Is it not worse talking about and acknowledging? But as I continue with the introduction of these articles focus on these words and phrases: RAPE, INCEST, TABOO, PROHIBITION, PSYCHOBIOLOGICAL, FORBIDDEN, CONSECRATED, VICTIM, SEXUAL INTERCOURSE. Because I know that the general public is probably not ready to feed on such a thing as this. Does it not exist? Is it not on youtube? If that's true! You therefore cannot say its not happening. It happens at the turn of a blind eye and behind closed doors. So, I asked you the question. What color is black or should I say whose the rat? There are a lot of things that we as parents and human beings do not know about, and therefore has no knowledge of or insight about. But those of you who are physically and active "you know what I'm taking about". Now that the cat is out the bag. Wouldn't you say its time to spill the beans? This my opinion; it's a crime against nature and should be dealt with, with tender loving care (without taking off the gloves).

It's not something that we should walk away from or assume its not happening. What are we talking about? "WOW"; Incest and taboo. Incest and taboo is something that most people probably don't want to hear about. Because it relates to sex, not just sex, but sexual intercourse, sexual affairs, with member of the same family to include children. Exploitation is a far cry from incest and taboo. However, two wrongs don't make a right. Some of this material you're about to read associates incest and taboo with various cultures, and religion. The purpose of these articles is to inform you the public just how blind and twisted we are as human beings. We turn a blind eye to what's wrong around us as if it doesn't exist. But if we don't do something about it. It will go away nor will it stop. A hardcore understanding expressing and explaining the meaning of these words will shock the world. It's not a normal thing a person would do. In essence its considered rape, rape in the worse way; and charges can and will be pressed against you. But, lets looks at this in another way. Keep in mind that this story is about "PREDATORS"; wouldn't you not say that whoever participates in incest and taboo is also a predator? Wouldn't you not say that? After all relatives and family members are being "Preyed" on sexually. This I would say is a wake up call to another form being a "PREDATOR". This is a predator of the worse kind (it lives with you). It could be anyone. The most frightening thing is that (it could be anyone). I asked that you pay attention to the articles that follows because this person could be you "giving" a new meaning to the word "PREDATOR".

https://en.wikipedia. Org/wiki/Taboo
The term "taboo", and I quote, comes from the Tongan tapu or Fijian tabu ("prohibited", "disallowed", "forbidden"), related among others to the Maori tapu and Hawaiian Kapu. Its English use dates to 1777 when

the British explorer James Cook visited "Tonga, and referred to the Tongans' use of the term "taboo: for "any thing is forbidden to be eaten, or made use of. The term was translated to him as "consecrated, inviolable, forbidden, unclean or cursed". Taboo itself has been derived from alleged Tongan morphemes ta ("mark") and bu ("especially"), but this may be a folk etymology (Tongan does not actually have a phoneme /b/), and tapu is usually treated as a unitary, non-compound word inherited from Proteo-Polynesian. *tapu, in turn inherited from Proto-Oceanic *tabu, with the reconstructed meaning "sacred, forbidden. In its current use on Tongan, the word tau means "sacred" or holy, often in the sense of being restricted or protected by custom or law.

Common taboo involve restrictions or ritual regulation of killing and hunting; sex and sexual relationships reproduction; the dead and their graves; as well as food and dining (primarily cannibalism and dietary laws such as vegetarianism, kashrut, and halal) or religious (trief and haram). In Madagascar, a strong code of taboos, known as fady, constantly change and are formed from new experiences. Each region, village, or tribe may have its own fady.

Incest itself has been pulled both ways with some seeking to normalize consensual adult relationships regardless of the degree of kinship, and others expanding the degrees of prohibited contact (notably in the United States.) although the term taboo usually implies negative connotations. It is sometime associated with entering propositions in proverbs such as forbidden fruit is the sweetest; unquoted.

https://en.wikipedia.org/wiki/Increst_taboo#Research_on_the_taboo
An incest taboo, and I quote, is any cultural rule or norm that prohibits sexual relations between certain members of the same family, mainly between individuals related by blood. All human cultures have norms that exclude certain close relatives from those considered suitable or permissible sexual or marriage partners, making such relationships taboo. However, different norms exist among cultures as to which blood relations are permissible as sexual partners and which are not. Sexual relations between related persons which are subject to the taboo are called incestuous relationships.
Some cultures prescribe sexual relations between clan-members, even when no traceable biological relationship exists, while member of other clans are permissible irrespective of the existence of a biological relationship. In many cultures, certain types of cousin relations are preferred as sexual and marital partners, whereas in others these are taboo.

One explanation sees the incest taboo as a cultural implementation of a biologically evolved preference for sexual partners with whom one is likely to share genes, since inbreeding may have detrimental outcomes. The most widely held hypothesis proposes that the so-called Westermarck effect discourages adults from engaging in sexual relations with individuals with whom they grew up.

LIMITS TO BIOLOGICAL EVOLUTION OF TABOO
While it is theoretically possible that natural selection may, under certain genetic circumstances, select for individuals that instinctively avoid mating with (close) relatives, biological evolution cannot select for punishing others for incest, since even genetically weakened, inbred individuals are better watchposts against PREDATORS than none at all, and weak individuals are useful for the stronger individuals in the group as looking, out for PREDATORS without being able to seriously compete with the stronger individuals.

RESEARCH ON THE TABOO
Incest is sexual intercourse between individuals related in certain prohibited degrees of kinship. In every society there are rules prohibited incestuous unions, both as to sexual intercourse and recognized marriage.

The two prohibitions do not necessarily coincide. There is no uniformity as to which degrees are involved in the prohibitions. The rules regulating incest must be investigated in every society by means of the genealogical method. The prohibition may be so narrow as to include only one type of parent-child relationship (though this is very rare), or classificatory kinship can be traced. The more usual practice is that unions with certain relatives only are considered incestuous, the relationships being regulated by the type of descent emphasized. In some societies unions with certain persons related by affinity are also considered incestuous. What penalties falls on (a) the individuals concerned; (b) the community as a whole? Are such penalties enforced by authority, or are they believed to ensure automatically by all action of supernatural force?

As this excerpt suggests, anthropologists distinguish between social norms and actual social behavior; much social theory explores the difference and relationship between the two. For example, what is the purpose of prohibitions that are routinely violated (as for example when people claim that incest is taboo yet engage in incestuous behavior)?

Moreover, the definition restricts itself to sexual intercourse, this does not mean that other forms of sexual contact do not occur, or are proscribed, or prescribed. For example, in some Inuit societies in the Arctic, and traditionally in Bali, mothers would routinely stroke the penises of their infant; such behavior was considered no more sexual than breast-feeding.

THIRD-PARTIES' OBJECTIONS

Another approach is looking at moral objections to third-party incest. This increases the longer a child has grown up together with another child of the opposite sex. This occurs even if the other child is genetically unrelated. Human have been argued to have a special kin detection system that besides the incest taboo also regulates a tendency towards altruism kin.

COUNTER ARGUMENTS

One objection against an instinctive and genetic basis for the incest taboo is that incest does occurs. Anthropologist have also argued that the social construct "incest" (and the incest taboo) is not the same thing as the biological phenomenon of "inbreeding". For example, there is equal genetic relation between a man and the daughter of his father's sister and between a man and the daughter of his mother's sister such that biologists would consider mating incestuous in both instance, but Trobrianders consider mating incestuous in one case and not in the other.

INCEST LAWS AND CRIMINAL CHARGES

An overview on the legalities of incest, different forms of acts of incest which are considered illegal, pressing charges for incest, defenses, penalties that may occur, and how a lawyer can help, by Ave Mince-Didier, and I quote, The crime of incest is committed when people who are related to one another engage in sexual activity, get married, or live together as man and wife. While the precise behavior that is considered incest varies across different states and cultures. Almost all societies consider some forms of incest taboo, and laws reflect those beliefs. In the United States, child sexual abuse is always a crime, and incest between adults is a crime in all but a few states.

HOW IS INCEST DEFINED?

Incest is defined differently in different states. In some states, incest is limited to sexual activity. In other states, people can commit the crime of incest by engaging in sexual activity, marrying, or living together romantically. Generally, in the U.S; incest laws ban intimate relations between children and parents, brothers and sisters,

grandchildren and grandparents. Some state's incest laws are limited to heterosexual relationships. For example, in Georgia, incest is defined as sexual intercourse between fathers and daughters and mothers and sons, including step-children and half-siblings; grandparents and grandchildren; aunt and nephews; and uncles.

PUNISHMENT

Incest between adults is a felony, punishable by five years' to life imprisonment, depending on state law. Incest against children is punished just as severely, if not more so, as other cases of child cases of child sexual abuse, usually by lengthy prison terms or life in prison. In some states, people convicted of sex crimes may also be committed to mental hospitals if they pose a danger to others.

STATUTORY RAPE LAWS AND CHARGES

A person who has sex with someone under the "age of consent" can face a variety of criminal charges depending on the state.

WHAT IS STATUTORY RAPE? HOW IS STATUTORY RAPE DEFINED?

Statutory rape is a crime that involves sexual contact with a person who is under an age specified by law, commonly referred to as the "aged of consent". The legal term for the crime varies from state to state and includes sexual intercourse with a minor, sexual assault of a child, criminal sexual penetration of a minor or a child under a certain age, and sexual abuse of a minor.

Statutory rape is based on the notion that a person under a certain age cannot consent to sexual contact or activity because he or she lacks the maturity or judgement necessary to make a knowing choice about sexual activity. This is a strict liability or statutory crime because the underage person's consent is irrelevant and the intentions of the defendant and what they believed about the age of the other person usually do not matter.

From state to state, statutory rape crimes can range from misdemeanors to serious felonies, depending on the age of the victim and the age different between the offender and victim. Other factors also can affect the level of the criminal charge, such as whether a pregnancy resulted, the involvement of drugs or alcohol in the sexual activity, and whether the defendant has a history of prior sexual offenses.

CONTROVERSY AROUND STATUTORY RAPE LAWS

Statutory rape laws are meant to protect children and teenagers from PREDATORY adults. The crime of statutory rape has been controversial because, historically, it has been applied primarily or exclusively to relationships where the female is under-age; unquoted.

https://www.scielo.br/scielo.php?pid=S0103-65642017000200287&script=sci_artTtext&tlng=em
INCEST AVOIDANCE AND PROHIBITION: PSYCHOLOGICAL AND CULTURAL FACTORS, by Francisco Wilson Noguiera Holanda Junior.

ABSTRACT

Although historically the incest prohibitive regulation is considered an almost ubiquitous cultural phenomenon that is not influenced by psychobiological factors related to the evolutionary history of human species, recent findings have challenged this traditional view and argued that the incest avoidance and prohibition are influenced by biological and cognitive factors along with cultural regulation.

The incest conceptual boundaries can vary according to the field of study or reference, formulates that behaviors referred to as incestuous in social sciences literature can be divided into three categories; incestuous endogamy, which is concerned to sexual intercourse between individuals with family relationship, that is, whose kinship is by direct descent (for instance, between parents and children or between siblings); the non-incestuous endogamy, which encompasses the sexual intercourse between individuals with more distant kinship (between cousins, for instance); and the sexual activity coming from the adultery between persons without genetic kinship in the familiar context (stepson and stepmother, for instance).

It is worth mentioning that endogamy and incest are terms that have been more commonly used in biological and social sciences, respectively, many times imprecisely. Specially, endogamy is linked to the idea of reproduction between the individuals with kinship, whereas incest emphasizes the sexual activity that may or not generate offspring. The prohibition of sexual intercourse between siblings or parents and children carries the smallest occurrence of this modality of kinship relationship, being understood that those are the genuine type of incest, in which social prohibitions act more strongly when compared with the relationships between relatives of second or third degrees.

According to a traditional portion of social sciences, the university (or almost universality) of the incest prohibition is predicated on a social -cultural basis that is independent from psychobiological processes compounding the evolutionary history of the human species. This approach emphasizes that the incest is socially interdict, once it somehow jeopardizes the social order. In this direction, according to, the incest prohibition expresses the passage from the natural fact of consanguinity to the cultural fact of alliance.

On the other hand, adopting a perspective that considers only either cultural or environmental variable of certain human beings' behavior, such as sexual behavior, results in falling into obsolete biology vs culture or innate vs learned dichotomies and neglecting that it is possible to describe, at least partially, the problems and adaptive solutions faced by the species ancestors.

ETHICAL AND LEGAL CONSIDERATIONS

In addition to the psychobiological and psychosocial factors previously discussed, incest t raises ethical and legal questions when practiced in such a way as it harms or threatens people's integrity, especially when there are abusive forms of coercion and without consent. The incest between an adult and a person below the age of consent is considered a form of sexual child abuse, what is identified as one of the most extreme forms of this kind of abuse and that generally results in serious lasting psychological traumas (especially if it is a case of incest between parents and children). The risk of incest between stepfather and stepdaughter is 15 times greater than between biological father and daughter. Daughters that are victims of incest with the father present problems regarding sexual esteem, depressive symptomatology and psychological suffering. The start age of this kind of incest is premature, with estimates from 5 to 8 eight years old for the daughter. More than 80% victims feel distant from both parents or only from the male progenitor, indicating affection damage.

Now that you have read the articles and without turning a blind eye to the disease of incest and taboo, and how it affects others especially children. How does it make you feel? How does it make you feel knowing that this is happening to children? How can you stomach such a thing? Isn't it enough to make you stroke? Do you not feel like vomiting? Do you not feel like whipping some ass? The question is; whose ass? You should of course get the authorities involve, maybe call a friend, clergy, whatever your religion belief is, call that person seeking help for your child especially if you're not involved in such an act. But of course you're going the try to hide the sinful act of those involved. Why; they're family members. And, yes of course it will be very embarrassing. But, what if anything would you do? Would you ignore it as if nothing ever happened? How could you live with yourself? Are you human enough to do the right thing? It's a question that I hope you'll never have to confront. But in back of your head remember these words "WHAT IF"?

Lets talk about something more that you should understand or at least should have some form of knowledge of. But hey, I could be wrong. Some people understands only what they want to understand. You tell me; who don't understand twisted seduction. What is twisted seduction? Simply means that nothing goes the way you thinks! let me just say this; how you presents yourself publicly attracts others. How you attracts others depends on the individual. What gratify him/she. What draws him/her to you; his needs, her needs, their needs. my speech to you; don't let your guard down. Be aware of your surrounding. Be aware of others watching and observing you. Be suspicious of anything and or anyone unintentionally wanting to be friends with you. When walking or driving home be aware / alert of who might be following you. Don't assumed its nothing. All of these things are warning signs alerting you of DANGER. Don't get seduce by the wrong person (s), and become a victim of an abduction / involved in a kidnapping situation. It can be ugly, painful, and very stressful. That brings me to the story at hand.

May I have your attention please; let talk about twist seduction. This story takes place in INDONESE. A man was talking to himself, love, fill you love. Talking to a white female and he tape up her mouth. The man was a white male, tall man, wearing mostly black. He would watch her at work a lot and follows her home. He attended office functions whenever she was there which wasn't very often. His work area wasn't very far away from hers. They would say Hi, from time to times but that's about it. He would politely say good morning as he smile down at her especially when offering her a cup of coffee. She would give him an unfriendly look and say; thanks but I will get my own. That would seriously pissed him off. His face turns blue and red as he stood there while she walked away. Under his breath you could here him saying "you bitch". He asked her out one day and very politely, and she said I'm sorry I don't go out. She dropped some papers to the floor and he pick them up for her. He would always leave work minutes after she did.

I GUESS you could say that she was anti-social because she barely interact with the other women. Other women would try being friends with her but she always had an excuse I'm busy. He took notice of her demeanor and purposely would try to talk to her. But as usually she would do everything to avoid him. You could say that he was attracted to her, maybe. She walked to his work area one morning and said; why have you been watching me? He said you're a beautiful woman. Don't take this the wrong way but I'm attracted to you. He tells the woman why she's there. He refused to let her use a phone. If you do what you're told you won't get hurt. I don't want to hurt you. She was 25 years of age, a very beautiful woman. Punch line; this man knew her from work. He observed her at work. He felt that she was anti-social. Especially when he found out that she pretended to be going on a trip. This man even has degree in psychology, and tells her that he knows how the mind works. in other words; don't play him for no fool.

He tries to feed her doing the first few days of her stay chain to the bed. She refuses to be fed by him spitting it out onto the bed, and tightly keeping her mouth closed. He says ok; we'll try again later. Get this; nothing she does make him angry, violence, and or piss off. He's actually very nice to her. He did warned her that if he take off the tape, she scream, the tape will be put back on. He took off the tape two days later, and sure enough she screamed and the tape was put back on. He shortly thereafter told the woman that he's leaving and will be back

within 24 hours. He returned bring her downstairs for food. He removed the tape from her mouth. She ate the food and they talk for a few minutes. She repeatedly called him a sick bastard. She said that you must be out of your (F) ing, mind. Your not going to get away with this. He told her that he was school in the U.S. He profile his potential victims. He pick women out base on comparability. He later gave her options; obey him -will not get hurt. He then gave her a change of clothes.

Told her to clean herself us. He unbind her from being tied to the bed. He went back upstairs giving her some privacy. She tried to escape. She pick up a stick and hit him across the head. She get caught. She is rebind secured to the bed. Shortly thereafter she falls asleep but later wakes up screaming. Teach her not to be anti-social and to choose her friends and associates more wisely. Stop pretending to be someone she's not. He made a shirt for her; saying "I have been kidnap. She fail in love with him at the end of the story. They made freely passage love together. She understood why he abducted and kidnapped her. Its's as if her life has changed. She press no charges against him. No police involvement. This woman was lucky that she was not brutally treated. That she was not raped. That she was not killed. Lets call her the "Lucky One". Hopefully something was learn from this story of events. Play it back in your mind and think about it. Two things did take place; she was abducted and kidnapped. In other words; taken against her will. The article that follows pertains to this story.

https://en.wikipediaorg/wiki/Seduction
Seduction is the process of deliberately enticing a person, to engage in a relationship, to lead astray, as from duty, rectitude, or the like; to corrupt, to persuade or induce into engaging in sexual behavior, Strategies of seduction include conversation and sexual scripts, paralingual features, non-verbal communication, and short-term behavioural strategies. The word seduction stems from Latin and means Literally "leading astray. As a result, the term may have a positive or negative connotation. The emergence of the Internet and technology has supported the availability and the existence of a seduction community, which is based on discourse about seduction. Seduction is also used within marketing to increase compliance and willingness. Seduction, seen negatively, involves temptation and enticement often sexual in nature, to lead someone astray into a behavioural choice they would not have made if they were not in a state of sexual arousal. Seen positively, seduction is a synonym for the act of charming someone----male or female----by an appeal to the senses, often with the goal of reducing unfounded fears and lending to their "sexual emancipation ". Some sides in contemporary academic debate state that the morality of seduction depends on the long-term impacts on the individuals concerned, rather than the act itself, and may not necessarily carry the negative connotations expressed in dictionary definitions. Males and females both implement the strategy of seduction as a method of negotiating their sexual relationships. This can often involver manipulation of other individuals. This is primarily bases on desire, normally physical, as well as attraction toward them. Popular phrases often used include; 'the language of love is universal'. These phases help to demonstrate the extensively pervasive and ubiquitous strategy use within love and relationships amongst humans. Individuals employing such strategies often do so subconsciously and will merely report the feelings and thoughts that they subjectively experienced and are colloquially comparable to 'attraction' or love. Evolutionary psychology suggests that this form of sexual enticement can be used in order to cajole desire individuals to engage in sexual intercourse and ultimately reproduce. Male declare that they adopt the strategy of seduction statically more frequently than females. Men more commonly wish to engage in more frequent short-term mating, which may require this strategy of seduction used to access the female for intercourse.

Human mate poaching
Seduction is related to human mate poaching. Human mate poaching refers to when either a male or female purposefully entices another individual who is already in an established relationship into sexual relations with them. This is akin to the definition of seduction in the introduction. This is a psychological mechanism which had unconscious and conscious manifestation, that in relation to evolutionary psychology has been adaptive to our ancestors in the past has continued to be functional in modern society. Human mate poaching is a form of seduction, and can be used as a short-term and long-term mating strategy among both sexes. Moreover, there are associated costs and benefits to poaching, Schmitt and Buss (2001) investigated the potential costs and benefits across sexes in relation to human mate poaching.

Costs for women engaging in poaching behaviours include unwanted pregnancy, transmitted infection and diseases, and insecurity about provisions (shelter, food, and financial security). However, the associated benefits include emotional support that she may not be receiving from her current partner, and access to 'good genes' that the male possesses, such as facial symmetry. Potential costs for males engaging in mate poaching can include resource depletion, violence and aggression from the female's current partner. who takes part in mate guarding behaviors used to protect their mate from other potential males or females).

Biosocial theory
Kenrick and Trost (1987) have formulated a Biosocial theory of heterosexual relationship which encompasses several stages of seduction. This includes five stages of natural progression:

Individuals identify a potential partner based on desired characteristics such as physical attraction
Both individuals establish contact
Other traits of the individual that are not necessarily explicit are analyzed to determine fitness
A physical relationship is established
The relationship is either successful and progresses or discontinued

Within these stages, both individuals are interacting in a game which is never explicit, this is because if either individual were to be rejected this would damage their self-esteem. Therefore, when seducing, the overarching aims and goals are never vocalized to the other desired individual. This is sometimes referred to as paradoxical exhibition.
The main goal of seduction whether it is active under conscious or unconscious mechanisms is to impress the desired partner and display positive characteristics that are likely to be attractive, and to repress undesirable characteristics.

Sexual Deviations; and I quote, In Australia and New Zealand homosexuality is regarded as a definite antisocial abnormality. The existing laws are not concerned with the concepts of homosexuality as a biological fact or as a neurosis curable by psychoanalysis. Offenses of this character are starkly and clearly defined as the following section shows; "Buggery and bestiality; Any person who has carnal knowledge of any person against the order of nature, or has carnal knowledge of an animal, or permits a male person to have carnal knowledge of him or her against the order of nature is liable…." In three of the six Australian states the penalty is imprisonment for fourteen years. Homosexual relations between males receive greater attention than homosexuality among females and are regarded more seriously by our lawmakers. According to psychiatrists and the police, there is much homosexuality in Australia, but it is impossible to quote any statistics. The true homosexual rarely seeks treatment but bisexual individuals do because of the heterosexual component.

Transvestism, or eonism, is identification with the other sex, particularly with regard to dress. In most states it is not an offense unless dressing as one of the opposite sex is used to deceive people and facilitate some illegal activity. In general, sexual deviations indicate a failure to reach full psychological development. The Coital Complex and Sex Deviation; as has been previously noted in this article, many people of the world, especially almost all those who have been seriously influenced by Juceo-Christian ideologies, define as deviational or perverted sex behavior human participation in any sex acts that are not strictly penile-vaginal, or that do not at least terminate with "normal" penile-vaginal coitus.

According to this way of thinking, oral, anal, heterosexually masturbatory, and other nonvaginal acts are perfectly proper when they are engaged in as forms of sexual foreplays; but when they are carried on up and including actual orgasm, without any penile-vaginal copulation actually having taken place, they are deviated or perverted acts; unquoted. I deviated from the subject of understanding in question to open your eyes and your mind into what bothers us the most. Because not everything is written in stone or in black and white. I have given you a lot of information to focus on with regard to taking care of your children and things to look out for. It is now up to you as parents, and soon to be parents now to do the right thing. I'm not here to hole your hands or to say you must do this or else. "USE YOUR OWN COMMON SENSE". I have made you aware of what could happen and what will happen if you do nothing. I notice months after my Book: evilness is he that sinfully preys on the heart of young children, was published, NOT MANY OF YOU BOTHER TO BUY IT. Why; wait, don't answer that. I don't want to know. "TELL IT LATER TO YOUR CHILD / CHILDREN" when it happen to them. Tell them that their Abduction \ Kidnapping could had been PREVENED; IF ONLY I HAD BOUGHT THIS BOOK. OH, YEAN, EXPLAIN IT TO THEM.

I'm giving you a second chance to do the right thing. By you buying this book a life hopefully will be block out of armsway. Do not feel guilty informing on someone who has abducted / kidnapped children. Because you need to understand what their going though. Children are not only being abducted / kidnapped but force into prostitution and raped repeatedly by their captures. They are being psychologically torture into a state of fear and madness to the point of no return. They will do anything their captures say to live, and to avoid being raped and killed. Children are sometime being taken into an underground cave. An abandon house. An abandon church. An abandon school. Even under your nose the house next door / and even the house across the street. You ask me how crazy is that? It could be the person you work with. It could be your best friend. It could be your neighbor. "IT COULD BE ANYONE". Do you know what to look for? 1. Different in demeanor, something out of place, facial expression, tone of voice, change in usual routines, secrecy, cuts and injuries, weapon on person, in vehicle that you know shouldn't be there. Excuses for everything, accidents that shouldn't had happened, bloody clothing, late nights, anything that don't make sense. "THESE THINGS ARE CALLED "RED FLAGS". "red flags" are warning signs that something is wrong. Please don't do what most people do. Don't let the other person know that you are suspicious of HIM / HER.

Please don't do that. If you have real evidence of a crime something you can prove to the police outside of suspicion "QUICKLY AND SECRETLY GO TO THE POLICE STATION. Do not let yourself be seen going there or leaving the police station. Because you have just put yourself on top of the list of next to be abducted / kidnapped. And, by the way you will be killed. Because they will fear that you know too much. I was watching a movie on television one night. A black middle age tall black man kidnapped a young black female. She was not from a broken home. That black man live within the community. he was well respected and admire by his neighbors. They didn't suspect a thing. He locked the young black female down stairs inside a bedroom without windows. He would tie her arms to the bed. And of course warn her not to try to escape.

He said if you know what's good for you! How did he get caught? An older man was suspicious of him. He knew the young black female. He knew her family. He started going from house to house looking for the girl. A woman peeping out of a third floor window told him that no one is going to help him. But hears what she did tell him. She told him about a man living across the street. When he went to knock on the door. Some sparked his memory. He grab something sharp and forced opened the door. He yelled for her. She answered. He quickly forced opened the bedroom door. He was attacked shortly thereafter from behind by the kidnapper but not before the girl was untired. The black young female seeing what was happening quickly picked up something and started hitting the kidnapper over the back until he was unconscious.

https://www.isbe.net/Pages/Child-Lures.aspx
Child Lures Prevention-teaching America's South to think first & stay safe! And I quote, Has your school implemented child lures prevention program yet? Illinois State board of Education is a proud partner of the Child Lures Prevention Initiative, a first-ever statewide effort to help safeguard students from predatory crimes. A Child Lures School Program kit has already been sent (free of charge)to all 3220 Illinois public elementary and middle schools. It is a turn-key program, complete with two videos, one to prepare teachers to present the program, and one to present to children, along with a Presenter's Guide and one copy of the Child Lures Parent Guide. We encourage implementation of this personal safety program within your health curriculum, school assembly programs or in whatever way best suits your school. Should you have questions regarding the program, please visit CHILD LURES PREVENTION'S WEBSITE-http://www.childlures prevention.com/) for information.

The Child Lures Prevention Initiative received statewide attention during an NBC5 Town Hall Meeting Telecast: "Smart Choices/Safe Kids" which features Child Lure Prevention creator, Kenneth Wooden demonstrating the lures most commonly used by predators. Program creator Ken Wooden states, "As an educator, I feel it is imperative to give children a perspective on personal safety which is both balanced and accurate. Child Lures Prevention does this with two messages. The first and most powerful message is that the vast majority of people are loving and caring and committed to the safety of all children. The second message is that there are some people, a small but active group, that try to lure young people into dangerous and abusive situations by using lures, but by teaching the various lures and prevention strategies, students can learn how to think first and stay safe; unquoted.

According to the Bible, and I quote, Why do you boast in EVIL, O mighty man? The goodness of God endures continually. Your tongue destruction, like a sharp razor, working deceitfully. You love EVIL more than good, lying rather than speaking righteousness. You love all devouring words, you deceitful tongue. God shall like wise destroy you forever; He shall take you away, and pluck you out of your dwelling place, and uproot you down from the land of the living. The righteous also shall see and fear, and shall laugh at him, saying, "Here is the man who did not make God his strength, but trusted in the abundance of his riches, and strengthened himself in his wickedness. The fool has said in his heart, "there is no God". There are corrupt, and have done abominable iniquity; there is none who does good. God looks down from heaven upon the children of men, to see if there are any who understand, who seek God. Every one of them has turned aside; there is none who does good, no, not one. Have the workers of iniquity no knowledge, who eat up my people as they eat bread, and do not call upon God? There they are in great fear when no fear was, for God has scattered the bones of him who encamps against you; you have put them to shame, because God has despised them. Unquoted.

I was watching a TV story, and a beeper, beeper, alert went off above the screen. I said what is this? Parents your children are not safe no matter where you choose to live. If you're not with your child my God I don't know. Get real parents I'm telling you that the ground you walk on is like sinking sand pulling the rub from under your feet as alligators attacks you from behind. Because the devil is watching hiding to prey ripping your soul out kidnapping and abducting your love ones. Their worse than evil itself. Their cling ball of sinful dirt dragging sterns into the body of the ungodly. Like an eagle they fly high seeking it prey of the night catching the weak, and pure in heart. I couldn't believe it someone had abducted a child. I'm so, so, sorry that the family didn't have my book. can I say? It's not published yet. Parents I can't stress it enough that you need to know where your child is at all times. I don't like to hear about dirty old men monsters of the worse kind preying on our young children, our future of tomorrow, and our young adults.

It makes my heart bleed and wants to cut out their cold, cold Infected disease so called heart pumping blood throughout their body. Come to me and I will give you peace. I will cut out your heart and feed it to the dogs. Who knows, maybe the dogs wouldn't want it. It's a parent worse nightmare. Parents listen to me and listen good. If I must pull you by the head to wake you up I will. I will do what I must to knock some senses into your head. The safety of your children depends on it. Depends on what! Depends on you. Parents too, too many children are being forced into prostitution, forced against their will to perform naughty sexual acts. Is this what you want? Parents don't close your eyes or walk away from the problem. Pull out your arsenal and see what makes predators ticks. Treat them the worse way you possibly can. Mercy, they don't deserve mercy. Who else must be abducted before we say enough is enough? No mercy, no mercy, no mercy. Nail them to the cross and let the blood of evil drain from their body until death do them part. Parents surely everyone has seen the stripe across the TV screen alerting you to a child by and adult has been kidnapped. The first thing comes to my mind is; it happened again. Why is it happening again, and again? What's wrong with people? Do they or do they not value the life of a child? Children are being abducted and kidnapped so very young is a scary situation. A spit into the mouth of a clinging snake without skin as the stink of death rises up to swallow you. The look into its eye is enough to say burn in hell snake your dead. Why can't we say the same thing to would be predators? Are they not like the snakes of the pit? Scream damn scream. Cry if you must. Just don't sit on your ass and do nothing. Call and pursue the would be predator male and or female alike to barrel its head into the sand of bloodiness until the water runs cold, and until the stink of death is no more as the wind of the south makes contact with the wind of the east casting out the smell off the face of the earth. Send a message to all that children life, health and welfare is not yours and never will be yours to tamper with. This I say will be the law of the land "an eye for an eye" casting out demon ways. Maybe its time to blow the whistle on whoever might be behind the abduction of children kidnapping them for personal fulfillment and for other reasons whatever that reason might be. Don't be afraid parents to seek the help of your local police, FBI, and other agencies whenever an abduction and or a kidnapping confronts you. Don't wait until another parent is face with the same problem. Don't wait until a shouting match starts. Don't wait until bloodshed take the life of another child by the hands of a would be predator. Don't wait parents because it could happen to you. And, it will! I stand before you parents planting a seed of terrible events involving the abduction and kidnapping of children providing you with the following articles taken from the internet. Thank God for the internet. Parents as you read these articles keep in mind that you could be reading about yourself.

www.koco.com/article/del-city-police-investigating-abduction-of....kids/9579800
Child Abduction Attempt In Del City, published January 07, 2016, by Ariana Gaza, and I quote, A Del City Elementary School student and Del City High School student were walking home Monday afternoon in the direction of Kerr Middle School when a man approached them near Southeast 23rd Street, between Epperly and Vickie drives, and asked them if they needed a ride, according to school district officials. The students were

unharmed and reported the incident to their parents, who then called the police. The district was not made aware of the situation until late Tuesday and sent out a letter notifying parents Wednesday, a school district spokeswoman said.

The man in the car was described as a Caucasian male, 40 to 50 years old, weighing 160 to 170 pounds, with long sideburns. He was wearing a black hat and sunglasses. He was driving a red Chevrolet Malilbu with a dent on the right of the car. Please discuss safety rules with your child at home and we will reinforce them at school, "school officials said in a letter to parents. Encourage your child to report any suspicious activity to you and to the adult at school."

https://www.wmbfnews.com/story/27826523/police-investigate-reported-child-abduction-attempt

Police Investigate Reported Child Abduction Attempt, posted Jan 12, 2015, By Jerilyn Gamble, and I quote, Myrtle Beach, SC (WMBF)- The Myrtle Beach Police Department responded to the area of Porcher Drive on January 11, in regards to a suspect allegedly attempting to entice a child into a vehicle. According to MBPD, the child reported that while walking her dog, an individual approached her and asked if she could help him find his dog. The child yelled "no" and ran toward her home. The child said, as she was running, the suspect pulled up beside her in a black, four door vehicle. The suspect reportedly yelled for the child to come with him, and told her if she didn't, he would hurt her. The child continued to run home and the suspect allegedly fled the scene, west on 73rd Avenue North.

The suspect was described as a white male, with blue eyes, and missing the corners of his top teeth. The male was wearing a red collared shirt with three buttons down the center, and a black basketball cap with a Nike symbol on the side. One nearby neighbor says the area is known as being safe so Sunday's incident is causing everyone to think twice. "I was once honestly shocked to hear something like that would even happen, "said Leah Belcher. She was impressed with how the young girl handled the man's request, but not everyone is ready for these type of situations. That's why the Myrtle Beach Police Department gives out these pointers to both kids and adults. "Please do not talk to strangers. If you do not know someone that's approaching you to ask you questions, again, find an adult that you trust, make your way home as quickly as possible. If you are outside, and for everyone, be aware of your surroundings, know what's going on around you, know who's around you, said Lt. Joey Crosby.

https://newsok.com/article/3934869

Arizona Father Arrested On Child Abduction Complaint In Oklahoma, by Robert Medley, published: February 18, 2014, and I quote, An Arizona man wanted on a child abduction complaint in Missouri was arrested in Oklahoma City Monday with his 11-year old daughter, the Oklahoma Highway Patrol reported. Andrew Smith, 46, was arrested at a restaurant at NE 122 and Interstate 35 about 5:30 p.m. Monday, according to a patrol news release. Smith had rented a car in Tulsa that was located in Oklahoma City near a truck stop. Aurora, Mo., police for the Oklahoma Highway Patrol's help finding Andrew Smith after his 11-year girl was taken from Marionville Elementary School Monday morning by Smith. Smith was taken to the Oklahoma County Jail Monday night. The girl was reunited with her mother. During the search for the girl and her father Monday, troopers arrested Smith's brother, I Oliver Smith, near Wellston during a traffic stop and took him to the Lincoln County jail, accused of helping his brother.

https://www.dallasnews.com/news/crime/2015/04/14/child-abduction-attempt-reported-in-watauga
Child Abduction Attempt Reported In Watauga 11 Dallas Morning News, and I quote, the 6100 block of Nelson Terrace, after an 11-year-old girl said a man tired to physically force her into his car before the girl escaped and ran home. The attacker hit her face on the car door as he forced her in, cutting the inside of her lip. She managed to struggle and escape, the girl's mother said. Investigators said the suspect was a black man in his 30's, approximately six-feet tall with an average build, wearing a tan or light-colored tight skull-cap type beanie, dark sweat pants and a long white T-shirt that hung below his waist. Anyone with information in related to either abduction attempt is asked to call detectives. Feature story of a Child Abduction Attempt Reported In Watauga, published: April 14, 2015, by KXAS-TV (NBC5), The Dallas Morning News, and I quote, Watauga police say the description of a reported child abduction attempt Monday matches a similar attempt near the same area last month.

https://newsok.com/article/5453176
DNA Links Oklahoma Man To 1997 Child Abduction, posted October 13, 2015, By Kyle Schwab, and I quote, MIDWEST CITY, Ok, ---Police and the FBI conducted an intensive national search for 8-year old Kirsten Renee Hatfield after she vanished from her bedroom in the middle of the night more than 18 years ago. No trace was ever found. On Monday, investigators arrested a neighbor who still lives only two doors down. "Oh my goodness, "said the victim's mother, Shannon Hazen, who learned about the arrest from The Oklahoman. "Yes!" she said, then began sobbing. Anthony Joseph Palma, 56, of Midwest City, Ok, was arrested in the second-grader's abduction after new DNA testing connected him to evidence found at the 1997 crime scene, police reported. Midwest City Police Chief Brandon Clabes on Monday night confirmed Palma's arrest. "This is a huge case......It's one of those cases you want to solve 'before you retire," said the chief, who said he has been with the department for 36 years and police chief for 16 years.

Palma was identified as a suspect in the cold case because his blood was found on the girl's bedroom window sill and on her ripped underwear, which were recovered in the backyard of her home, police reported. Investigators conduded the blood belonged to Palma after he consented in June to give a DNA sample. The match was one in 293 sextillion, "police reported. "There have been no verified sightings or contact from Kirsten since May......of 1997, "Midwest City Police detective Damell Miller wrote in a request for an arrest warrant. "Therefore, it can be conduded that she was killed shortly after her abduction....." It is likely that Palma has been motivated to stay in the same home to conceal evidence of the crime and/or the location of Kirsten's body, "the detective wrote.

The police chief said that investigators searched Palma's home Monday and will resume Tuesday. After the disappearance, the victim's mother told police she had tucked Kirsten into bed May 13, 1997. When she checked on her daughter the next morning, she was gone. Palma was questioned about the disappearance in 1997 and again in June. Palma said both times he was home the night of the incident. He denied in June having any involvement, the detective reported. Some of the information Palma provided in 1997 was inconsistent with what he told investigators in June, the detective reported. He is a longtime groundkeeper and reportedly works for the state at lake Thunderbird State Park. Palma went to prison in 1985 for more than a year for a 1982 assault case, record show. It was unclear Monday night whether Palma has an attorney.

QUESTIONS FOR PARENTS AS FOLLOWS:

* Parents how does reading of the articles at hand grabs you?
* Is it frightening, scary, and shocking?

*   How safe does it make you feel?
*   Who's child do you think will be next?
*   Do you feel that the local authorities ie. police department / sheriff department, can protect your child from would be predators?
*   Do you feel that your child is safe walking to and from school?
*   What if anything has told you that children life are in danger?
*   What in particularly grabs you by the hand in the articles?
*   What as a parent would you do different now knowing what you know?
*   Would you as a parent partition the government to do more to protect your children?
*   Do you feel that predators male and or females alike should be consider a threat with regard to children safety?
*   What does you as a parent intends to do to protect your own children from the evilness of potential predators?
*   What was going through your mind if anything while reading these articles?
*   When you look at your children knowing there is a predator preying on your children as they walks out of the door. What is the first thing that you asks yourself?
*   What would you do if the next child abducted and or kidnapped is your child?
*   Is it not something to think about?
*   What would you do if someone knocks on your door and tells you that your child has been abducted, sexually assaulted, and or killed?

* Do you see other parents as potential would be potential predators, if not, why, if so, why?
www.nbc-2.com/story/....police-investigating-reported-child-abduction-in-fort-myers
Police Investigating Reported Child Abduction In Fort Myers, posted: April, 2014, By Member Center, and I quote, FORT MYERS, FL- A Fort Myers mother says when she saw her son walk out her front door. She thought he boarded the school bus at his stop at Franklin Street and Central Avenue. "The school never called me. I never heard anything. "said his mother. The 10-year-old never arrived at school. Instead, he reported he was taken by two men in an SUV and driven around for three hours until he was able to escape. She said the boy is not revealing what happened during the drive. But he was able to get away near Fort Myers Middle Academy and run home.

"He was devastated. Shirt off, pants pulled up, face swollen, crying. He said he thought he wasn't going to see us again, "she said. We did some digging to find out why she wasn't told her son didn't make it to school. A spokesperson for Lee County School says they send out robo-calls to parents about absences at the end of the school day. They say those notifications go out later in the day to account for tardies. His mother says she thought the threat had passed. Two weeks ago a different ten year old reported someone approaching him at his bus stop near the Sunterra Apartment. The man also offered that boy two dollars. Police are looking into whether the incidents are connected. Other parents say they are keeping a closer eye on their kids at the bus stop. "I just hope nobody" child get taken, because that is something very sad. If that did happen, that shocking," said Jacara Byrd.

Police say they have stepped up patrols in the neighborhood where this happened.
https://www.facebook.com/public/DeAnn-Smith
School Employee Allegedly Shot Springfield Girl After Abduction, posted: Feb 19, 2014, By DeAnn Smith, Chris Oberholtz, and Erka Tallan, Reporter, and I quote, SPRINGFIELD, MO (KCTV) – Greene County Prosecutor Dan Patterson announced Wednesday afternoon that he has filed first-degree murder and child

kidnapping charges in the death of a 10-year-old Springfield girl abducted while walking to a friend's home. Craig Michael Wood, 45, a Springfield school district employee, has been charged with first-degree murder, child kidnapping and armed criminal action. He is accused of planning to kidnap Hailey M. Owens, and then fatally shooting her. "My office is committed to seeking justice for Hailey, "Patterson said. Under Missouri law, the child-kidnapping charge could Patterson to seek the death penalty against Wood if he is convicted of first-degree murder. The only other punishment for a first-degree murder conviction is life behind bars. Patterson said he will consult with Hailey's family before deciding whether to seek the death penalty. "That decision is a way off. "Patterson said during an evening news conference. The child's material grandmother, Delinda Fereby, remembered her granddaughter as a "real girly-girl" who was full of joy and life. "She was always laughing, dancing, and she was a big hugger," she recalled. "If she didn't know you, she'd get to know you right away." Hailey has an older brother.

"All I can say right now is I missed her and I love her. Her father, Markus Owens told a Springfield television station. Police believe they found early Wednesday Hailey's body inside the home where Wood was staying. A medical examiner will conduct an autopsy to formally confirm the identity of Hailey. Wood is being held in the Greene County Jail, and bond is unlikely to be set on a first-degree murder charge. Authorities say Wood was a "STRANGER" to Hailey. But Wood was an employee and coach in the school district where she was a fourth grader. Hailey's body was found inside the house at 1538 E. Stanford Street where Wood was living. Police Chief Paul Williams said. "It's tragic. It's horrific, "Williams said.

WARNING: THE FOLLOWING DETAILS FROM COURT DOCUMENTS ARE UPSETTING.
A medical examiner examined the body at Wood's home and determined she was shot in the base of her skull, according to the court records. Her arms had also been bound. A spent.22 shell casing was found inside Wood's residence. After obtaining a search warrant, crime scene technicians found Hailey's body into two trash bags and crammed into a plastic tote. Wood apparently tried to conceal the tote in the basement, according to court records. The smell of bleach was strong in the basement and authorities said they found evidence that Wood had used bottles of bleach in the basement. Wood was arrested after a three-state manhunt for the girl.

Williams said Wood is refusing to speak to investigator, and so they don't have a motive. Court documents say Wood denied any contact with Hailey. Neighbors who saw the abduction called 911 at 4:48 p.m. Tuesday. Officers took 10 minutes to get there. After interviewing witnesses, police quickly determined that it was a STRANGER abduction and issued an Amber Alert to the Springfield area within an hour. The Missouri Highway Patrol issued its Amber Alert about 7 p.m. Tuesday, and it was extended about 9:30 p.m. to include Kansas and Oklahoma. The Amber Alert was canceled Wednesday morning after her body was found. Family members were told about 5:30 a.m. Wednesday.

Authorities are searching Wood's home as well as Dutch Maid Laundry at 526 S. National Ave. FBI Agents are looking through washers and dryers at the laundromat. Workers said a man matching Wood's description used a washer and two dryers to clean sheets, blankets, and other clothing items. FBI agents seized bags of laundry. Hailey was walking from her home to a friend's house when witnesses described seeing Wood pull up in a pickup truck, and try to speak to the girl. This was in the area of Lombard Street and laurel Avenue. Carlos and Michelle Edwards were enjoying the warm evening while sitting in their garage. They saw a man in a gold-colored 2008 Ford Ranger pickup drive up and down the street several time before approaching Hailey. He allegedly sought directions. The girl initially resisted his overtures, according to witnesses, however, as he continued to press for help with directions, witnesses said she eventually got close enough that Wood jumped out and threw her into

the truck before taking off. Witnesses described the vehicle as gold-colored 2008 Ford Ranger. "She initially ignored (his attempts at conversation)and then came back and spoke to the driver, and at which time he suddenly jumped out and grabbed here, and pulled her into the vehicle. Our witnesses said it happened just that quick, "Williams said. "The vehicle spend off with her inside the vehicle." Michelle Edwards described Wood pounding when Hailey took a step or two toward the vehicle. "She said the male funged out of the vehicle, grabbed the girl with his left hand, and threw her in the truck like a rag doll.

Michelle said the suspect then fled the area at a very high rate of speed," according to court documents. Michelle Edwards remembered the exact license plate. This allowed police to find Wood's father, who was the registered owner and lived in a nearby community. "He's my son, and he's in a lot of trouble," Jim Wood told the Springfield News-Leader. Police zeroed in on Wood and arrested him by 8:30 p.m., authorities said Wednesday morning. He was found sitting in the pickup truck outside the home where he was staying. Wood was booked into jail at 11:30 p.m. Police looked through the home and did not see Hailey. After getting a search warrant, they combed the house and found her body. Court records show Wood has a drug conviction from about 25 years ago in Missouri. The police chief said others witnesses the abduction and also alerted authorities. Williams praised the couple.

"There were a couple of very good witnesses," the police chief said. The fact that people are paying attention and actually tried to stop the abduction.....is to be commended. The prosecutor became choked up and emotional as he thanked those who tried to save Hailey from harm. Several witnesses chased on foot after the vehicle while one person hopped in a car and took off, but lost sight of the Ranger, Williams said. After running the plates, police found Wood's father, who owned the vehicle, Wood's father directed police to his son and his residence. Williams said Wood pulled up to the house while officers surreptitiously were watching it, and was arrested without issues. Hailey was a student at Westport Elementary and last year she attended Bowerman Elementary. Hailey was less than two blocks from her home when she was abducted, Williams said. He urged parents to be vigilant. This should just help people realize they should heighten their awareness. It can happen anywhere to anyone in a blink of an eye," he said. "Its not something we like to admit. It's something I'd like to be able to prevent. You can protect your kids as best as you can." https://kmox.radio.com/articles/15-apps-predators-use-target-children; Police: Child predators are using these 15 apps to target children, and I quote; MeetMe, It helps you find new people nearby that shares your interest and wants to chat.
https://kidshealth.org/en/parents/911.html?WT.ac=p-ra
Teaching Your Child How To Use 911, by Elana Pearl Ben-Joseh.MD; and I quote, Everyone need to know about calling 911 in an emergency. But kids also need to know the specifics about what an emergency is. Asking them questions likes, "What would you do if we had a fire in our house? or "What would you do if you saw someone trying to break in? gives you a chance to discuss emergencies and what to do if one happens.

For young children, it might also help to talk about who the emergency workers are in your community--- police officers, firefighters, paramedics, doctors, nurses, and so on – and what kind of things they do to help people who are in trouble.

When to Call 911; Teach kids that a 911 emergency is when someone needs help right away because of an injury or an immediate danger. For example, they could call 911 if:

*   there is a fire
*   someone is unconscious after an accident, drinking too much, or an overdose of pills or drugs.
*   someone has trouble breathing, like during an asthma flare-up or seizure

*   someone is choking
*   they see a crime happening, like a break-in, mugging, ETC.
*   there's a serious accident

Kids may feel scared or nervous if they have to call 911. Tell them that the emergency operators who answer the phone talk to too a lot of kids who are nervous or worried when they call. tell they to stay calm as they can. Make sure your kids know that even though they shouldn't give personal information to strangers, it's ok to trust the 911 operator. Explain that the emergency operator will ask them what, where, and who questions such as;

* What is the emergency?" or "What happened?'
* Where are you?" "Where do you live?"
* "Who needs help?" or "Who is with you?"

They should give the operator all the information they can about what the emergency is and how it happened. If they're old enough to understand, also explain that the emergency dispatcher may give first aid instruction before emergency workers arrive at the scene.

Other Things to Know About 911

* Make sure your kids understand that calling 911 as a joke is a crime in many places. Every prank call or unnecessary call to 911 can be delay a response to.
* Although most 911 calls are now traced. It's still important for your kids to have your street address and phone number memorized.

For Parents:

* Always refer to the emergency number as "nine-one-one" not "nine-eleven." in an emergency. a child may not call the number correctly if trying to find the *11* button on the phone.
* Make sure your house number is clearly visible from the street so that police, fire, or ambulance workers can easily locate your address.
* If you live in an apartment building, make sure your child knows the apartment number and floor you live on.
* Keep a list of emergency phone numbers handy near each phone for your kids or babysitter.
* Keep a first aid kit hand and make sure your kids and babysitter know where to find it. When kids are old enough, teach them basic first aid; unquoted.

Parents, I'm speaking to you. Open up your blind eyes and close your mouth. It's time for reality to set in. You sit on your ass all day watching television and talking on the phone. Talking bull shit all day with others. What you fail to do the most "paying attention to your children". Why is that? Because its all about you. You, your friends and others. What a damn shame. Something must happen for you to get off your ass putting something in place protecting your most valuable possession-your children. Go to hail because its now too late. Listen parents, this brings me to a movie that I was watching Sunday morning the 9th day of August 2020. Close your mouth. Close your legs. Put down the phone. "Above all listen". This movie isn't about you. It's about what can happen to your children. For reference, I will call this conversation; A SNAKE IN THE GRASS. First of all this was an old movie. I had to research to find it. a black and white movie. Both family were white with children. They met in church doing church service. They became very good friends days later and agreed to spend a lot of time together.

I will called them family A, and family B. Family A, was visited daily by family B. They went shopping and had dinner together a lot to include sleep overs. Each family had at least four (3) children. Family A, had two young girls and a son. Family B, had three son's and a girl. They all became like one big happy family. The father of family B, wanted to be more than friends with family A, oldest daughter who was only twelve (12) years of age. While at the house of family A, he would not only laugh and joke with the parents but also focus on their oldest daughter a lot. They played games of fun and took pictures together especially pictures of the oldest daughter. Their oldest daughter would pose for him wearing at that time a dress. She thinking only that he was simply nice occasionally show too much. He asked the mother one night if he take their daughter horse back riding. She told him it's a school night maybe tomorrow if its not too late. The father of family B, said ok, and started to leave.

He turned to the mother of family A, and said maybe I could pick her up from practice. The mother said ok but have my daughter back before seven (7:00) p.m. The father of family B, picked up the daughter of family A, from practice and went on their merry way somewhere but it wasn't horse back riding. He literally abducted and kidnapper the girl. The wife of family B, asked the parents of family A, not to involve the authorities. The wife of family B, was convenience that her husband would bring their daughter back. And, she was not being kidnap. Both family were thinking maybe something just happened. Fat tire or an accident. Well, that wasn't the case. The father of family B, did in fact abducted and kidnap the daughter of family A. He stage a crime scene miles outside of town making people think that they were kidnap by abandoning the car, and breaking of the driver side window. He was very created thinking after the authorities finds the car they would stop looking for them. The parents of family A, waited five (5) days before calling the authorities.

The father of family B, after picking up the daughter of family A, from practice gave her a pill to take. Their daughter trusting the him took the pill without hesitation. It turn out to be a sleeping pill. "He had a lot of them". Once the authorities were called and initiate an investigation others wanted to help. The authorities told the parents of family A, their child has been abducted and kidnap. The authorities observing the abandoned car was suspicious due to the method of how the driver side window was broken and tire track leaving away from the crime scene. The wife of family B, told authorities that they have a small trailer parked in the garage. But when the authorities checked the garage their trailer was gone. The father of family B, was in his forties, again, the daughter of family A, was only twelve (12) years of age. He repeatedly gave her a sleeping pill and forcing himself sexually on her. Note: not once in the movie did she resist him. Why; because she was under the influence of a sleeping pill.

The father of family B, called the parents of family A, from somewhere in Mexico, telling them that their daughter and him are married. And, he would like to return home but didn't want to get arrested asking for their blessing, and not to press kidnaping charges. The mother of family A, said no way will they not press charges. Our daughter is too young to marry. You had no rights to take her. We trusted you. How could you do that to us? He became angry and told the mother of family A, that her husband is homosexual. He warned her that if she don't agree he would tell others. "She did not agree". The parents of family A, called the authorities after learning the whereabout of their daughter. Note: This was a small town. Everyone knew and trusted each other. You could even leave your door open and unlock. It was all about trust. Everyone was so surprise when they found out who the kidnapper was. "They were shock". Red Flag; The brother of the wife of family B, told the authorities that his brother is attracted to young children.

The Mexican authorities found out where they were, and arrested him. They took the girl to what look like a dungeon until she was taken home by the FBI. RED FLAG; He warned the girl not to say anything. Not to talk

about what they did. Not to tell anyone that he sexually force himself on her. Not to tell anyone that he gave her sleeping pills. Why? To shut her up. To avoid going to prison. He wanted the authorities to think that they were vacating together. He made it clear to the girl that if she did say something her parents would suffer. The oldest daughter of family A, out of fear never reveal to her parents or to authorities what really happened to her. She was checked my medical professionals but there was no sign of sexual penetration or intercourse. You will be surprise of what happened later. No, you will be shock. Because the oldest daughter of family A, refused to talk her abductor and kidnapper was spare prison time. He bought some property in another state. He wanted the oldest daughter of family A, to come and stay with him.

Don't say anything "yet". Their daughter beg her parents to let her go and stay with him. According to their daughter she love him. What a crock of shit. She love him! Well, if that don't bike the snake in the ass. Of course the parents said no. But later her mother said yes, and drove her to the airport. Why? Because their daughter was threatening to leave without their permission. The relationship didn't last long. She and the man started having problems and their daughter requested a divorce. CAN YOU IMAGINE YOUR DAUGHTER MARRY THE MAN WHO ABDUCTED AND KIDNAPPER HER, AND LATER WANTING TO TAKE HER AWAY AS HIS WIFE? WHO GAVE HER SLEEPING PILLS AND REPEATEDLY RAPED HER UNCONSCIOUSLY AGAINST HER WILL UNDER THE INFLUENCE OF IN HER CASE UNKNOWN SUBSTANCE AT SUCH A YOUNG AGE?

https://www.nbcnecs.com/news/us-news/former-oklahoma-state-senator-sentenced-15-years-child-sex-trafficking-n910516
Former Oklahoma state senator sentenced to 15 years on child sex trafficking charges, By Associate Press, and I quote, OKLAHOMA CITY—A former Republican state senator in Oklahoma was sentenced to 15 years in federal prison Monday on a child sex trafficking charge.

U.S. District Judge Timothy DeGiusti handed down the sentence to Ralph Shortey, 36, who faced sentences of between 10 years and life in prison. DeGiusti also ordered Shortey to serve 10 years supervised probation once he is released from prison and said he will impose a fine on the two years lawmaker at a later date. The fine could be up to $250,000. Ralph Shortey is seen in 2017 photo release by the Cleveland County Sheriff's Office. Cleveland County Sheriff's Office via AP.

Shortey was arrested in March 2017 after police found him in a suburban Oklahoma City motel room with a then-17- year-old boy. Police were acting on a tip from the teen's father when they went to the motel and said they smelled marijuana coming from the room. Police accused the married father of four of hiring the teen for sex. Shortey resigned shortly after the arrest. His wife obtained a divorce earlier this year.

A police report indicated a search of the teen's tablet computer uncovered a series of sexually explicit exchanges for "sexual stuff".

The FBI also found that Shortey had previously used fake names to send and receive child pornography and to go on Craigslist to seek casual encounters with male, the "younger the better."

By John Paul Brammer, and I quote, Ralph Shortey, a former Oklahoma state senator who last year served as Donald Trump's campaign chair in the state, was meticulous about keeping up his reputation as a pious man, according to several fellow Oklahoma. That reputation, however, has all but disappeared. According to Shortey's attorney, the former Republican lawmaker will plead guilty to one count of child sex trafficking on Nov. 30.

Ralph Shortey is facing felony child prostitution charges after police say he solicited sex from a 17-year old boy. Cleveland County Sheriff's Office via ap.

Shortey, a 35 -year-old married father of three, resigned from the state Legislature in March after being charged with several felonies, including engaging in child prostitution, after police found him in a hotel room with a 17-year-old male. Shortey's attorney, Ed Blau, confirmed that his client will plead guilty to a charge of child sex trafficking in exchange for U.S. prosecutor's dropping the child pornography charge against him. Mr. Shortey feels this is a necessary step in putting this painful and humiliating ordeal behind him, for both himself, his family and for the state of Oklahoma. The Morning RundownGet a head start on the morning's top stories a tip from John Doe's father, police went looking for the teen at a Super 8 Motel in Moore, Oklahoma, on March 9, at a room rented with Shortey's driver's license and credit card. When officers knocked, Shortey told them he and the teen were getting dressed.

"When Shortey opened the door, Doe left the room with his backpack, which contained a bottle of lotion," the police report stated. "Inside the room, Moore Police offers found Shortey's backpack. Shortey's backpack contained an open box of condoms and a laptop computer."

The report also stated Shortey was in possession of child pornography that "depicts a man engaging in sexually explicit conduct with a prepubescent girl."

For LGBTQ advocates in heartland, Shortey's fall from grace exposed the "family values" politician as a hypocrite. Troy Stevenson, executive director of the LGBTQ organization Freedom Oklahoma, said he knew Shortey as a person who cared a great deal about maintaining his image as a good Christian lawmaker.

Steven described one encounter with Shortey ahead of a vote on an ant-transgender bill" in which the lawmaker allegedly told Stevenson that while he couldn't vote against the measure because it would inflame his Christian base, he would abstain.

Then, not 12 hours later, he sits in the committee and voted in the bill, "Stevenson lamented.

This was not the first time Shortey voted against the state's LGBTQ community because of his Goodman, a Republican and first-term state representative in Ohio, resigned on Nov. 14 because of "inappropriate behavior." Several local news outlets, including the Cleveland Plain Dealer and The Columbus Dispatch, reported Goodman-a vocal proponent of "natural marriage"—was caught engaging in sexual activity with a male visitor in his legislative office.
Stevenson said he does not believe Shortey's sexual orientation is delving into. "We've made it very clear that this isn't about him being gay. It's about him being as CHILD PREDATOR and a sex trafficker and a hypocrite. He was also caught with child pornography of both males and females of a much younger age. He's an equal OPPORTUNITY PREDATOR."

Oklahoma Pol Hit With Prostitution Charges Quits State Senate, by U.S. NEWS – Corky Siemaszko, and I quote, The Oklahoma lawmaker who was charged with child prostitution after being caught in a motel room with a teenage boy resigned Wednesday from the state senate.

Ralph Shortey said he was quitting because he did not want to be a "distraction" to his colleagues in Mary Fallin and State Sen. Mike Schulz. "My resignation is evidence of my respect for public service and the duties of our elected officials," the 35-year old Republican said in a statement.

Shortey was already being shunned by his peers. Even before he was charged with a crime, the Oklahoma Senate passed a resolution that suspended nearly all his privileges and scrubbed his name off any legislation he had a hand in – as well as his office door.

Ostensibly a conservative-family-values politician, Shortey was busted after police were notified that he had checked into a Super 8 Motel in Moore, Oklahoma – using his own name -around midnight on March 9 and a boy was with him. Shortey insisted they were "just hanging out," but police discovered a graphic online exchange in which the disgraced lawmaker asked the 17-year-old if he would be "interested in sexual stuff". The married dad is also charged with engaging in prostitution within 1,000 feet of a church, and transporting a minor for prostitution /lewdness, according to the Cleveland County District Attorney's Office.

State Sen. Ralph Shortey was charged a day after the Oklahoma Senate- by a vote of 43-0- passed a resolution that suspended nearly all his privileges. It remained to be seen whether Oklahoma would move to impeach Shortey, who represents parts of Oklahoma City, now that he has been formally charged. They have already stripped him of his capitol office, his parking space and state-owned laptop, scrubbed his name off any legislation he authored or co-authored- as well as his office door; unquoted.

https://www.hollywoodreporter.com/thr-esq/harvey-weinstein-leaves-rikers-island-state-prison-facility-1284504

March 18, 2020 by Jeremy Bar; and I quote, Harvey Weinstein Leaves
Rikers Island for State
Prison Facility

After a short stay on the island prison, he is headed to the Wende Correctional Facility in Alden, New York. Harvey Weinstein is leaving the Rikers Island prison and will be transferred to the Wende Correctional Facility in Alden, New York, a spokesperson for the New York State Department of Collections and Community Supervision told the Hollywood Reporter on Wednesday afternoon.

Long-term correctional facility "meets his or her security, medical, mental health and other needs," according to the general guidelines for prisoners. The considerations includes: whether the crime (or crimes) committed was violent, prior criminal history, the length of a prisoner's sentence, prior employment, "extensive notoriety" and the inmate's behavior in the local prison.

While housed at the Reception/Classification Center, Weinstein ---like all inmates-----will receive a shower, a delousing treatment, a shave and a haircut. He will watch an orientation video, a suicide prevention video and a "general—specific Orientation."

Weinstein's prison consultant, Craig Rothfeld, said that Weinstein will spend between two and eight weeks at the Wende Facility before getting his long-term assignment. "A normal stay is four weeks, "he said. "He will have two weeks of intake and processing right now."

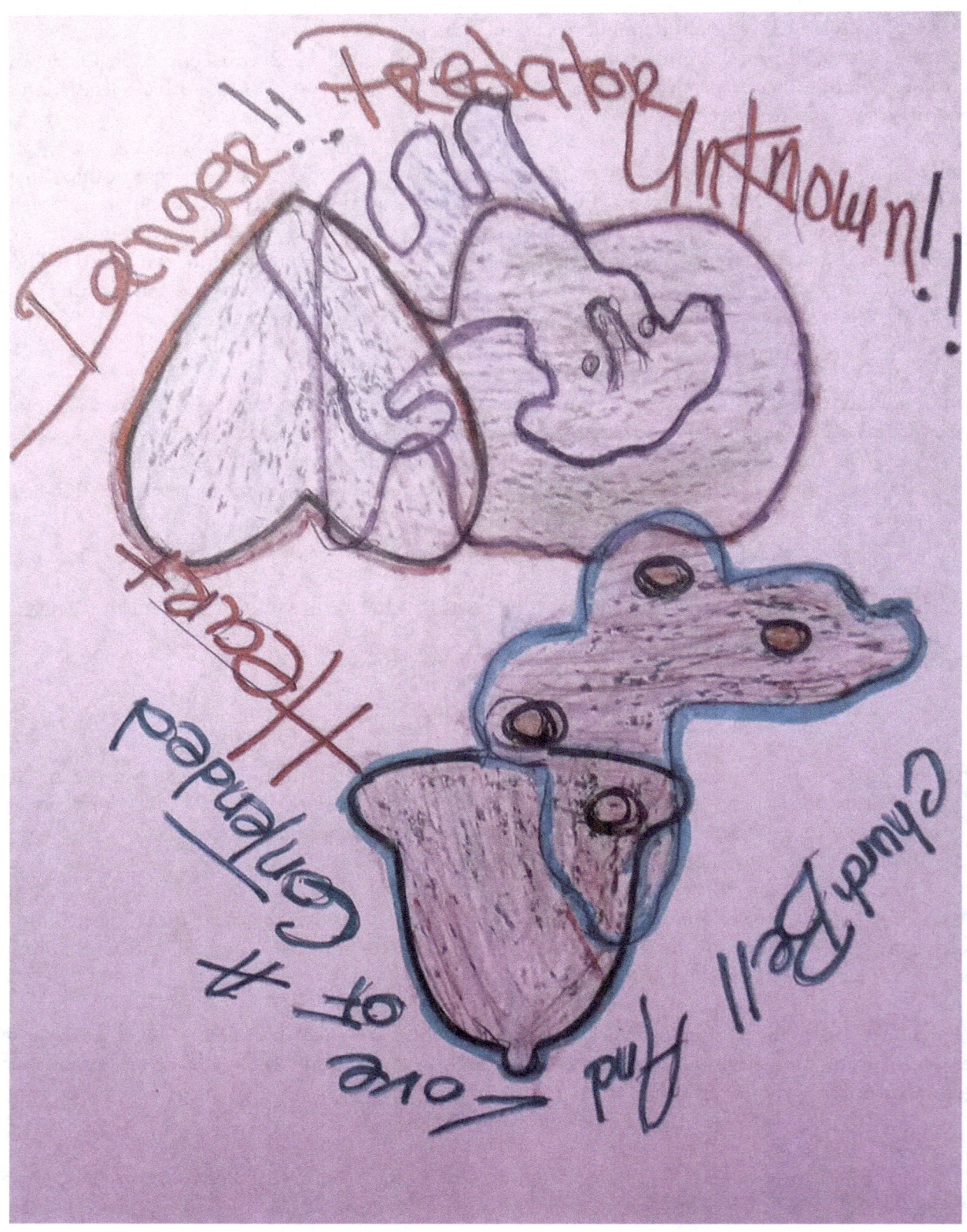

Rothfeld said there are limited options for Reception/Classification Center in New York State. As a general guideline, prisoners who face more than six more years in prison are housed in maximum—security facilities, a state spokesperson said. Weinstein was sentenced last Wednesday to term of 23 years in prison, plus several more years of supervised released after that. Weinstein, according to lawyer Donna Rotunno, has a "multitude of medicals issues" that require further treatment and monitoring.

Juda Engeimayer, a spokesperson for Weinstein, said previously that his client go to the Downstate Correctional Facility----though the state spokesperson previously said they do not comment on transfer locations. "That is the first place he will go to be received into the system," Engeimayer told THR. "We would hope he can stay there." Arthur Aidala, Weinstein's New York-based lawyer, said on the day of his sentencing that the Fishkill Correctional Center would be an ideal long-term facility for his client because it has a hospital. The Wende facility is about a six hour and 20 minute drive from New York City. Martin Horn, a former commissioner of the New York Department of Correction who now teaches at John Jay College, said that Weinstein could be at his Reception/Classification Center "for two weeks—or it could take longer."

"Depending on his medical and mental health and security needs, it could take longer to find the appropriate place, "he told THR. "He's obviously different from the run-of-the-mill, the average prisoner….they've got a pretty sophisticated way of doing it and they do pretty well. they get it right most of the time." Horn said that all state correctional facilities have medical units, though some have more sophisticated levels of care than others and some have more mental health services than others.
Weinstein, "Horn said. "He may be a target." Horn guessed that Weinstein won't be of much interest to other New York State prisoners. "I think they're probably going to be indifferent to him for the most part, "he said. In addition to the Fishkill Correctional Center, another possible long-term home for Weinstein is the Sing Sing Prison, which the New York Post recently called "the Plaza Hotel of prisons. In an ironic twist, considering Weinstein's Hollywood background, Sing Sing Prison has been featured in multiple motion pictures, including Breakfast at Tiffany's and Analyze That.

Harvey Weinstein, by DEADLINE, and I quote, convicted of rape and sexual assault in a New York courthouse on February 24, and sentenced to 23 years in prison, has been transferred from Rikers Island to a state prison in Fishkill, N.Y., Deadline has confirmed. A spokesperson for Weinstein said the move was requested because the Downstate Correctional Facility in Fishkill, N.Y., about 60 miles north of New York City, has a medical facility to handle Weinstein's ongoing heart ailments and other health issues. The former mogul recently underwent a stent procedure. Weinstein's stay at the notoriously dangerous Rikers was brief; only two days. Prior to that he was held at Bellevue Hospital in Manhattan. Exactly how long Weinstein will remain in Fishkill is unclear.
Harvey Weinstein hit with new sexual battery charges by L. A. District Attorney. By Dominic Patten, Erik Pedersen, and I quote, Harvey Weinstein tests positive for Coronavirus in NY State Prison; Convicted Producer in Isolation. Harvey Weinstein back in Bellevue Hospital with "Chest Pains" after 23-year rape sentence. Harvey Weinstein accusers speak out: "23 years! We did it." Irate Harvey Weinstein Attorney still says evidence presented irreconcilable with 'Normal, Regular Rape Victims'. Harvey Weinstein 23-year prison sentence gives "Hope to Survivors of sexual violence," says Manhattan D.A.

https://deadline.com /2020/02/Harvey-weinstein-guilty-rape-trail-new-york-appeal-assured-1202862551/

DEADLINE

Harvey Weinstein Says "But I'm Innocent" After Guilty Verdicts In Rape Trial; Sentencing Set For March 11, by Grey Evans, and I quote, Updated with Harvey Weinstein reaction: Harvey Weinstein has been found guilty of rape in the third degree and criminal sexual acts in the first degree, bringing his seven-week New York trail to a conviction in the central criminal case of the #Me Too movement.

Weinstein was remanded to custody by New York Supreme Court Judge James Burke pending sentencing on Wednesday, March 11. His defense attorney Donna Rotunno made an unsuccessful last-ditch plea to keep Weinstein free on bail due, in part, to his ill health and pain as a result of an auto accident last summer, but the judge did not grant the request. Weinstein was remanded to a medical unit, likely on Rikers Island.

Four New York court marshals immediately surrounded Weinstein, seated at the defense table. As many as nine other officers were stationed alongside walls and doors in the Lower Manhattan courtroom as the seemingly stunned former producer was led out of the courtroom in handcuffs. Weinstein remained immobile throughout the verdict delivery, staring forward toward the judge's bench. In a post-verdict press conference, Manhattan District Attorney Cyrus Vance Jr, called Weinstein a vicious, serial sexual predator who used his power to threaten, rape, assault, trick, humiliate and silence his victims. "He praised the women who testified as "brave" and "heroic," saying the accusers, including the trial's primary complainants Miriam "Mimi" Haley and Jessica Mann, have "changed the course of history.

"This is the new landscape for sexual assault survivors in America, I believe, and this is a new day, "Vance said at a news conference following the verdict announcement. "It's a new day because Harvey Weinstein has finally been held accountable for crimes he committed. The women who came forward courageously and at great risk made that happened. He's been found guilty of a criminal sexual act in the first degree and will face on that court a state prison sentence of no less than five years and up to 25 years." Rose McGowan, Mira Sorvino, Rosanna Arquette and Other "Silence Breaker" React To Harvey Weinstein Verdict. "Rape is rape, "Vance said, whether committed "in a dark alley by a stranger" or by "a man of immense power and privilege," Outside the courthouse, defense attorney Arthur Aidala expressed confidence for an appeal, telling reporters that the ground for an appeal are so strong that appellate judges would overturn this case in five minutes." Aidala said Weinstein has been the target of" a calculated campaign "since 2017," and I think the jury felt that pressure. A poll of the jury found unanimity, including on the not guilty verdicts returned for two predatory sexual assault charges involving actress Annabella Sciorra. The third degree rape count, based on a 2013 rape allegation by Weinstein's former hairstylist and aspiring actress Mann, could bring up to four years in prison, though probation on that count is possible. A third degree rape conviction means the jury found Weinstein guilty of SEXUAL INTERCOURSE WITHOUT CONSENT. A third-degree conviction required the use of PHYSICAL FORCE OR THE THREAT OF DEATH OR PHYSICAL INJURY. Mann, 34, claimed Weinstein raped her on March 18, 2013 at the Double Tree Hotel in Midtown Manhattan. Her case, like that of Haley's presented CRUCIAL CHALLENGES TO THE PROSECUTION due to the women's continued and seemingly affectionate contract with Weinstein following their encounters—contact that the defense team used to portray the accusers as mercenary careerists willingly to trade sex for

Hollywood breaks. But those challenges were met by the prosecutors, who repeatedly referenced expert testimony indicating that rape victims often maintain contact with their abusers for any number of reasons, including fear and urge to rationalize away past traumatic events. Mann provided one of the lengthy trial's most emotional and dramatic moments when she broke into sobs and left the witness stand during what she described to the judge as a panic attack. Testimony was halted for the day, and she returned to the stand the following morning carrying a squeezable stress ball. With a combined 29-year maximum sentence, the verdict could see the 67-year old Weinstein spend the rest of his life in prison. He also faces a SEXUAL MISCONDUCT TRIAL in Los Angeles involving two women, one of whom—Lauren Marie Young—testified in New York to bolster the Hadley and Mann cases.

Harvey Weinstein Guilty Verdict "Historic Moment, "Time's Up Says
The New York jury found Weinstein not guilty on two counts of PREDATORY SEXUAL ASSAULT, apparently dismissing or deadlocking on a rape allegation made by actress Annabella Ssciorra. In order to convict on the predatory counts, the jury had to find that Weinstein was guilty in the cases of Mann and/ or Haley, plus Sciorr. The criminal sexual assault (against Haley) carries a possible prison sentence of five to 25 years; the third-degree rape conviction (in the Mann case) carries a sentence from probation to four years in prison. Haley, now 42, was a Project Runway production assistant in 2006 when, she says, Weinstein forcibly performed oral sex on her in his Soho apartment on a July night in 2006. (Haley's account of having sex with Weinstein later that month at the TriBeCa Grand Hotel, under duress but not physically forced, did not produce criminal charges.

Although Sciorra's rape allegation against Weinstein couldn't be tried due to exceeding the statute of limitation—she says the incident occurred in her Gramercy Park apartment during the winter of 1993-1994—New York law allowed her testimony to be used to conjunction with that of Haley and Mann to establish predatory behavior. Three other women, including Young, testified to their own accounts of sexual misconduct involving Weinstein, as the Manhattan District Attorney's Office attempted to portray the producer as a longtime abuser who prayed on young woman attempting to gain a foothold in the film industry.

In addition to requesting to re-hear the January 24 testimony of actress Rosie Perez—including her account of a phone call in the early 1990s in which her friend Sciorra spoke of a rape—the jury requesting all Sciorra-related emails, including those between Weinstein and his private investigators Black Cube and Guidepost Solutions. The Miramax co-creator hired the companies in 2017 to investigate Sciorra and other women he suspected were co-operating with Ronan Farrow for what turned out to be the journalist's blockbuster Weinstein expose in The New Yorker. Anita Hill Says The Hollywood Commission Intends "To Chang The System" That Allows Harassment And Bias.
Anonymous; So happy the lengthy deliberations did not end in a hung jury. These jurors, obviously, took their responsibility seriously with many questions for the judge and evidence review. The die is now finally cast for Harvey even though he has LA and NY Appeal. The way this seems to be going is that sooner or later, Harvey Weinstein will spend the rest of his life in jail with much of his fortune spend on his defense. By the time he gets to LA…he will be in a wheelchair continuously decaying right before the eyes of the world. Karma.

https://en.wikipedia.org/wiki/Rikers-island
Rikers Island, by Wikipedia, and I quote, is a 413-17-acre island in the East River between Queens and the Bronx that is home to New York City's main jail complex. Supposedly named after Abraham Rycken, who bought the island in 1664, the island was originally under 100 acres in size, but has since grown to more than 400 acres. The first stages of expansion were accomplished largely by convict labor hauling in ashes for landfill. The island is politically part of the Bronx although bridge access is from Queens Community Board and uses an East Elmhurt, Queens, Zip Code of 11370 for mail. The island is home to one of the world's largest correctional institutions and mental institution, and has been described as New York's most famous jail. The complex, operated by the New York City Department of Correction, has a budget of $860 million a year, a staff of 9,000

officers and 1,500 civilians managing 100,000 admissions per year and an average daily population of 10,000 inmates. The majority (85%) of detainees are pretrial defendants, either held on bail or remanded in custody. The rest of the population have been convicted and are serving short sentences. According to a study done in 2015 by the Vera Institute of Justice, it cost the city approximately $209,000 to obtain one person for one year at Rikers Island.

Rikers Island has a reputation for violence, both abuse and neglect of inmates, attracting increased medial and judicial scrutiny that has resulted in numerous rulings against the New York City government, and numerous assaults by inmates on uniformed and civilian staff, resulting in often serious injuries. In May 2013, Rikers Island ranked as one of the ten worst correctional facilities in the United States, based on reporting in Mother Jones Magazine. Violence on Rikers Island has been increasing in recent years. In 2015 there were 9,424 assaults, the highest number in five years. The Rikers Island complex, which consists of ten jails, holds local offenders who are awaiting trial, serving sentences of one year or less, or are temporarily placed there pending transfer to another facility. Rikers Island is therefore not a prison by US terminology, which typically holds offenders serving longer-term sentences. It is home to ten of the New York City Department of Correction's fifteen facilities and can accommodate up to 15,000 prisoners.

Facilities located on the island include Otis Bantum Correctional Center (OBCC), Robert N. Davoren Complex (RNDC), formerly ARDC), Anna M. Kross Center (AMKC), George Motchan Detention Center (GMDC), North Infirmary Command (NIC), Rose M. Singer Center (RSMC), Eric M. Taylor Center (EMTC), formerly CIFM), James A. Thomas Center (JATC) (no longer used to house inmates), George R. vierno Center (GRVC) and West Facility (WF). The Bantum, Kross, Motchan, and Vierno facilities house detained male adults. Taylor houses sentenced male adolescents and adults. Davoren primarily houses male inmates who are of ages 18 through 21. Singer houses detained and sentenced female adolescents and adults. North Infirmary primarily houses inmates who require medical attention from an infirmary. The only road access to the island is from Queens, over the 4,200 foot three -lane Francis Buono Bridge, dedicated on November 22, 1966, by Mayor John Lindsay. The actual street address is 15 Hazen St. E. Elmhurst, NY 11370. Before the bridge was constructed, the only access to the island was by ferry. Transportation is also provided the Q100 MTA Regional Bus Operations route. There are also privately operated shuttles that connect the parking lot at the south end to the island. Bus services within the island for visitors visiting inmates is provided by the New York City Department of Correction on Fridays through Sundays.
Rikers Island has been referred to as the world's largest penal colony. For comparison, Europe's largest correctional facility, Silivri Prison in European Turkey, sit on 250 acres, and houses 10,904 prisoners.

https://www.yahoo.com/lifestyle/family-impacted-harvey-weinstein-scandal-004138354.html
The family affected most by the Harvey Weinstein scandal, by Taryn Rider. Writer, Yahoo Entertainment, and I quote, Harvey Weinstein is "profoundly devastated" following reports of sexual assault and harassment. Over the past week, dozen of women have come forward accusing the producer of sexual misconduct, and Weinstein's wife. Georgina Chapman, has announced she is leaving him. I have lost my wife and kids, whom I love more than anything else," Weinstein told Page six. "I fully support her decision. I didn't stand in Georgina's way when we discussed a separation. I encouraged her to do what was in her heart. I know she has to do what is best for the children, for herself considering his statement, let's take a look at that family.

Weinstein's first wife was Eve Chilton. In 1986, Chilton, worked as her future husband's assistant at Miramax. By the following year, he married her and placed her in charge of the children's division of the studio. Former Miramax employee Mark Lipsky spoke about their relationship in a 2004 book, Down and Dirty Pictures. "It

seemed like not even a day (passed0 before he was all over her ", Lipsky, who was head of distribution at the time. alleged. "For possibly a couple of weeks or so there were a dozen roses on her desk when we walked in to work, to the point where we had to confront him and say: You can't do this, it's an office not your personal, sexual playground.'
According to the Daily Mail, Chilton is the well-off daughter of a prominent New England family who summered on Martha's Vineyard. In the book, she is described as loving devoted and selfless.

While there are photos of Chilton supporting her husband at various red carpet events during their two decades long marriage, she reportedly preferred to live her life out of the spotlight. After the couple divorced in 2004, she remarried and moved to the suburbs for a quieter life. Weinstein and Chilton's divorce settlement was kept private, but they had joint custody of their three daughters Lily, 22, Emma 19, and Ruth, 14. Many of the harassment and assault allegations against Weinstein supposedly took place around the time when Chilton gave birth (1995-1998), 2002. The girls also live their life primarily out of the public eye, however, Weinstein's oldest daughter, Remy (formerly Lily), was dragged into the headlines on Thursday. Cops were called to her home in Los Angeles when she believed her father was "depressed and suicidal".

"Remy overreacted at the situation.....This situation is of course very hard for Harvey, but he is not suicidal---his heart is breaking for his kids ", an insider claimed to Page Six, adding Weinstein doesn't want them "to be drawn into the media maelstrom ". Those aren't the only kids he wants to protect. Weinstein also has two young children with his second wife, Marchesa co-founder Georgina Chapman. The producer met Chapman, then an aspiring designer, at a party in 2004. "I had no idea who he was," she recalled to Vogue years later. "He's not a person you can sort of ignore or brush off. He's incredibly charming and so charismatic, it sort of draws you in." Weinstein and Chapman began dating shortly after his divorce and pair married in 2007. In an interview two years later, Chapman brushed off their 24-year age gap and reacted to rumors she had and his infamous temper. "He is warm....and he is very funny, "she told the Evening Standard. "You can't stop people commending. Can you? You can choose to react or not react and as long as no one's life is at risk, and the children are ok, what does it matter? The There's genuine mutual respect. "He added. "Harvey is an incredibly powerful man and very talented and tenacious at what he does. And Georgina is the same, but their approaches are different. Georgina is far more firm-footed, yet they come out with the same result, which is to be the best at what they do." Chapman gave birth to their first child, daughter India, in 2010.

They welcomed a son, Dashiell, three years later. In April, the designer told Forbes she's also fiercely protective of her children. "Yes, I like my kids to know that I'm there for them, "she explained. "During the week, everyone's rushing around between activities and school, and then dinner, bath and bed....the weekends I like to be peaceful. My daughter's very keen on horse riding, so we spend a lot of time at the stables." Family on the weekends often included Weinstein's daughters from his first marriage too. Growing up, the girls would visit his home with Chapman in Connecticut every other weekend, according to a profile in Vogue. They would also participate in family vacations. Although Weinstein initially stated that Chapman was standing by him, she released a statement this week that they are separating. "My heart breaks for all the women who have suffered tremendous pain because of these unforgivable actions. I have chosen to leave my husband. Caring for my young children is my first priority and I ask the media for privacy at this time, "she said.

Georgina Chapman's Net Worth Before Her Split from Harvey Weinstein:
Weinstein responded to news of the separation by saying that he supports his wife's decision. "I am in counseling and perhaps, when I am better, we can rebuild," he said in a statement. "There has been a lot of pain for my family that I take full responsibility for.' Chapman, 41, was born in London and the Chelsea College of Art and

Design, where she met her future business partner, Keren Craig. The two co-foundered Marchesa together in 2004, the year that Chapman started dating Weinstein, 24 years her senior; unquoted.

https://www.theguardian.com/global-development/2020/jun/26/fury-in-colombia-as-admit-of-12-year-old-indigenous-girl

Fury in Colombia as soldiers admit rape of 13-years – old indigenous girl, according to The Guardian, and I quote; Several soldiers confessed to raping child from the embera tribe.

Your privacy: We and our partners use your information - collected through cookies and similar technologies – to improve your experience on our site, analyse how you use it and show you personalized advertising. You can find out more in our privacy policy and cookie policy, and manage your consent at any time by going to 'Privacy settings' at the bottom of any page. Information that may be used Purposes; I'm OK with that Options.

We know that this is not an isolation issue, it is structural, "said Aida Quilcue, a human rights adviser at the National Indigenous Organization of Colombia (ONIC), at a press conference on Wednesday, when news that authorities were investigating the rape broke. "I want to repudiate this atrocious fact that goes against the rights of women and the indigenous people of Colombia."

As the fallout continued on Thursday, some were remined of a similarly brutal act of sexual violence. In 2016, Yuliana Samboni, a seven-year-old indigenous girl, was raped and murdered in Bogota by Rafael Uribe Noguera, a wealthy architect.

This is a line that can be drawn through every act of violence against women, whether committed by a soldier, a police officer, a rich man or otherwise: and that line is the abuse of power to deny a woman the right to her own body," said Olga Amparo Sanchez, director of Casa de la Mujer, a Bogota-based women's rights organization. "The fundamental issue is that a woman's life has no value in this country.

"The seven soldiers accepted the charge of "unlawful sexual abuse of a minor under 14 years old", the age of consent in Colombia. The country's attorney general, Francisco Barbosa, said that the men could receive a sentence of between 16 and 30 years in prison.

Colombia's vice- president, Marta Lucia Ramirez, called for a speedy judicial process on Thursday. "Colombia must be merciless with sexual abusers of minors, adolescents and women," the country's first female vice-president tweeted. "Ou: Pr solidarity with the girl and her family."

The Embera community, to which the girl belongs, had previously requested that the perpetrators be subject to their own laws, which Colombia's constitution grants to autonomous indigenous reserves. Colombia is home to about 2 million indigenous people from 115 different groups. Some observers say that the horrific episode reveals systemic cruelty within the military. "It's something systematic, and if their security training and doctrine doesn't change and doesn't include a serious human rights component, we can expect to see crimes like this becoming normalized," said Mafe Carrascal, a Bogota-based activist. Others see an alarming pattern of violence against women, particularly during the nationwide lockdown against the coronavirus pandemic that began on 20 March. Colombia has seen 110 femicides this year, with 50 during lockdown; unquoted.

www.vaches.com/help_text/sexual_assault.html

Sexual Assault Resources, and I quote, ……. These are Sexual Assault Resources
Please also see
Acquaintance/Date Rape 11 Drugs-Facilitated Rape 11 Prison "Rape Culture" 11 Sexual Harassment

Articles/Information/Research
(click here for Organizat_ons/agencies)
(click here for Commentary and Opinion)

Canada to pay C $ 1 bn to sexual misconduct victims in military "Canada's government will pay nearly C$ 1 bn ($770m) to members of the military who took part in class-action lawsuits alleging widespread sexual misconduct. "No one should feel unsafe in their place of work, in their communities," Justin Trudeau told reporters on Thursday, according to the CBC. "There are a lot of negotiation and discussions with both the people concerned and their representatives and we were pleased that we got a settlement that was acceptable to the people involved ", the prime minister said. A 2016 survey found that 27% of women in the armed forces had been sexually assaulted during their career, while members of the military were twice as likely to be sexually assaulted than the general population of working Canadians".

The Guardian, July 19, 2019
Thompson Man Charged with kidnapping and Sexually Assaulting Massachusetts Girl. "As alleged in the complaint, on May 31, 2019, Besaw encountered a 12-year old girl ("minor victim") at a park in Webster, Massachusetts, and enticed the minor victim to enter his vehicle. Besaw, who identified himself as "Chuck" then drove the minor victim to a wooded area in Thompson, Connecticut, where he sexually assaulted her. After the assault, Besaw drove the minor to Dudley, Massachusetts, where he released the minor victim in a neighborhood that was unfamiliar to her. The minor victim then borrowed a phone from a stranger to contact her parents who picked her up and brought her to the police station to report the incident. Later that day, a sexual assault examination of the victim was conducted at a medical facility. It is alleged that Besaw was identified as a suspect after an extensive investigation led by Webster Police with support from the Connecticut State Police, which included analysis of surveillance video collected from numerous residences and businesses in Connecticut and Massachusetts. On July 10, 2019, investigators conducting surveillance of Besaw collected cigarette butts that Besaw had discarded. It alleged that DNA evidence collected from the discarded cigarette butts matched DNA evidence collected from the minor victim on May 31, 2019.

U.S. Attorney's Office (CT), July 17, 2019
Three-decade prison term for man guilty in rape, imprisonment of girl on Lake County pot farm. 'A Lake County man accused in 2013 of imprisoning a 15- year-old girl in a tool box and sexually abusing her on an illegal marijuana farm was sentenced to 31 years in federal prison Wednesday, the U.S. Attorney's Office said. Ryan Balletto, 36, of Lakeport, pleaded guilty last year in U.S. District Court in San Francisco to charges stemming from the investigation, which revealed he and his partner were growing about 1,300 marijuana plants illegally and had forced the girl to work for them, according to federal prosecutors. The sentence was just one year short of the 32 years requested by federal prosecutors because of the severity of Balletto's admitted crimes, which included "sadistic physical, sexual, and psychological abuse of a 15-year-old girl over a prolonged period of time, "according to a July 3 sentencing memorandum filed by the U.S. Attorney's Office ".

St. Bernard sheriff pays $200k to settle girl's claim of sexual abuse by jail deputy. "St. Bernard Parish Sheriff James Pohimann in March for $200,000 a lawsuit brought by a teenage girl who claimed she was subjected to persistent sexual abuse by a St. Bernard jail deputy. The settlement, which has not previously been reported, resolved a claim from the girl that a veteran deputy in the jail's juvenile division ordered her to masturbate for him and to disrobe in front of a surveillance camera while she was incarcerated from June 2015 to January 2016. The deputy, Eddie Williams, 69, remains on Pohlmann's staff but in the fleet maintenance division.

New Orleans Advocate, June 10, 2019
City schools see 2,000 percent rise in 'forcible-sex offenses'. "City schools are facing a sickening epidemic of sexual misconduct. In just the past year, the number of "forcible-sex offenses" reported by educators has risen nearly 2,000 percent----from just 21 in 2016-17- to 447 last year, according to a Post analysis of state data. By comparison, the entire rest of the state logged only 49 such incidents last year, the figures show. The offenses involve "completed or attempted" sexual contact from rape to forced groping, and seven involved victims and perpetrators as young as elementary school students, according to the data". Suspect accused of raping 3-year-old girl, infecting her with his STDs "According to court records, the victim's mother noticed discharge in her diaper and took her to a local hospital for treatment. The doctor confirmed she was infected with the STDs, and police began investigating. During polygraph test, Perkins allegedly admitted to raping the girl in January while he was doing drugs. He said he assaulted the girl at his apartment while her mother was at work. The affidavit also notes Perkins has the same STDs that the girl was found to have contracted". March 6, 2019. Chargers: McDonald's manager in Twin Cities raped 14-year-old employee in cooler, elsewhere. "A manager at a McDonald's restaurant in Maple Grove raped a 14-year-old employee in the cooler and assaulted her elsewhere for weeks afterward according to chargers. Andrew Otero Albertorio, 24, of Maple Grove was charged last week in Hennepin County District Court with five counts of first-degree criminal sexual conduct and remains jailed in lieu of $100, 000 bail. An employee at the McDonald's location near Base Lake Road and interstate 494, said Tuesday that Albertorio no longer works there.
January 22, 2019.

Havertoman was convicted for child sexual assault
"|Media Courthouse—A Havertoman man was convicted on four counts Friday for the sexual abuse of a 4-year-old boy last year." The horrific actions of the defendant, Michael Kaminsky are deplorable, abhorrent and reprehensible, as he sexually abused an innocent 4-year old child who was entrusted in his care ", said Delaware County District Attorney Kateyoun M. Copeland following the conviction. "As he is currently incarcerated, and will likely be so for a long time, he can cause no more harm to this victim or any other children. November 16, 2018.

Man admits to raping, killing at least nine young girls
"New Delh – A jobless 20-year-old Indian man has confessed to raping and killing at least nine girls aged between three and seven in New Delhi, the capital, and three other cities over the past two years, police said on Wednesday. The case spotlights the number of young children who go missing every year in India and raises the question of whether the police have sufficient resources to investigate such brutal sex crimes". Reuters, November 21, 2018.

Two men sexually assaulted a 9-month-old girl and filmed it, authorities say "Memphis, Tenn, ---two men in Tennessee accused of sexually assaulting a 9-month-old girl and recording the sexual acts on a phone were indicated by a jury Tuesday. Authorities said 19-year-old Isiah Hayes was sexually aroused and performing acts on the child while 22-year-old Daireus Ice filmed a series of videos, WREG-TV reported. Advertisement the victim's mother later discovered the Hayes in the video after searching on Facebook and gave the information to police. WHBQ-TV reported, Hayes admitted to the crime after he was arrested earlier this year, police said. October 10, 2018.

CHP officer in Amador County arrested on suspicion of raping 12-year-old girl.
A California Highway Patrol officer in Amador County was arrested Monday afternoon on suspicion of raping a 12-year-old girl, the Amador County Sheriff's Office said. Michael Joslin, 36, is suspected of molesting the child for about a year. Undersheriff Gary Redman said in a news release. A church pastor called officers Sunday afternoon and told them that the girl's mother told the pastor that the girl had been molested. Redman said, Joslin was located Monday in Placer County and arrested on suspicious of oral copulation with a minor under 14, lewd acts with a child under 14, continuous sexual abuse of a child, penetration with a foreign object and rape, Redman said. August 15, 2018.
Man caught having sex with stroke victim shrugs off rape allegations; 'C'mon, she could nod her head'. "A man caught having sex with an incapacitated stroke victim at Bronx Lebanon Hospital shrugged off the rape allegations he's facing, claiming that the bed-ridden woman was a prostitute he had patronized before, authorities said Tuesday. "C'mon she could nod her head, she could say 'No'. She could say 'Yes', "suspect Keith Nembhard, 37, told cops after a nurse at Bronx Lebanon Hospital found him on top of the 32-year-old patient around 5:30 p.m. Saturday, police said. Nembhard said he was visiting the woman at the hospital when she consented to having sex with him—even though doctors said she suffered a stroke and multiple seizures". September 5, 2017.
Man accused of deadly hammer attack faces new charge: lewd act with child Read more here:

http://www.sacbee.com/news/crime/article173643211.html#storylink=cpy
"They stared down Deandre Chaney Jr. from their seats Friday afternoon as he faced a judge from his courtroom cell – his former girlfriend, a protective plastic collar around her neck, now mourning the death of her eldest child; her mother and other family members calling out "coward" and "he killed my grandson" through their tears. Their glares soon turned to sobs. Prosecutors on Friday added a new charge at Deandre Chaney Jr.'s arraignment on murder and attempted murder charges in the Sept. 15, 2017.

Former teacher found guilty of abducting, raping and killing 10-year-old Hailey Owens, may face death penalty. "Springfield, Mo. – A former middle school football coach was found guilty on Thursday of snatching a 10-year-old girl from a quiet Missouri neighborhood in front of horrified witnesses and then raping and killing her. Jurors convicted Craig Wood of first-degree in the February 2014 death of Hailey Owens. Jurors will hear more arguments before deciding whether to recommended the death sentence. Wood's attorney, Patrick Berrigan, didn't dispute that Wood killed Hailey, but contended that Wood didn't deliberate first, as prosecutors allege. Berrigan described the abduction as impulsive, saying Wood had "no disguise whatsoever ". Berrigan blamed long-suppressed sexual urges and methamphetamine". November 2, 2017. Brooklyn man busted for repeatedly raping pre-teen member of extended family. "An 18-year-old Brooklyn man raped a pre-teen member of his extended family, authorities said Monday. Police arrested David Teitelbaum late Sunday and charged him with rape, sex abuse and acting in a manner to a child younger than 17. Teitelbaum, who has no previous arrest record, was arraigned on $15,000 cash bail Monday night. His defense attorney denied all the allegations, noting that his client has no history of trouble with the law". November 13, 2017.

Warrants: Mom sought men to sexually assault daughter, 10. "The mother of a 10-year-old girl found dead and dismembered in her New Mexico home told that she sought men online to sexually assault her daughter. The Albuquerque Journal reports that Michelle martens told police she had set up encounters with at least three men. The child's brutal death sparked vigils and outcry across New Mexico. September 14, 2016.

Georgia man gets life in prison for sexually assaulting fiancee's 12-year-old daughter, tells judge he was 'a good father until then'. "Shalin Ren Payne, who has ink covering his entire face, was babysitting the girl while his fiancée was at work when he attacked her in October. The girl's 4-year-old brother was close by". August 11, 2016.

Jail ordered for sexual assault.
"McCook, Nab. – A McCook man charged with sexually assaulting two young children, with alleged offenses dating back to 2003 and as recent as 2012, will serve less than two years in county jail following his sentencing earlier this week. The offender, 66-year-old Benito Garcia of 906 E. Fifth Street, was convicted on two misdemeanor offenses and ordered to serve 300 days in jail stemming from a Red Willow County assault and a consecutive 300 days stemming from an assault occurring in Frontier County". October 8, 2015.

HIV-positive rapist jailed for filmed sex with 6-year-old boy.
"An Hiv positive Pennsylvania man is charged with raping a 6-year-old, recording the sickening act and spreading it on the internet, cops said. Ira S. Task, who told the cops he was HIV- positive for over 20 years, was busted after cops saw footage of him and another man raping a 6-year-old on a third pervert's phone. October 21, 2015.

Kansas women dies after being raped, set on fire at park.
"Neighbors discovered the screaming ignited in flames last week at a Wichita park, but she succumbed to her injuries Saturday morning.Police have arrested Cornell A. McNeal, 26, in connection to the attack. "Wichita, Kan.---A 36---year-old woman who had been sexually assaulted and set on fire died Saturday morning, police said, just over a week after she was found in a Wichita park with several burns on more than half her body and cuts on her head". November 22, 2014.

Girl, 15 with low IQ gang-raped under desk during class in Elmont: suit A mentally challenged 15-year-old girl was gang-raped beneath her desk during class---only feet away from her teachers---at an Elmont, N. Y., school, according to a lawsuit filed Friday. When the girl reported the horrific incident the next day.. School officials failed to it. The victim's mother claimed in the suit.
January 12, 2013. 'I'm a dirty rapist, 'Queens man tells cops after arrest for alleged sex assault. "A tattooed man accused of waving a fake gun and raping a woman in Queens told cops he was a "sex addict," and blamed drugs for his behavior, a prosecutor said Thursday. "I'm a dirty rapist," says defendant George Persaud in a taped conversation with cops, according to a prosecutor at Persaud's arraignment in Queens Criminal Court.

That's clearly me. I guess I raped her." January 10, 2019. 'Girl in the closet' Lauren Kavanaugh jailed after she's accused of sexually assaulting teen girl, Lewisville police say. "Lauren Kavanaugh, who became known as the "Girl in the Closet" after surviving years of torture and abuse at the hands her family, has been charged with sexual assault of a child, Lewisville police said Wednesday. Police received a tip Monday that a 14-year-old girl had been in a "sexual assaulted by Kavanaugh. The girl told officers that she had been in a relationship with Kavanaugh for two months, police said. Detectives determined that the victim met Kavanaugh, 25, through a

Facebook account titled "the |Lauren Kavanaugh Story", which Kavanaugh used to offer friendship and support to victims of abuse, police said. December 20, 2018.

Woman who was raped as a Teenager is Awarded $1 Billion in Damages.
"Hope Cheston was 14 when, outside a friend's birthday party in October 2012 in Jonesboro, Ga; an armed security guard at an apartment complex raped her on a picnic table. For years, she thought she'd be forgotten like countless other sexual assault victims. But on Tuesday, jurors in Clayton County, Ga; awarded her $ 1 billion in compensatory damages in a civil lawsuit against Crime Prevention Agency Inc., the security company that employed her rapist. Her lawyers believe it is, by far, the largest jury verdict ever awarded in the United States in a sexual assault case." May 23, 2018.

Kidnapped California girl, 13, jumps out of moving truck to escape captor who allegedly drugged, raped her. "The unarmed victim, 13, apparently agreed to an offered ride from Timothy Lee Marbie, 50, outside at a Napa Shell gas station after she ran away from home following a fallout with her mother Friday morning. April 4, 2017; unquoted.

When the sky changes people tends to change blaming it on the moon as in the life of a wolf but not of human species. We seek out to blame others when things don't go our way. We think of excuses to take the place of what really happened in our life. We use these excuses to exploit temptation gaining the attention of others. We wonder later down the road what went wrong. Why did I do that? Did I need money that bad? Could I have waited? What are we talking about? Who are we talking about? Well, that takes us into a story about two good friends both females in high school. One of them has been going online looking at "Porn" advertisement, wanting young girls to Audition for a part. But what drives her the most is the all mighty dollar called "Big Butts". The younger girl tries to talk her out of it; hey girl friend don't do it. But of course, she don't listen.

She would rush home every day from school to go online "Porn" star advertisement. More and more she's drawn into it stronger then before. One day she set up a camera system posting videos of herself striping taking off her blouse, bra, and sometime panties. Other times she would take off everything and sexually seduce men getting them sexually arouse. She didn't stop there, Oh no. She would spread her legs widely open from time to time twisting into multiple positions. One day she received an acknowledgement inviting her to a motel. She didn't even tell her best friend. She told no one. Because she knew that her best friend would had tried to talk her out of going. Men were putting hundredth of dollars into her online account. She came home from school the next day and started preparing for her big day view. She dressed hot and sexy. She was indeed a very beautiful young lady.

But young and foolish. She didn't know her ass from her feet. It was all about the money. Hard head, soft ass, lesson learned. She is about to learn a very good lesson. She goes to the motel later that night. She walk to the door. She knock on the door. There is a sign on the door that says will be back soon. She push on the door and it opens. She goes inside looks and walk around for a few minute and sits down. She stands up after hearing noise outside and goes to the door. A man appears outside of the door as she attempts to leave forcing her back into the room. He tied up her arms, legs, and tape up her mouth. She now realizes there is something wrong. He doesn't hurt her or anything. He goes online to his buyer advertising her for a price. But at no time does she see his face. Days past no one has heard from her. No one has seen her.

Her friend and family begins to worry that something is wrong. Her mother and father are divorce. The mother calls the father reporting their daughter missing. He comes over to the house angry and pissed the (F) off. He asked her how long has it been? What was she wearing? Have you call the police? He said, don't worry about it.

I've do it. He called the police. They came over to the house. The mother gave the police a description of her daughter and also a picture of her. The police organized a search days later looking for their daughter. The police later that week got the News Network involved and put out a missing person alert. The girl best friend Beckey, and a male school friend name Jason, decided to try things their way. Jason was also a friend of the missing girl Nancy. She knew Jason but not that well.

Jason and Beckey plotted an act of mercy to track down Nancy by posting herself online as a "Porn" sex star. Jason, you could say very smart when it came to computers and electronic equipment. He monitor her online when presenting herself as a porn sex star, and recorded everything. Whoever that person was he knew that their conversation was being recorded. Because the second time she went online he block her friend Jason so that they couldn't be monitor or recorded. Beckey received an acknowledgement inviting her to the same hotel that Nancy went to. Beckey was not abducted or kidnap that night maybe because he knew it was a trap. But later in the story the abductor/ kidnapper turns out to be Nancy, Jason, and Beckey, high school English teacher, Mr. David Aborade.

He was married and have a ten (10) year old boy. The next day at school Beckey was asked by Mr. Aborade to stay for a few minutes. Beckey notice as they were talking "familiar words of expression was used. I'm not sure how she kept a straight face but he to caught on quickly that she knew that he was the kidnapper. But of course, being in school he didn't try anything. She called her mother but everything "Voice mail". So, she left her mother a voice message telling her mother about the teacher; and that she's going to follow him. Beckey followed Mr. Aborade to where her friend Nancy might be. He went into the house as if he didn't know that Beckey was watching him. Beckey got out of her car and very quickly ran to the left side of the house.

Mr. Aborade, the English teacher came up from behind her putting something over her head taking her to an enclosed container. He tied Beckey to the bed and gage her mouth. After Beckey mother listen to the recording on her phone. She went to the high school and spoke to the principle. The principle gave Beckey's mother the address of the English teacher Mr. Aborade. The mother, Miss. Boaldrin, went to Mr. Aborade house. She knock on the door. His wife came to the door. She said Mrs. Aborade, I believe that your husband have my daughter. Please, may I come in? Mr. Standfort, the father was waiting in the car. Miss Boaldrin was inside the house for at least a good ten to fifteen minutes. Mr. Aborade wife gave her his other address. She and Mr. Standfort, the father drove there quickly but first called and formed the police. They saw their daughter car parked on his property. They knock on his door. Mr. Aborade came to the door with a gun behind his back. They identify themselves as the girl parents. He asked them would they like to look around? Of course they did but there was no sign of their daughter or the other girl. Mr. Aborade gave the other girl something to put her to sleep. But, they only look into room where door were already open.

Common sense should had told them to open doors that were not already open. But apparently that didn't happen. Lets called that the blind leaving the blind. The mother went in one direction and the father went in the other direction. I thought at one time he was going to open a door. He would had saw the other girl lying on the floor asleep. "That didn't happen". Good news, as they were getting ready to leave. They heard noise, a female voice coming from an enclosed metal container. It was their daughter. Minute late, Mr. Aborade came outside with the other girl pointing a gun at them. He said; get back, don't come near me. I will kill her. The girl fought Mr. Aborade knocking the gun out of his hands. He got into his car and drove away but didn't get far. They quickly untied the other girl and freed their daughter from out of that metal container.

https://en.wilkipedia.org/Webcam_model

The article in which you are about to sink your teeth into relates to the story above showing that Webcam is real, and can harm young people minds attracting the wrong audient fulfilling their mind with false hope and dreams. Webcam model, and I quote, colloquial gender-neutral; camodel; female camgirl; male; camboy) is a video performer who is streamed upon the internet with a live webcam model often performs erotic acts online, such as stripping, masturbation, or sex in exchange for money, goods, or attention. They may also sell videos of their performances. Since many webcam models operate from their homes, they are free to choose the amount of sexual contents for their broadcasts. While most display nudity and sexually provocative behavior, some choose to remain mostly clothed and merely talk about various topics while still soliciting payment as tips from their fans. Webcam models include "women, men, straight, gay, and trans" performers. Once viewed as a small niche in the world of adult entertainment, by 2016, camming because "the engine of the porn industry", according to Alec Helmy, the publisher of XBIZ., a sex-trade industry journal.

In 1996 an American college student and conceptual artist, Jenny Ringley, created a website called "JenniCam." Her web camera was located in her dorm room and automatically photographed her every few minutes. The camera captured Rilngley doing almost everything—brushing her teeth, doing her laundry, doing stripteases – and then broadcast its images live over the internet. Later in 1998 she divided her website's access into free and paying. Also in 1998, a commercial site called AmadaCam was launched. Amanda's site, like Ringley's had multiple camera around her house which allowed people to look in on her. However Amanda made an important early discovery that would influenced the camming industry for decades to come -- that a website's popularity could be greatly increased by enabling viewers to chat with a performer while online. Within her members section, Amanda made it a point to chat with her viewers for over three hours a day. Since the early days of live webcasts by Ringley and Amanda, the phenomenon of camming has grown to become a multibillion—dollar industry which has an average of at least 12,500 cam models online at any given time.

Payment systems define format

A camming website acts as a middleman and talent aggregator by hosting, hundreds of independent models, and verifies that all are at least 18 years old. Camming, websites typically fall into two main categories, dependent upon whether their video chat rooms are free or private. In private chat rooms, viewers pay by the minute for a private show. However, in free chat rooms payment is voluntary and is in the form of tips, thus providing the model with an income at a minimal cost for the multiple viewers of her chat room's video stream.

Tips are electronic tokens that viewers can buy from a camming website, and then given to the models during live performances to show appreciation. Tokens can also be used to buy access to private shows, operate a Teledidonic device that a model may be wearing, or used to buy videos and souvenirs from a model. The website provides the transactional platform and then collects and distributes a percentage of the tips to the models. Within public chat rooms the audience can see tips and viewers comments as scrolling text which appears next to the real-time video stream. Camgirls will frequently read and respond to the scrolling viewer comments.

Much of the success of camming owes to its ability to move beyond the borders of erotic videos performance, and into the everyday social lives of camming customers. Webcam performers are often highly entrepreneurial, and use mainstream social networking, sites such as Twitter, Instagram, Snapchat, Skype, and Tumblr to build and maintain relationships with their customers. Camming sites specify rules and restrictions for their cam models, which in turn tend to give the camming site a distinct style and format. For example, one major free-access site, which only allows female models, fosters an environment where the camgirls are not necessarily obligated to do Masturbation shows, or even display nudity.

Resources for performers:
Cam studios allow models to rent facilities outside of their home. These businesses can supply model with video equipment, Internet service, computer, lighting, and furniture. Within some studios the cam models can work by the percentage of business they bring in, instead of renting studio time. The cam models do not have to pay to join this type of studio, but they ae also not guaranteed a salary.
Another workplace option is called a "camgirl mansion" which is a place that provides equipment and broadcast rooms where multiple camgirls can live and share expenses, but without a studio owner.

RISKS
While the conduct of webcam model's clients in chat rooms has been described as generally civil and polite, some model have faced "aggressive sexual language" and online harassment. In 2012, a group of chan users harassed a webcam model about her weight until she began crying on camera. Even clients who are polite can behave in ways that makes models feel uncomfortable, such as when clients become overly attached to, or obsessive, about a models; if the client is a regular customer and a heavy tipper, this can make the model feel pressured to give in to the client's requests. Webcam models have occasionally been the targets of cybers and blackmailers. If they don't comply, they run the risk of having their real identity exposed. Internet trolls revealed the real name, address and phone number of a webcam performer and posted this information, along with explicit photos of her, on social medial, and the account was forwarded to her friends and family. Another issue faced by cam models is that viewers may record streams or images of the model without their consent and then redistribute them on pornography websites. Unauthorized use has been likened to theft of the model's property, since the porn site will earn money from the video an not the cam model; unquoted.

I find myself with pretty of time on my hands due to CoviD 19, and therefore watches a lot of television movies. But that's not a bad thing. I have a story of interest for you Moms and Fathers. You may also want to watch this movie. It painfully hits home. What you're about to read will bring tears to your eyes. The movie itself is a bitch meaning the lives of the characters will suffer a terrible end of torture at the hand of a serial killer the worse predator of all enemy of young beautiful helpless women. This guy told each of the women that he can't get women. No matter how hard he tries they prefer someone else.

Whatever you do don't feed into his feelings, emotions, or his demeanor. He is a snake in the grass and the worse kind. He hangs at a bar the same bar all the time trying to pick up women. He looks like someone very unhappy, tall, medium built, angry looking, and never smiles. You'll be surprise where he lives. Although a predator an enemy of women can live any where. This guy live outside of the city remote country built up area away from everyone. You could say that he don't want to be disturb. Total isolation and strictly privacy. Well, lets get into the story especially now that I have your attention. This guy name was Gerimery Wilton. One night he was sitting at the bar. To the left end of the bar was two young women. He bought one of the women a drink. She gave him a note on the way out saying; you must be dreaming. He was very pissed off. He stake out her housing area. He saw her the next morning jogging and going into her house. While she was taking a shower he quietly invited himself into her house searching up everything including her bedroom. He even took one of her undees (pants) and put it into his left side pocket. She thought that she heard a noise while taking a shower but apparently there was no one. Well, that's what she thought. I thought that she was going to be kidnap right then and there but that didn't happen. Gerimery Wilton made his move the following morning. She came out of her house heading to her car. She opened the car door and started putting her sport bag into the car. Before she could close the car door he grabbed her from behind from the back seat putting something over her nose stopping her from screaming.

"Both the kidnapper and the young girl were white. This guy had a certain taste in women; young and beauty, and white. Why white only; I don't know. Gerimery Wilton tied her up in his basement both arms and legs. He injected her with something every time she awaken screaming and yelling at least six (6) different times. He tries several times to feed her what look like hot cereal. She initially rejected the food. He tried to sweet talk her getting her to feel sorry for him. She later in the week calm down getting him to untie her stopping the injections. They shortly thereafter started talking especially about his father. She saw a picture of his father the police officer in the background of the room. She said tell me about your father. He replied do you really want to know? She said yes. Tell me about him. So he started talking about his father while touching her hair. She looked up at him. He smile. Gerimery Wilton continued talking about his father saying that his father was a man of standards and had a voice that demand attention.

Gerimery said that he respected him for that.
She asked Gerimery what happened to his father. He replied I buried him. Her eyes ball up like stars in the sky. Her mouth became the size of a small soft ball in shock of what to say next fearing that something would happen to her. She froze like ice couldn't move a muscle as he stared down at her. She said softly please continue. He said after my Mom died his father changed caring only about his job. A twist of fresh air kicked in small talk between the two of them. She and Gerimery started talking about love and women. Why you feel that women don't like you? Women are not that way. They like all men. Your tall and handsome and very muscular. That put a smile on his face. He said why did you say that to me? Gerimery said that's not true and you knows. She said look at you. Gerimery left the room and went again to the bar. The conversation was starting to make him feel uncomfortable.

While at the bar drinking a young beautiful woman caught his attention. He was looking hard down on her. Remember; he like them young and beautiful. Gerimery asked the bartender who is she. The bartender told Gerimeray that you don't want to mess with her. Gerimery replied I don't remember asking for your opinion. It so happen that the young lady in question of attraction boy friend was there. Her boy friend was much more built, heavily built and taller than him. Geirmery got his ass kicked. The other man also got his ass kicked when he turned his back on Gerimery thinking that he was out for the count too unconscious to move. Gerimery after slowly getting onto his feet he stole the man truck and drove home with it. He was hurt and bleeding from the forehead. The girl whom he abducted and kidnapped treated his wounds.

She said O' my God, what happened to you? He later laid onto the bed next beside. Gerimery awaked hours later feeling better went and fixed something for them to eat. He was starting to feel differently toward her not that she treated his wounds. She asked him what happened at the bar? He said that I wanted a another woman someone like yourself. What a "blow", what a shock? Another woman he said. But it didn't happen. His little adventure turned into a house of pain. His gratification for another woman seeking twice the pleasure was a wake up call leave women at a bar alone. Gerimery and the girl became more and more comfortable together days later as he stared into her eyes, kissing her, and touching her sexually. It seem as if she was loving the sexual fulfillment coming from him. The revealing of my eyes to yours as he sexually went down fucking her causing

her to scream openly in gratification. Soon thereafter she got dress and started up the stairs. She saw him sitting in a chair corner of a wall. Gerimery told her that she is free to leave. She acted as if she didn't want to leave him.

BECAUSE THEY HAVE JUST HAD PASSAGE SEX. She didn't want to leave. She said I don't want to leave. I love you. Why are you making me leave? He said to her leave. Leave now; I can't stay here. I kidnapped you. The police will be looking for me. Go, go now. He had to forced her outside in order for her to leave. FBI, CASE FILE PART 11, Stockholm Syndrome; The FBI Agent assigned to the case was puzzled as he looked into this young lady eyes as he was questioning her. She at first refused to cooperate with him staying that she was not kidnap and that Gerimery Wilton has done nothing wrong. "Hm"; what's going on inside of her head? Lets take you back on the day of her being physically forced out of Gerimery's house refusing to leave as insisted by him. A woman was driving down the road listening to rock music spotted her along side the road. She cautiously approached the girl to avoid any sudden movement. The girl awaken slowly and looked at her. She was asked are you alright? She being tired, weak, and unconsciously not knowing where she was spoke softly help me. The woman driving the car helped the girl to her vehicle. She was later seen being question by the FBI. The FBI Agent asked her, what do we remember about the man? What does he look like, and how tall is he? Where does he live? Again, she refused to cooperate saying I'm not going to tell you. The FBI Agent, showed her pictures of other girls that Gerimery Wilton had abducted and kidnapped. Some of the women had been brutally killed with multiple stabbing wounds, beating to death, and amputation of body parts. There were found buried in a field near by not far from where Gerimery lives. The FBI Agent, told her if you must keep quiet just answer this one question; did he tell you about his father?

She said yes. The FBI Agent, told the girl that he is wanted in connection with the disappearance and murder of his father in Stockholm. He said that this case is called the Stockholm Syndrome due to the death of his father disappearance. What you don't is that shortly after she was forced to leave Gerimery Wilton's house he abducted and kidnapped another girl. Shortly after having a fulfillment of sexual pleasure he told the girl that she could leave. Really, well, bite the lips and close your legs. He followed her minutes later grabbing a knife as his killing weapon of choice. He later saw a Crowbar, grabbed it and chased her into the field, far into the field where an old building was. He yelled come out where ever you are. Can you imagine being killed so viciously? She was tall, beautiful, and wearing only pants.

Gerimery chased this poor young beautiful girl down and hit her three time in the Belly with that Crowbar until she was dead. And, get this; Gerimery Wilton, blamed her forcing him to killed her saying; "Look what you made me do". He put her decease body, naked dead body, on back of that stolen truck and drove it to her final resting place an isolated field out of sight and out of mind. He told the girl thanks for wasting my time. You are free to go. Think about Mothers, and Fathers that could had been your daughter. What would you had done? Where would you had look? What questions would you had ask? These missing girls identity was plastered on poles, doors, and an on just about every news station. Yes, people were talking about them but no one really took an active interest to find them. like in western movies where trails goes cold the pursuit stops. NO ONE CARES ANYMORE. But you know who does? The parents of those missing children. What follows is an article with respect to what the FBI Agent, in the story called Stockholm Syndrome.

https://en.wikipedia.org/wiki/Stockholm_syndrome
Stockholm syndrome, and I quote, has been defined as a condition in which hostages develop a psychological alliance with their captors during captivity. Emotional bonds may be formed between captor and captives, during intimate time together, but there are generally considered irrational in light of the danger or risk endured by the victims. Stockholm syndrome has never been included in the Diagnostic and Statistical Manual of Mental

Disorders or DSM, the standard tool for diagnostic of psychiatric illnesses and disorders, mainly due to the lack of a consistent body of academic research.

The syndrome is extremely rare as noted by the U.S. Federal Bureau of Investigation's Hostage Barricade Database System and Law Enforcement Bulletin estimating that fewer than 5% of kidnaping victims show evidence of Stockholm syndrome. This term was first used by the medial in 1973 when four hostages were taken during a bank robbery in Stockholm, Sweden. The hostages defended their captors after being released and would not agree to testify in court against them. It was noted that in this case, however, the police were perceived to have acted with little care for the hostages safety, providing an alternative reason for their unwillingness to testify. Stockholm syndrome is paradoxical because the sympathetic sentiments that captives feel forwards their captors are the opposite of the fear and disdain which an onlooker might feel towards the captors.

There are four key components that characterize Stockholm syndrome:
- A hostage's development of positive feelings towards the captor
- No previous relationship between hostage and captor
- A refusal by hostages to cooperate with police and other government authorities (unless the captors themselves happen to be members of police forces or government authorities).
- A hostage's belief in the humanity of the captor because they cease to perceive the captor as a threat when the victim holds the same value as the aggressor.

Stockholm syndrome is a "contested illness" due to doubt about the legitimacy of the condition. It has also come to describe the reactions of some abuse victims beyond the context of kidnapping or hostage-taking. Actions and attitudes similar to those suffering from Stockholm syndrome have also been found in victims of sexual abuse, human trafficking, terror, and political and religious oppression.

Mary McElroy, was abducted from her home in 1933 at the age 25 by four men who held a gun to her, demanding her compliance, took her to an abandoned farmhouse, and chained her to a wall. She defended her kidnappers when she was released, explaining that they were only businessmen. She continued to visit her captors while they were in jail. She eventually committed suicide and left the following note; "My four kidnappers are probably the only people on Earth who don't consider me an utter fool. You have your death penalty now—so, please give them a chance.

Natascha Kampusch, was kidnapped in 1998 at age 10 and kept in an insulted, dark room under the garage of Wolfgang Priklopil. She would receive a variation of kind, physically and sexually abusive, controlling, and permissive treatment from her captor. Eight years after her kidnaping, Kampusch left and Priklopil committed suicide. After her kidnapper's death, Police reported that Kampusch lamented and kept a picture of him in her wallet. Kampusch, however, has expressed frustration at others, including psychologists and media, for supposing what might have motivated her.

Kampusch now owns the house in which she was imprisoned, saying, "I know it's grotesque--- I must now pay for electricity, water, and taxes on a house I never wanted to live in. It was reported that she claimed the house from Priklopil's estate because she wanted to protect it from vandals and being torn down; she also noted that she has visited it since her escape. When the third anniversary of her escape approached, it was revealed she had become a regular visitor at the property and was cleaning it out, possibly to move in herself.

In a 2010 interview with The Guardian, Kampusch rejected the label of Stockholm syndrome, explaining that it does not take into account the rational choices make people in particular situations, saying; I find it very natural that you would adapt yourself to identify with your kidanpper ", she says. "Especially if you spend a great deal of time with that person. It's about empathy, communication. Looking for normality within the framework of a crime is not a syndrome. It is survival strategy.

In 1977, Colleen Stan was hitchhiking to visit a friend in southern California when she was kidnapped by Cameron Hooker and his wife Janice and forced to live in a wooden restraining box underneath their bed. For seven years, she was repeatedly raped and tortured by Camercn and forced to live life as a sort of domestic / sex slave. Even though she was allowed to socialize with Janice and even visit her mother, she still continued to live in the box and did not attempt to escape. She was eventually freed by Janice, who asked Colleen to not disclose her abuse, as Janice was attempting to reform Cameron.

Colleen remained silent until Janice finally decided to turn Cameron over to the police. abuse victims
There is evidence that some victims of childhood sexual abuse come to feel a connection with their abuser. They often feel flattered by the adult attention or are afraid that disclosure will create family disruption. In childhood, they resist disclosure for emotional and personal reasons.

Lima syndrome
An inversion of Stockholm syndrome, called Lima syndrome, has been proposed, in which abductors develop sympathy for their hostages. An abductor may also have second thoughts or experience empathy towards their victims. It was named after an abduction at the Japanese embassy in Lima, Peru, in 1996, when members of a militant movement took hostage hundreds of people attending a party at the official residence of Japan's ambassador.

Symptoms and Behaviors
Victims of the formal definition of Stockholm syndrome develop "positive feelings toward their captors and sympathy for their causes and goals, and negative feelings toward the police or authorities. These symptoms often follow escaped victims back into their previously ordinary lives.

Physical and Psychological Effects
- Cognitive: confusion, blurred memory, delusion, and recurring flashbacks.
- Emotional: lack of feeling, fear, helplessness, hopelessness, aggression, depression, guilt, dependence on captor, and development of post—traumatic stress disorder (PTSD).
- Social: anxiety irritability, cautiousness, and estrangement.
- Physical: increase in effects of pre-existing conditions; development of health conditions due to the following from food, sleep, and exposure to outdoors.

Fairbairn's Object Relations Theory of Attachment to the Abuser
Ronald Fairbairn wrote a complete psychoanalytic model in a series of papers (1940-1944) which are collected in his 1952 text Psychoanalytic Studies of the Personality. His model explains the surprising psychological reality that abused children become deeply attached to their abusers. He saw that lack of love, chronic indifference and abuse led to a counter-intuitive emotional attachment to the very parent who was abusing them. The child's unmet dependency needs from chronic emotional deprivation, as well as the complete lack of other human alternatives in his \ her environment, leaves the child stuck at an earlier emotional age, as they have not been able to continue their developmental progress in the absence of parental help and support. "Thus the child may

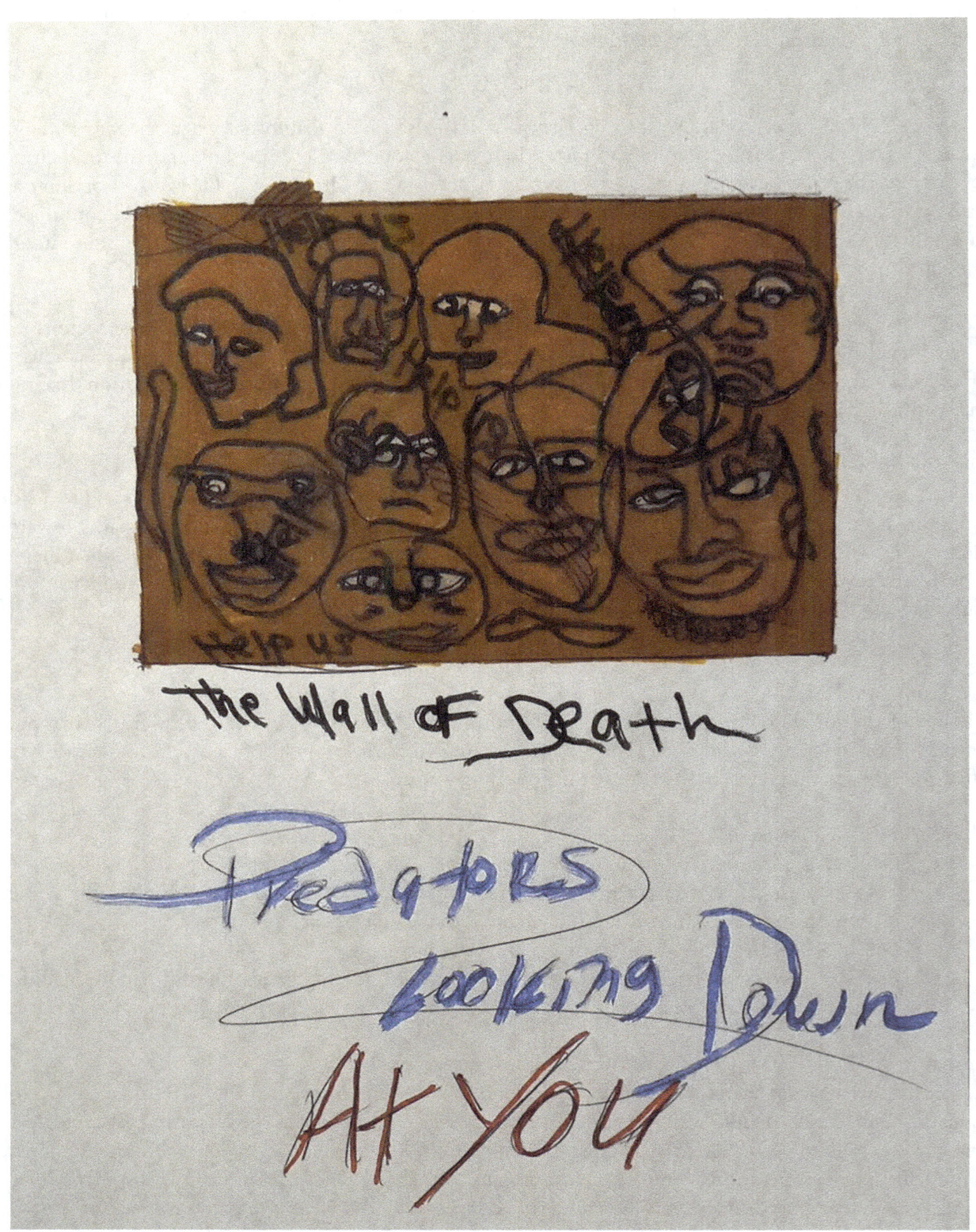

be 12, but emotionally and needs forces him to focus on the abuser's welfare because his developmental progress hinges upon on the whims, moods and emotional state of the abusive parent. In addition to the pressure from unmet developmental needs, the child also aware of the potential danger that can emerge from the volatile and aggressive parent, and anything that he can do to placate, or draw praise from the abuser increases his chance of survival.

The neglected or abused child's utter helplessness and absolute dependency upon the goodwill of their parents prevents him / her from "seeing" or remembering those interpersonal events in which they have faced indifference or physical abuse, as this awareness would overwhelm them and submerge them in a torrent of dread. This feeling of dread is most often experienced as a massive abandonment panic during those moments when the child realizes that he /she is living in constant danger with no one to help him / her to survive. The solution to this enormous problem is for the child to encase himself / herself within a thick psychological cocoon of denial and fantasy that creates a false reality in which he /she believes that they are living in a loving and caring family.

The first way that the child protects itself is by using the greatest reality—altering defense that humans have at their disposal, which is the defense of Dissociation. The dissociative defense that is seen in adults who have suffered a life—threatening trauma, and dissociation prevents them from fully realizing what has happened. In children, the same defense protects the child by forcing parents into memories of neglect, abuse, or total indifference that they suffered at the hands of their parents into their unconscious, where these memories will not disturb the child's illusion that he /she lives in a safe and loving family. The dissociative defense is the basis of what is commonly called denial. The more frequent the abuse, the more frequently dissociation is required and the larger the number of intolerable memories are forced into the unconscious; unquoted.

https://www.thesun.com/news/1055949/child-snatcher-girl-berlin-playground/?utm_medium=browser_notifications&utm_source=pushly

ARK SNATCH HORROR Chilling moment child snatcher abducts little girl, 2, while mum was distracted talking to another parent, by Chara Florillo, and I quote, Not all can be told. videos blocking material details of what transpired. Therefore only bits and piece can be viewed. IE, The man holding the child. Luckily, a woman spotted the man holding the child and chased him. The 27- year – old woman. Heike said she called for help and a kiosk operator named in reports as Zoran Z, 44, came to her aid. She added: "I was lucky he was there". Zoran sprinted after the man and caught up with him, before asking him: "Is this your child?"

Children Playground

The suspect reportedly answered: "No. I love children. I can't understand how mothers and fathers leave their children at home with some caregivers." Pictures show the man holding the girl firmly on his shoulders, before Zoran convinces him to take the child back to the playground. As they were waling back toward the playground. Zoran asked the suspect: "Why did you take the child with you?"

The suspected kidnapper said: "I think children are simply the most important thing. Children are our future, aren't they?" When they arrived at the playground in the park, he asked the girl on his shoulder' "Is your mum here in the park?"

A kiosk operator named in reports as Zoran Z helped bring the child back to her mum (credit:Newsflash)

He added: "All right, that's where we're going, right? We're going to mum, right? You sit up there. You have to look for where she is. You have the best view, OK? Where's mum? Oh, damn, a lot of people. We have to look closely." In the meantime, a crowed of people had formed in the playground, with concerned parents surrounding the distraught mother of the missing girl.

Zoran later told local media: "The mother was panicked. Another mother was already on the phone with the police. The guy then put the child in her arms. She was probably in such a state of shock that she spoke to him normally."

Police arrested the suspected kidnapper, 44, who was already known to officers and was reportedly drunk. A blood sample was ordered because he refused to take a breathalyzer test. A police spokeman told local media: "After the arrest, the suspect was taken into police custody and was processed for identification. Conditions for issuing an. Which is why he had to. The police forwarded the. responsible for "child offender kidnapping. (Sorry for missing information. due to posted videos). They found that there was paedophile. They determined that there was no evidence or a sexual motivation or of malicious intent; unquoted.

https://www.the-sun.com/news/1055132/soldiers-columbia-gang-rape/?utm_medium=browser_notifications_7utm_source=pushly
Seven Colombian soldiers face up to 30 years in prison after the sickening gang-rape of a 13-year-old girl. The servicemen admitted to the rape of the child from the indigenous Embera tribe on June 21st. She had gone missing from her rural reserve in Northern Colombia before being found the next day by a nearby school.

The army had been dispatched to enforce lockdown measures to help halt the spread of coronavirus. The leader of the Embera tribe, Juan de Dios Queragama, said in a statement that the girl had been taken to hospital after her shocking ordeal. He said: "it appears that some friends from (the rural settlement of) Santa Cecilia found her, because her mother was looking for her as she had been lost.

"When she went to look for her, she found the child at her school. When they picked her up, the child couldn't walk. They took her directly to the hospital and from the hospital they took her to forensic services." The incident has shocked the nation and services, as the latest example for campaigners against sexual violence toward indigenous women in South America. Demonstrators took to the streets over the weekend in a sit-in protest to condemn the vile actions of the army men; unquoted.

Parents, shut up, don't say anything, just listen. I want your heart to skip a beat. I want your eyes on me. I want you to fully focus on the events of this story. I therefore want your full attention. Some of you don't know your left foot from your middle finger. Why, because you're so distracted by other things. You forget to place value where value should be. Why, because you're too busy focusing on yourself. Parents, there are danger outside the home. There is danger outside the work place. There is danger on the streets. What have you to say for yourself? This story that you're about to read is base on a true story about a woman so desperately wanted a story so we became the story. She was a white female reporter a reporter that stage her own abduction and kidnapping.

(The Queen Bitch), very approaches don't you think? That's what I'm calling her. This young reporter according to the story told other reporters after she was found that she was kidnapped but eventually escape their capture. She ran into the streets yelling for help. She was seeing later talking to her co-workers a man and a woman. She wanted to report on her own abduction and kidnapping. Her supervisor said no, its not a very good ideal. The story was given to another female reporter. Sasha didn't like that decision at all. She wanted everyone to recognize her as a well-rounded reporter, a reporter with a great story, a story that would get her notice by all television stations and most importantly her sick father.

Sasha love her father, sick or not, she would do anything to impress him on the air. Sasha wanted her father to see just how good of a reporter she was. The female reporter that was given the story didn't believe Sasha abduction and kidnapping story. She started sphereheading spiking her own investigation asking questions. She would also follow Sasha from work and stake out her apartment. She would monitor Sasha movements and photograph where ever she was. She even went to Sasha's father house to learn whatever she could about Sasha. That wasn't a very smart thing because Sasha shortly thereafter show up at her father's house.

She saw that her co-worker the reporter was there watching a video of her. Her sick father was a sleep lend back into a chair. Sasha told her co-worker the other reporter to leave. She said; how dare you come to my father's house. Get the (F) out. She told Sasha that she's just doing her job. Sasha told her get out. The other reporter learned later that Sasha fake her own abduction and kidnapping with help from her male supervisor, and his female friend. Her male supervisor was a Professor. Sasha after regaining her freedom acted as if nothing had happen to her. How she kept a straight face is beyond me. She show no sign stress, no sign of fear, no sign of being batter, and or any form of mistreatment. There was nothing to indicate that she was abducted and or kidnap. That is why the other reporter was very suspicious of her.

Sasha has a co-worker, a good friend named Alex. He let Sasha stay at his house days later following her fake abduction and kidnapping. She was feeling stressed out and very upset. Because of what the other female reporter was dong invasion her privacy. She was starting to worry and fear that the other reporter would find out too much. Alex told Sasha that she could stay at his house as long as she like. Sasha of course said yes. She slept on the couch that night. She awaked doing the night and was seeing taking a knife out of the kitchen drawer. She made a cut across her right hand and bloody her dress. Sasha change clothes putting the dress into Alex washer. She left before her friend Alex awaken. Hours later Alex was seen being arrested by the police. He didn't even know what was going on. But the other female reporter had a very good ideal of what really happened just couldn't prove it. Sasha made it look like her friend Alex was her abductor and kidnapper. She even had the police convent. How could she do it framing the man? She used him as her escape goat to lure the other reporter off her trail. But it didn't work. Sasha was later seen kissing and hugging her Professor embracing him tenderly. Bragging about Alex being arrested. Sasha while on the air was being asked; how did she know it was a man?

Sasha dream that she saw pictures. Report of blood found on the man clothes. Her report was that she didn't know. The Professor, her supervisor was please with the respond from Sasha. Again, the other female reporter didn't believe Sasha story no matter how convenience it sound. She would tail Sasha everyday, day and night. That was starting to make Sasha feel very piss off and angry. Not even now has Sasha show any emotion She doesn't scream or cry. Nothing has been acknowledge by her things that a victim of an abduction and being kidnapped would do. Sasha doesn't now that three strikes you're out. * Fake the abduction an kidnapping

    * Frame her friend/co-worker Alex
    * Fake a home invasion

The wife of the Professor approached Sasha in the middle of the night, where, I don't know. She made Sasha aware that she know about them; the affair between the two of them. The wife told Sasha; you don't think that I would protect my husband? The wife said; I don't know about you? Think about that when the police comes to arrest you. The wife told Sasha to stop seeing her husband. Stop the affair or she will go to the police. Sasha

didn't like that one bit. I thought just maybe Sasha was going to kill the wife. The wife after returning home approached her husband. He was sitting in a chair watching television. The wife told her husband that she know about his and Sasha affair. She warned him to stop. Well, to my surprise; he and Sasha met later that same night. They were both pissed off that his wife knew about them. But that didn't change anything. Someone posted a video of Sasha at work in the middle of the night She seeing the video and gets afraid. Sasha calls the Professor, her supervisor, and sexual lover. She tells him that they meaning the other reporter and his wife know about them, and what actually happened on the day she disappeared. She asked him, the Professor; how much did his wife pay to protect him? We\re now at the point of Sasha being arrested. You can probably imagine how that feels. How embarrassing that will be. Sasha threatened the Professor's wife brutally threatening to kill her.

But killing his wife, Sasha fear that
the Professor will turn against her. He will go to the police. Well, out of fear Sasha pick up something knocking the Professor seriously unconscious thinking that he is dead. She goes immediately to the Professor's house knocking on the door to confront and kill his wife. Remember, all this is taking place in the middle of the night. The Professor wife didn't come to the door but instead called the police. Sasha was later seen on the air giving a story when she got a surprise visit by the other female reporter and the guy, her friend, whom she frame for her abduction and kidnapping. And of course, her love, the Professor whom she thought she killed. Sasha was taken into custody by the police while on the air.

https://www.the-sun.com/news/1070148/child-predator-exposed-himself-child-easter-bunny-north-dakota/?utm_medium=brower_notifications&utm_s....
From jail, by Flonnuala Oleary, and I quote, A child sex predator was jailed for exposing himself to a ten-year-old girl worked as a mall Easter Bunny when he got out. Daniel Sanderson pleaded guilty to the sick act he inflicted on a child described as an "acquaintance" in 2015.

Sanderson was jailed for exposing himself to a 10-year-old. Cops in North Dakota Square Mall in Minot back in March 2016 for two weeks, violating his parole. Sanderson's job there involved working with lots of children who visited the center with their parents and got their photograph taken with him.

Sanderson's probation was then revoked and he was sentenced to prison for felony failure to register as a sex offender. The child predator was released at the end of June 2020, prompting the Fargo Police Department to issue a warning to locals in his new neighborhood.

He is considered to be a "high risk sex offender" and his disturbing convictions means he will be on the sex offenders register for his entire life.

Following his arrest over the Bunny job, cops discovered photos of Sanderson's wearing the costume on his cellphone. They said he used two phones to search for "graphic and disturbing" pornography and the West Fargo Pioneer reported that his mom had found soiled kids' underwear in his apartment.

Sanderson claimed he couldn't remember those internet searches and wasn't responsible for the item found in his house. His arrest at the mall sparked mass outrage amongst concerned local parents. A spokeperson for the Dakota Square Mall said a private contractor was responsible for all their hired staff. When he was released from jail, he then violated his probation again.

The North Dakota Sex Offender Registry listed Elwell as at moderate risk to reoffend and he had to register until at least 2040; unquoted.

https://www.the-sun.com/news/1073552/ghislaine-maxwell-arrested-jeffrey-epstein-fbi-court-latest/?utm_medium=browser_notifications&utm_source....
Epstein 'pimp' Arrested Ghislaine Maxwell arrested: Jeffrey Epstein's ex-lover detained by FBI in child sex probe, by Rebecca Husselbee, and I quote, note; bits and pieces of this article blocked by videos. not all completed paragraph are available. Sush as; Ghislaine Maxwell was. for her alleged 'unspea. Girls into the hands of. Maxwell's arrest comes. arrested and then killed. Ghislaine Maxwell was a confidante and ex girlfriend of sex abuser Jeffrey Epstein. Prince Andrew with his arrest. Virginia Roberts, while Ghislaine.

Over the pervert as he carried out his sick abuse. She was arrested on Thursday morning on charges of conspiring with Epstein to sexually abuse minors and is expected to appear in a federal court later today. The place of her arrest is understood to be close to the home of her alleged boyfriend Scott Borgerson in Bedford, New Hampshire.

And at a dramatic press conference in New York this afternoon, prosecutor Audrey Strauss said she would "welcome" Prince Andrew- to make a statement and "help the investigation ". The Prince has faced backlash over his friendship with the disgraced financier and faced allegations from victim Virginia Roberts, who claims she had sex with the royal on several occasions.

Andrew, who denies the claims, has been locked in a six-month stand-off with authorities in America, who claim the prince has declined their request for an interview. But the Duke of York insists he has offered three times to be a witness in the case. The acting Manhattan US Attorney said today; "Our doors remain open and. and have the benefit of.

In describing Maxwell, she said; "Maxwell played a critical role in helping Epstein to identify, befriend and groom minor victims for abuse. "In some cases, Maxwell participated in the abuse herself." The FBI's William Sweeney today branded Maxwell "a villain" and said she had been arrested without incident.

He added: "We have been. Maxwell's whereabouts and more recently we g. to a gorgeous property. "She continued to live a. victims lived with the tr. Years ago. Count two: Enticement of a minor to travel to engage in illegal sex acts Count three: Conspiracy to transport minors with intent to engage in criminal sexual activity
Count four: Transportation of a minor with intent to engage in criminal activity
Count five and six; Perjury – the offence of willfully telling an untruth or making a misrepresentation under oath.

Maxwell had not been officially accused of criminal wrongdoing until today. Her presence "helped put the victims at ease because an adult women was present" during their interactions with Epstein. the 18-page indictment says. She has been accused of pretending to be a "woman they could trust" while setting the victims up to be abused by herself and Epstein. Ms Strauss said; "Maxwell and Epstein worked together to entice these minor victims to travel to Epstein's residence – his residence in New York City on the Upper East Side, as well as Palm Beach, Florida, and Santa Fe, New Mexico.

"Some of the acts of ab. Residence in London, En. Maxwell also "compound. Lying in 2016 when she. Strauss said. She continued; "Maxwell. alleged was almost unsp. Minor girls, got them to. into the trap that she a.

Maxwell's arrest means some justice for survivors can exist. "For years, I feared Epstein and his ring. Maxwell was the center of that sex trafficking ring. Now that the ring has been taken down. I know that I can't be hurt anymore. "Day after day, I have wanted for the news that Maxwell would be arrested and held accountable for her actions.

"Her arrest is a step in that direction, and it truly means that the justice system didn't forget about us". A jury returned a six-count indictment dating back to 1994 which involve three unnamed victims. The document claimed the three female victims were as young as 14 when they were allegedly recruited, groomed and abused by Maxwell and Epstein. It adds that the pair "knew for certain" the victims' ages. Maxwell is said to have repeatedly lied when questioned about her conduct in order to conceal her alleged crimes. The indictment says the. relationship with disgrace. Mid-90s and was paid to. By 1994 she is accused of. Multiple minors girls to. Epstein. Her methods are said to. befriend victims by ask. The indictment says Maxwell and Epstein would attempt to create time alone with their victims. Maxwell is accused of massaging Epstein in front of the victims and encouraging them to give Epstein massages – during which the victim would be fully or partially nude.

After developing a rapport with the victims, Maxwell is accused of normalizing sexual abuse by "discussing sexual topic, undressing in front of the victim, being present when a minor was undressed, and/or being present for sex acts involving the minor victim and Epstein.

Maxwell is accused of being present for and participating in sexual abuse of minor victims and knowing that Epstein had a preference for underage girls. The indictment goes on to say that many of those massages resulted in Epstein sexually abusing the minor victims.

Maxwell encouraged certain victims to accept Epstein's assistance when he offered to pay for travel and/or educational opportunities. The indictment says that. made to feel indebted. Epstein were trying to. Epstein's resulting abuse. "touching a victim's breath. placing a sex toy such as. genitals, directing a victim. masturbated, and direc. genitals".

Maxwell is accused of perjuring herself when she said she was unaware that Epstein was having sexual relations with anyone other than herself and two other people. Today, my fellow Epstein survivors and 1 are able to take a breath of relief, as Maxwell's arrest means some justice for survivors can exist.

Jeffery Epstein Survivor Jennifer Araoz
It comes two weeks after the New York attorney who was investigating Epstein was fired because he reportedly refused to drop his demands to interview Price Andrew. Epstein, a registered sex offender, was arrested last summer on new federal charges of exploiting dozens of underage girls in New York and Florida in the early 2000s. He attempted suicide in custody in late July, and then died after another suicide in early August. Two of the guards tasked. face federal charges for. before his death. One day before his suicide. released the transcript. Epstein repeatedly refused. procured young girls fo. Spokespeople for the FBI. in Manhattan declined.

The last public sighting of Maxwell was last August, when she was photographed at In-N-Out Burger in LA reading a book about CIA spies. (credit: the mega agency). Bill Clinton and Ghislaine N. Epstein's Lolita Epstein' Je. Ghislaine Maxwell, longtime associate of accused sex trafficker Jeffrey Epstein. The place of Maxwell's arrest. home of her alleged boyfriend.

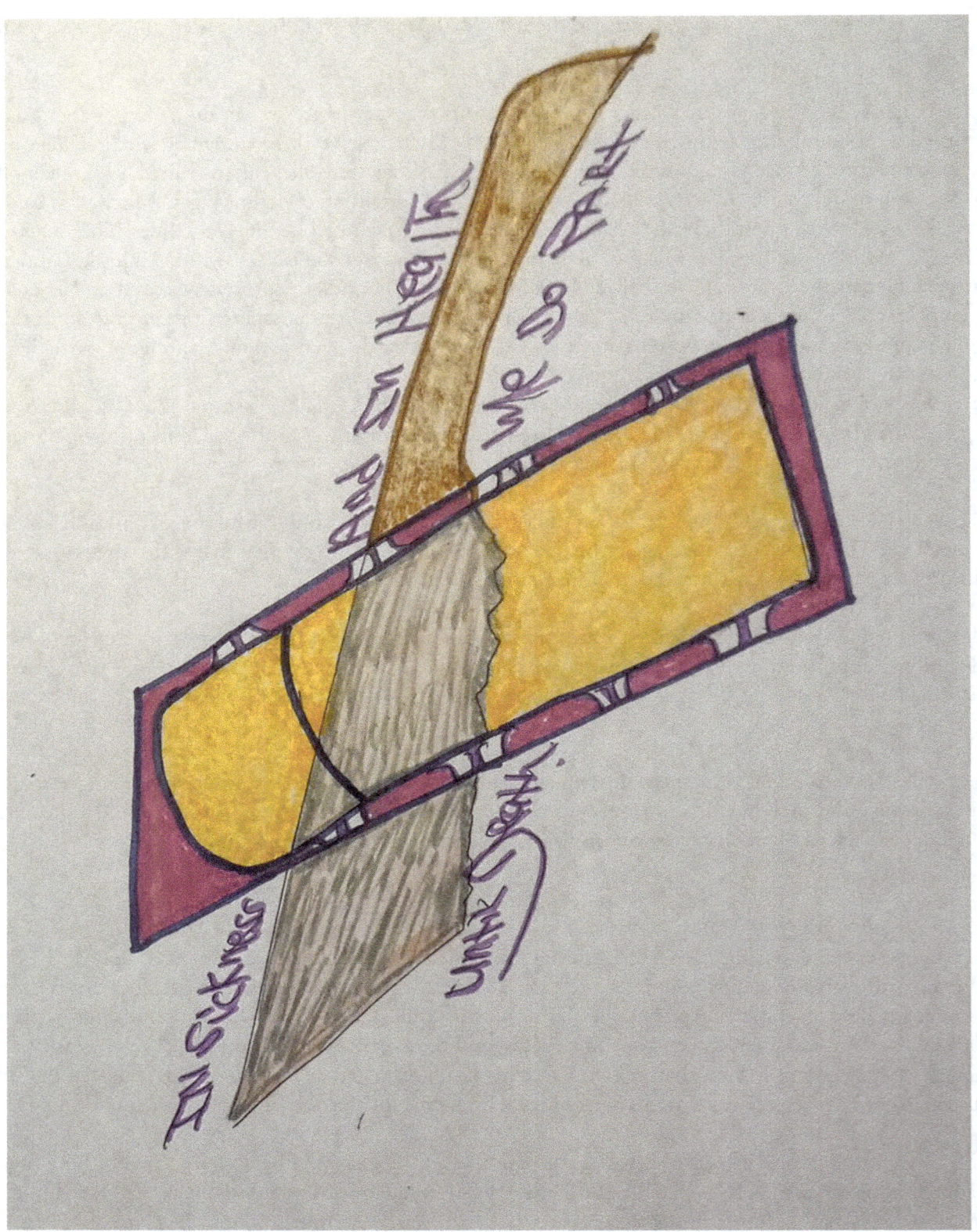

The FBI also wants to quiz Maxwell over her links to Epstein, whose have been detailed in Netflix documentary Filthy Rich. She was last seen in August 2-19 at a takeout burger restaurant in Los Angeles after remaining in hiding since Epstein was arrested in last June. It is claimed she also introduced Prince Andrew to US "sex slave" Virginia Roberts, now known as Virginia Gluffre. Roberts has accused Maxwell of recruiting her to work as Epstein's masseuse when she was 15.

She claims Maxwell directed her to give erotic massages and engage in sexual activities with Price Andrew and others, and says she had sex with the royal "three times, including one orgy". The first encounter allegedly took place in Maxwell's London home when Virginia was 17. In April, Epstein accuser. Sworn affidavit alleging. were sexually abused by. then to be abused by Epstein and his pals. While Maxwell was missing. The Sun offered a E10,000 reward for information on her location. Maxwell is accused of facilitating abuse at Epstein's New York mansion. (credit: Getty images – Getty)One victim was allegedly a. Mexico (credit: Reuters)

Even Maxwell's own lawyers are said not to have her exact location. The indictment says Maxwell facilitated Epstein's access to the victim at his Palm Beach, Florida home. (credit: Splash News).Virigina Roberts has accus. Work as Epstein's masseus.

https://www.the-sun.com/news/1075931/ghislaine-maxwell-same-prison-epstein-suicide-new-york/?utm_medium=browser_notifications&utm_souce...
AADAM' IN MANHATTAN Ghislaine Maxwell could be locked-up in same prison where Epstein killed himself after brief first court appearance, by Fionnuala O'leary, News Reporter, and I quote, Jeffrey Epstein's alleged "madam" Ghislaine Maxwell could eb locked up in the same jail where the disgraced billionaire killed himself. On Thursday, Maxwell, 58, faced a New York City judge remotely after prosecutors accused her of building a rapport with girls as young as 14 before allegedly.

Note; bits and pieces of this article is block out due to posted videos. Therefore information will be left out with stops and go part of meanings. As you will see in the following passages and others.

Ghislaine Maxwell was arrested on Thursday in New Hampshire credit: Getty Images. Jeffrey Epstein and Ghislaine Maxwell attend Batman Forever/R. Mcdonald Event on June 13, 1995 in New York City credit: Getty – Contributor.

The Metropolitan Correctional Center where Epstein took his own life credit: AP: Associated Press. Earlier, she was arrested in New Hampshire for allegedly luring girls as young as 14 years old to a number of Epstein's residences – including his mansions in New York City and Florida. Prosecutors said investigators found her "hiding" on a 156 – acre property she bought in cash back in Decembe 2019. Maxwell and her Attorney Lawrence Vogelman faced the Concord courtroom via video link shortly after 3:30 pm for 20 – minutes, after agreeing to a remote hearing. Magistrate Judge Andrea Johnstone told Maxwell she would be temporarily detained and "transported to the charging district" – the United States District Court for the Southern District of New York (SDNY) – where hearings would begin accordingly.

If she's brought to New York, she would be transferred to either the Metropolitan Correctional Center (MCC) In Lower Manhattan or the Metropolitan Detention Center in Brooklyn, Bloomberg reported, citing legal experts. The MCC is where Epstein was found hanging in his cell ahead of his sex – trafficking trial after being charged with the sex trafficking of minors.

Maxwell helped Epstein choose and procure his victims, New. The 58 – year-old British socialite allegedly convinced young women to give Epstein massages partially or fully nude credit: Getty Images – Getty. But the US government fear Maxwell, faced with the prospect of 35 years behind bars, is "an extreme flight risk" meaning she could be denied bail, according to court filings.

"The Government respectfully submits that Ghislaine Maxwell, the defendant, poses an extreme risk of flight", the prosecution's legal memorandum read. Citing her alleged "disturbing and callous" conduct, prosecutors listed her international ties, dual citizenship, wealth, and lack of meaningful ties to the United States as reasons she may flee. "She has no children, does not reside with any immediate family members, and does not appear to have any employment that would require her to.

Federal prosecutors announced the charges against Maxwell at a press conference on Thursday credit: AP: Associated Press. It's claimed that she also introduced Prince Andrew to 'sex slave' Virginia Roberts (pictured here with the royal) credit:Rex Features. "You're remanded to the custody of the United States Marshall," Judge Johnstone concluded this afternoon. Maxwell is facing a alew of charges for allegedly conspiring with Epstein to abuse minors, as well as perjury for lying during a sworn deposition.

Speaking at the US Attorney's office in Manhattan three hours before the hearing, prosecutor Audrey Strauss described the "unspeakable truth" and role Maxwell allegedly played in recruiting girls for Epstein. NYPD Commissioner Shea was also present at the conference earlier today and praised the joint efforts of police and the FBI credit: EPA.

FBI Assistant director Sweeney addressed the victims directly earlier today. credit: United States Attorney for the Southern District of New York.

She acknowledged concerns for Maxwell's safety once she's behind bars, saying "we are sensitive to that concern and certainly we'll be in dialogue with the Bureau of Prisons about it" three hours before her court appearance. But Strauss also told reporters how Maxwell would "befriend young girls" as part of her alleged grooming process.

The attorney described how the alleged madam would take them to the movies, ask about their families, and "develop a rapport with them". "She pretended to be a woman they could trust", Strauss said during the NYC conference, which was also attended by William Sweeney, assistant director of the FBI's NY office, and NYPD Commission Dermot Shea.

Maxwell, the daughter of a British media tycoon, moved to New York in 1991 and dated Epstein a year later credit: PA. Press Association. During the shocking Q&A portion of the briefing, Strauss told journalists that investigators would "welcome" Prince Andrew- who was a friend of Epstein's – coming in for a chat with police. Strauss also told reporters "we would welcome Prince Andrew coming to talk with us to have the benefit of his statement". The accusations against Maxwell were laid out in a federal filing which was unsealed earlier this morning.

It stated that from 1994 to 1997, she allegedly "assisted, facilitated, and contributed to Jeffrey Epstein's abuse of minor girls", by helping him to "recruit, groom, and ultimately abuse" underage victims. After grooming these victims, Maxwell then encouraged them to give Epstein massages when they were fully or partially nude, these filing alleged.

https://kidshealth.org/en/parents/net-safety.hetml
Getting Involved in Kids Online Activities, and I quote, More important than blocking objectionable material is teaching your kids safe and responsible online behavior, and keeping an eye on their internet use.

Basic guidelines to shave with your kids for safe online use:

- Follow the family rules, and those set by the Internet service provider.
- Never post or trade personal pictures.
- Never reveal personal information, such as address, phone numbers, or school name or location.

Babysitter Instructions

Before you leave. prepare the sitter. Be sure to:

- Go over your child's usual routine (homework, bedtime, meal times) talk about your general house rules, including any limits on TV, computer use, video games, playing outside, etc.
- Tell the sitter where you will be and how to reach you at all times, and under what circumstances to call 911 before contacting you.
- Text or write your own phone number and address.
- Show the babysitter where emergency exits, smoke detectors, and fire extinguishers are.
- Show the babysitter how to enable the alarm system if you have one.
- Show the babysitter where you keep the inside door keys in case a child locks himself or herself inside a room.

Things To Consider It's obvious that a 5-year old can't go it alone. But that most 16 -year-olds can. But what about those school-aged kids in the middle? It can be hard to know when kids are ready to handle home alone. Its comes down to your judgement about what your child is ready for.

In general, it's not a good idea to leave kids younger than 10 years old home alone. Every child is different, but at that age, most kids don't have this maturity and skills to respond to an emergency if they're alone.

It's also important to consider how your child handles various situations. Here are a few questions to think about:

- How does your child show signs of responsibility with things like homework, household chores, and following directions?
- How does your child handle unexpected situations? Does your child stay calm when things don't go as planned?
- Does your child understand and follows rules?
- Can your child understand and follows safety measures?
- Does your child use good judgement?

WHEN BEING KIDNAPPED AND ABDUCTED DO SOMETHING BUT DO NOT PANIC .
ANYTHING TOI GET OTHERS ATTENTION

SCREAM

THROW SOMETHING   KICK SOMETHNG

DO SOMETHING EVEN WHEN YOU'RE TOLD NOT TO

Handling the Unexpected

Before being left home alone. your child should know:

- When and how to call 911 and what address information to give the dispatcher
- How to work the home security system, if you have one, and what to do if the alarm is accidentally set off
- How to lock and unlock doors
- How to work the phone/cellphone (in some areas, you have to dial 1 or the area code to dial out)
- How to turn lights off and on
- How to operate the microwave
- What to do if;
  There's a small fire in the kitchen
  The smoke alarm goes off
  There's a tornado or other severe weather
  A stranger comes to do door
  Someone calls for a parent who isn't home
  There's a power outage

WhatsApp: This app works like a phone, allowing users to call, text and share photos and videos worldwide. Bumble: Similar to the dating app Tinder, except women initiate contract. Kid have accessed this app with fake names and ages. LiveMe: This livestreaming video app uses geolocation to share the exact location of users. the app uses a vital currency called "coins", which can be used to "pay" minors for photos. Ask.fm: this site that allows other users to ask questions is known for cyberbullying. Grindr: A dating app aimed toward gay, bisexual and transgender people. there are options to chat and share videos. users can also use their phone's GPS function to find nearby users. Tik Tok: A new app for creating and sharing short videos. Users are vulnerable to seeing explicit content and bullying as there are few privacy measures. SnapChat: This popular app promises that shared photos and videos will disappear once they are seen.

This app also shares the geographic location of users. Holla: An app that allows users to instantly video connect with users all over the world. However, some users report being exposed to explicit content, racial slurs and more. Skout: A location-based dating app where users under 17 are not able to share photos, but kids have found their way around the restriction. Badoo: A dating and social networking app where users can chat, share photos and videos, and connect based on location. Though intended for adults, children and teenagers have used it. Kik: A texting app that allows users to direct message others. the app is known for preserving the anonymity of its users. Whisper; An anonymous social media app allows users to share secrets with strangers.

It also shares user's location information. Hot or Not: Another dating app that allows users to rate profiles and find other users in the area. SECRET CALULATOR VAULT(there are many versions of the same thing) Calculator% A secret app that allows users to hide photos, videos, files, and their browser history. Look: A live video and text message app that is unfiltered and contains inappropriate content. It also encourages users to connect with strangers nearby. Comvo: The Free Speech Social Network: A platform that offers unfiltered posting. The makers encourage users to speak freely and post whatever they want. This app also allows users to "expire" their posts so they cannot be accessed after a certain date. BYF: Unfiltered Social Media app that offers people an unfiltered experience. there are no restrictions or filtering, which means unlimited access to pornographic images and conversations. This app also poses a risk to cyberbullying, trolling, and encouraging self-harm; and Unquoted.

"Child" Fly Like An Eagle

Child fly like an eagle. Fly high into the sky.
Fly as far as you can into that safety net above.
Don't look back I say. Don't look back.
Because the bully man awaits you -your return flight back.
Child waiting to capture you when you get home.

Whatever you do my child do not come back alone.
I would welcome you home my child but this is not the time.
There are too many predators lurking around. I know it must be
hard for you my child wondering when. My child I ask that you
be patience and wait my call. Until it is safe my child stay
where you are. I'm hoping in the meantime that the law will

intervene. I don't want to do the wrong thing stepping on their
toes. The law doesn't work that way and don't want to be told.
They come when they can down that long, long road. However
Long it takes them my child I will not give up on you. The law
Has the authority, the badge, and the gun. Let them do what

they must do to rid the predators of the streets. I don't have a
Problem with that my child as long as they help me. Please
understand my child I can't do it alone. Other parents my child
must be willing to tag alone. Its hard my child staying away
From you. But until the law steps in the sky will be blue.
Let them shoot the beast in the streets as long as they get rid of
The predators they seek. So please be patience my child as long
As you can. I will soon welcome you home once again.

QUESTIONS FOR PARENTS AS FOLLOWS:

* Parents how does reading these articles at hand grabs you?
* Is it frightening, scary, and shocking?
* How safe does it make you feel?
* Who's child do you think will be next?
* Do you feel that the local authorities can protect your child from would be predators?
* Do you feel that your child is safe walking to and from school?
* What if anything has told you that children life are in danger?
* What in particularly grab you by the hand in these articles?
* What as a parent would you do different now knowing what you know?
* Would you as a parent partition the government to do more to protect your children?

* As a parent do you feel that predators male and or female should be consider a threat with regard to children safety, if yes, why, if not, why not?
* What does you intend to do as a parent to protect your children from potential predators?
* What was going through your mind if anything while reading these articles?
* When you look at your children knowing there is a predator preying on them as they walks out the door. What is the first thing if anything at all are you thinking about and asking yourself?
* What would you do if the next child abducted and or kidnapped is your child?
* Is it not something to think about?
* What would you do if there was a knock on your door and someone tells you that your child has has been abducted, kidnapped, sexually assaulted, and cr killed?
* How would you handle it?
• Parent knowing what you know do you see other parents as a potential predator, if yes, why, if not, why?

WORDS OF INTEREST

The definition of such words are taken from THE AMERICAN HERITAGE STUDENT DICTIONARY, written by HOUGHTON MIF

Passivity: The quality or condition of being passive; submissiveness.

Password: A secret word or phrase that one uses to get into a place or gain access to information.

Passion: A powerful feeling such as love. Joy, or hatred. The object of such enthusiasm.

Path: A small piece of land, usually with plants growing on it.

Abduct: To carry away by force; kidnap.

Kidnap: To seize and detain.

Prey: A person or thing that is defenseless against attack; victim.

Torture: Infliction of severe physical pain in order to punish someone or force someone to do something or provide information.

Touch: To cause a part of the body, especially the hand or fingers to feel. To lay hands on in violent. To effect the emotions of; move to tender response.

Molests: To subject to unwanted or improper sexual activity.

Bind: To fasten, tie, or secure by tying, as with a rope or cord.

Danger: The chance or risk or harm or destruct

Blindfold: A piece of cloth put over the eyes and tied around the head to keep someone from seeing

Trickster: A person who swindles or plays tricks

Vicissitude: One of the sudden or unexpected changes or shifts often encountered in one's life or surroundings.

Vicious: Having the nature of vice; evil, immoral, or depraved.

Victim: A person who is harmed or killed by another or by an act, an or condition.

Exploitation: The act of using to the greatest possible advantage. The use of a person or group for selfish purposes.

Lure: A strong attraction, charm, or enticement.

Deceive: To make a person believe something that is not true; mislead; trick.

Disappeared: To pass out of sight; vanish.

Boundary: A border or limit.

Evil: Morally bad or wrong; wicked.

Fixation: An obsessive preoccupation

Creepy: Producing a tinging sensation of uneasiness or fear.

Suspicious: Arousing suspicious; distrust. Tending to suspect; distrustful.

Afraid: Filled with fear; fearful. Full of concern; regretful.

Body Language: Gestures and postures of the body and facial expressions by which an individual communicates with others.

Lurking: To wait out of view; lie in wait. To move about secret

Stigmatizing: To brand or characterize as shameful or dishonorable.

Subconsciously: Not wholly conscious; partially or imperfectly conscious.

Stranger Danger
Safety Song Lyrics and Sound Clip
Healthy Start Publishing.....By Songs For Teaching
.....and I quote.
Stranger danger, stranger danger
Don't be fooled. Stranger danger, listen to the rules

Stranger danger, stranger danger
Don't be fooled, Stranger danger, listen to the rules

Don't go with strangers they are not your friends.
This is a rule that only parents can bend.

Strangers don't love you like your parents do.

Don't go with strangers their not good for you.

Stranger danger, stranger danger
Don't be fooled. Stranger danger, listen to the rules.

A stranger is a person that you don't know.
Even if they seem like fun.

If a stranger tries to take you and make you go.
You just have to run, run, run!

Don't go with strangers they are not your friends.
This is a rule that only parents can bend.

Don't go with strangers no matter how they sound.
Don't go with strangers when parents aren't around.

Never, never ever be afraid to stream.
Tell somebody dial 9 – 1 – 1.

It doesn't matter how strange it seems
Shout it loudly as you run.

This is not my mother
Shout it girls and boys

This is not my father
Make some noise come on

This is not my mother.
It's a stranger.
We call it stranger danger.

We won't walk with strangers
We won't talk to strangers
We won't listen to strangers
We run away from strangers
We won't ride with strangers
We won't hide with strangers
We won't play with strangers

We stay away from strangers. Unquoted

CHILDREN PLAYING

We all enjoyed being outside as a child growing up. It was something to look forward to especially after school and on the week end. It was a time to have fun and be with friends. A time to be a child. To run and play all about with others. Parents didn't like it so much especially when our clothes got dirty. The bath tub awaits us and taking a bath felt good. But of course that wasn't the problem. In those days one would say that you could go pretty much anywhere day or night. Your parents didn't have reason to keep an eye on you so much. Why is that you asked; neighbors would also watch out for you. Not only, they would spank your butt real bad, having of course permission from your parents. That's just the way it was. Neighbors looked out for each other.

But now things has changed. That safety net is no more. Children now are being target by would- be -predators, and they could be anyone. What a scary thought but true. You can't put your child outside for a minute (turn your back) and they will be gone. Child gone missing a parent worse nightmare. A child can be taken right from under your nose. Yes, it can happen that fast. Parents, watch your child whenever you take them to the park, woods, and or to the supermarket. Watch them closely.
They are not safe. Speaking of safe; be aware of strangers. Be aware of others approaching your child / children. Stop, yell, scream, if you much. Just don't stand there and do nothing. Never assume that your child / children are ok when their not with you. To assume is a thought of the mind, a mind of false hope, a mind believing that everything is alright, a mind causing you to think that your child /children are safe. Know where your child / children are at all times. What questions should be ask? What mouth should be open? What Red-Flag should be raise? What word should be spoked? What should you do if anything at all? Whatever you do; don't panic.

Roses are red "yes" but children are blue, please keep them safe from predators like you. They don't know no better. They can't see beyond the clouds. Your children are not safe so keep them near your side. Take care of them whatever you do keep them inside and safe from "you know who". Predators whoever they are will abduct and kidnap your child causing you to scream and cry. Your children is a heart beat away keep them close and keep them safe. You should know where your child is at all times communicating with them especially when their not around.

Never assume your child is safe because you will open the parry gate of hell. A gate that you will regret for the rest of your life kicking and hating yourself, each and everyday psychologically wondering where they are, awaiting for a call from him or her telling you that your child is alive and well, just pay the ranson and will return her in a few days but only if you pay the ranson without delay.

So, I asked; What have you learn? What have you to say? What would you have done if it had went the other way? So, let me say this to all you parents. Children being abducted and kidnap means their not safe. Trust no one but yourself but to ask for help nevertheless. Your child don't let her out of your sight. She could get kidnap; "is that not right"? Laugh if you want but is it not true! But whatever you do parents don't stand around scratching your ass wondering who's who? It's too late for that don't you think? Scratch your ass later when your child is back. Your child is young, very young can't you see? So don't leave her outside alone playing by herself. Others could be watching just to take her away. To take someone away is to steal them. To steal them is to take without permission. To take without their knowledge. To take without their consent. To take without knowing is to take without feelings. Lack of trust and understanding. No sense of care for another human being.

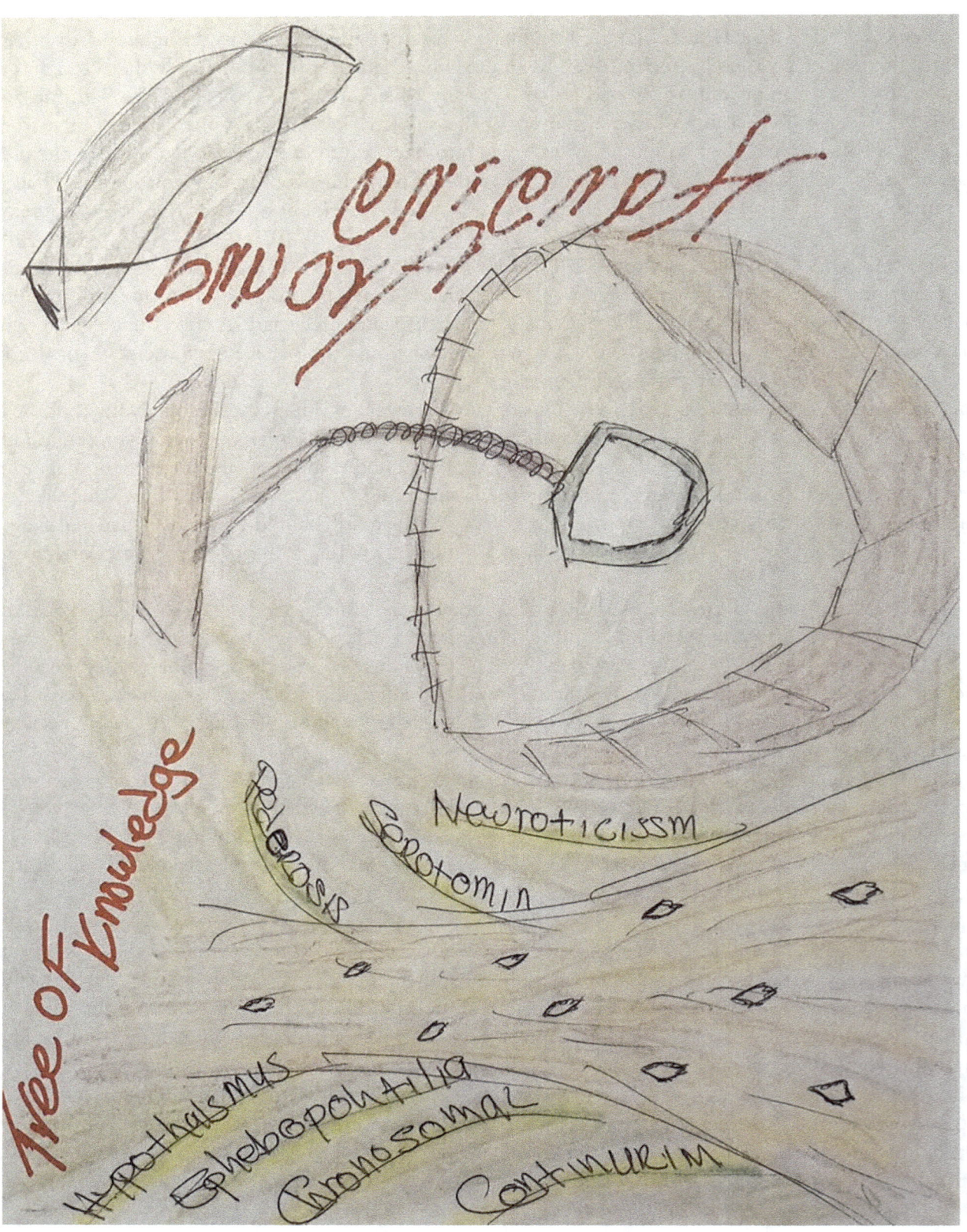

https://kidshealth.org/en/parents/stranger-smarts.html?WT.ac=p-ra
Kidhealth for parents: About Strangers?

Although I'd like my kids to be polite. I also want to teach them not to talk to strangers. How can I avoid sending mixed messages? "Don't to strangers" has been the rule for many parents for generations. But sometimes it's a good idea for kids to talk to strangers. Why else will they turn to if they're lost and need help?

So instead of making a rule, it's better to teach kids when it's appropriate to talk to strangers, and when it is not. When your kids are out with you, it's fine to let them say hello, and talk to new people. You are watching the situation and will protect them.

But if your child is alone and approached by a stranger, that's a different story. Tell your kids that if a stranger ever approaches and offers a ride or treats (like candy or toys) or asks for help with a task (like helping to find a lost dog), they should step away, yell "No!" and leave the area immediately. Your child should tell you or another trusted adult (like a teacher or childcare worker) what happened. The same goes if anyone----whether a stranger, family member, or friend-----ask your child to keep a secret, tries to touch your child's private area, or ask your child to touch theirs.

Most kids are likely to be wary of strangers who are mean—looking or appears scary in some way. But most child molesters and abductors are regular people, and many go out of their way to look friendly, safe, and appealing to children. So, instead of judging a person by appearance, teach kids to judge people by their actions.

It's also important to encourage kids to trust their own instincts. Teach them that if someone make them feel uncomfortable or if they feel like something's just not right---even if they can't explain why----they need to walk away immediately.

So, what happens if your kids are alone and need to approach a strange for help? First, they should try to find a person in uniform, like a police officer, security guard, or store employee. If there are no uniformed people, look for grandparents, women, and people with children who may be able to help. And again, remind them about instincts: If they don't have a good feeling about a certain person. They should approach someone else.

It's not possible to protect kids from strangers at all times. But it is possible to teach them about appropriate behaviors and what to do if somebody crosses the line. Keeping these tips in mind can help your kids stay safe while they're out and about; unquoted.

This song about Danger, danger, inspired me to write this song, and its a tribute to our future generation, our young children and young adults.

Hello stranger, stranger don't you see, Hello stranger don't bother me.
I'm playing out side trying to have some fun.
I mean you no disrespect stranger and that's the truth.

Stranger, stranger, please leave me along
As you can see stranger its very nice out here.
Let me have my fun stranger and play with my friends.
We won't bother your stranger, we'll go away, we'll go in side stranger and play another day.

If that pleases you stranger just walk away.
My friends and I stranger would like to play.
Look around, look around stranger tell me what you see.
Other children are having fun stranger playing in the sea.
I asked you this last time stranger what are you going to do?
Are you going to kill me stranger or let me be?
If not, if not stranger, please let me go.
My friends are waiting stranger that much I know.
Stranger, stranger, lets end this now.
I'm tired waiting stranger wondering what you're going to do.
Let me go home stranger and I'll be free of you.

www.abajournal.com
Recent Cases and Questions for Parents and the American Bar Association By Martha Neil and I quote, the Seattle Schools agreed to pay $3.05 million to two students molested by a former 5th grade teacher during his 20-year education career, involving multiple victims. According to the attorney representing the two students: "It was kind of the open secret within Broadview-Thompson elementary School. The teachers knew about it, but parents didn't know about it. The police didn't know about it."

How would you feel if teachers and administrators at your child's school knew or reasonably suspected that your daughter/son was being sexually abused, along with other students by a predatory teacher, but they never reported the suspected criminal conduct to the police or told you about it? And what if this had been going on for years?

According to a Government Accountability office (GAO) report on educator sexual misconduct (2010), a middle school teacher in Ohio agreed to resign because of inappropriate sexual conduct with students, in exchange for a positive letter of reference from the school superintendent describing him as an "outstanding teacher". Neither the police nor parents were notified. The predatory teacher was subsequently hired by a neighboring school district, where he was convicted of sexual battery against a 6th -grade girl.

How would you feel if a predatory teacher who had been sexually abusing your child and other children but a secret "passing the trash" deal was worked out between the sexual predator, school superintendent, and union rep in which:

1. No one reported the criminal behavior to the police,
2. The sexual predator was not disciplined in any way,
3. No one reported the criminal conduct to parents,
4. No one attempted to help current and past child victims of the predator's criminal sexual abuse,
5. The superintendent provided a positive letter of reference to the predator for the next school, and,
6. The predator greed to voluntarily resign and leave quickly and quietly.

The vigilance of one mother in a recent case in California helped uncover a teacher's sexual abused. On a periodic basis, she visited her daughter's elementary school to observe educational activities and how her child was performing. On one particular day while intending to observe her daughter's outdoor gym class, she noticed that neither her daughter nor the male gym teacher were present. Her inquiry as to their whereabouts led to the discovery of the teacher and her daughter in a storage room, playing the "lollipop game". This involved the little girl and then having her give him oral sex while he videotaped everything.

In January of 2012, I was doing research for a school edition of my 2002 book on sexual harassment in higher education when I came across several references that completely changed my thinking about the problem of sexual abuse/harassment of students in kindergarten through 12th grade (K-12). I had naively assumed that incidence rate of sexual abuse/ harassment in K-12 would be substantially lower than in college for two main reasons:

First, given that any sexual contact between teachers (or other school employees)and students constitutes a criminal offense punishable by prison time. I believed that this would deter educators from sexually abusing students.

1. Second, I assumed that the closer, more direct supervision of students in K-12 would substantially limit opportunities for educators to abusing students.

Below is a brief summary of the evidence I received that documents this horrendous problem.

- more than 4.5 million (emphasis added) students are subject to sexual misconduct by an employee (most often teachers) of a school sometime between Kindergarten and 12th grade".
- the 4.5 million victims represent 9.6% of all school-age children.
- "teachers who sexually abuse belie the stereotype of an abuser as an easily identifiable danger to children"; many are the most celebrated in their profession"; many are chronic (repeat) predators" most are men.
- many educators who abuses, work at being recognized as good professionals in order to be able to Sexually abuse children.
- the process of "grooming" is described as, "where an abuser selects a student, gives the student Attention and rewards, provides the student with support and understanding, all the while slowly increasing the amount of touch or other sexual students."
- Students who are more likely to be sexually abused include: girls, especially girl of color (African-American, Native American, and Hispanic-American); children with disabilities; children who are estranged from their parents, unsure of themselves, and/or engage in high risk behaviors.
- "For most children, being the victim of sexual misconduct does Damage that lasts well into adult-Hood, and for most it is never fully repaired.
- Concerning education/training for students; "like staff, students need to understand the boundaries That educators should not cross. This is important both for students who might be targeted and for students who observe such behaviors. Both sets of students need to know that such behavior is prohibited and that there is a person to whom they can and should report such incidents. Materials and programs that have been developed to protect students from sexual abuse rarely include examples of predators who are educators.

Virtually all sexual abuse of K-12 students takes place behind closed doors, in private settings. Thus, to insure that this does not happen to your daughter or son, inform (verbally and in writing) your child's principal and teachers that she/he is not to be alone with any school employee. You can offer to make yourself, your spouse, or another adult family member /friend available to come to school to be present with your child if 1-on-1 interaction with a school employee is needed. Schools should have official policies that prohibit employees from being alone with students.

If you suspect that your daughter or son been sexually abused, it is imperative that you quickly identify a qualified mental health professional and schedule an appointment. Even though signs of trauma might not be apparent, considerable Psychological Damage may have already occurred. Qualified mental health professionals include psychiatrists (MD's with additional psychological training), or clinical social workers with master's degrees. If you filed a complaint alleging criminal child sexual abuse against a school employee, strongly recommend that you consider securing legal counsel. Given the legal complexities associated with filing a criminal complaint on behalf of your child and potentially filing civil complaint against the alleged sexual predator and school officials; unquoted.

It's unfortunate that Coyote Predatory teachers preys on students of all ages taking advantage of their immaturity for their own personal satisfaction and pleasure forcing themselves sexually on such young children at a tender young age hoping that parents, and others would not find out about their sickness.

But what bothers me the most is when educators- teachers are aware of their co-worker sexual advances on students, and does nothing about it turning a blind eye looking the other way. It becomes as the article reveals a hush, hush, involvement predatory violation of self fulfillment against students.

The cover of secrecy spreading the blanket over evil; do not tell your parents, do you understand kicks in as the child believe that whatever is happening is ok. The teacher therefore is emotionally controlling the child causing the child to feel entangle within His or Her sickness thinking its alright.

But, what happens when the child becomes older? The teacher in reality is brain washing the child. Therefore in years to come that child is going to have some serious problems with regard t o sexual relationships. This article clearly support everything that has been said. Parents, wake up, wake up, keep eyes close on your children.

Listen to your children. You can always form your own opinion later with regard to what has been told to you by your child. Don't be so quickly to dismiss accusations no matter how unreal it may sound. We as parents are so quickly to jump to the conclusion that the child is lying. That is not always the case. Give your child at least the benefit of the doubt.

IN THE ARTICLE

In the article the writer applauds and addresses concerns for children safety in schools under the supervision of educators-teachers. Key factors of concerns:

- teachers having sex with students
- other teachers aware of the affair turn a blind eye to what's going on

- parents were not inform
- local law enforcement were not inform
- the board of education were not inform

The questions that follows: Whose the blame? Where do we go from here? How do we tell the parents that their children rights were has been violated as a student being force to have sex with a teacher? Note; saying I'm sorry is not enough. Enough is enough.

How do we deal with this type of a problem? turn a blind eye. act as if nothing happen, do nothing, say nothing. "OR', raise hell and speak out, prosecute predators to the full extents of the law, publicly embarrass them and their family Publicly embarrass the school, put predators in jail and throw away the key, bring back the electric chair as a means of punishment awakening the devil inside of them.

RED ALERT

Signs that might be given by children whether that child is a student or not telegraphing a message if you will telling the parent that something is wrong:

- child doesn't want to go back to school
- child is scare, frighten, and afraid
- appears nervous
- locks the bed room door
- don't want t be touch
- scream for no reason
- doesn't eat -just stares at the food
- child gets angry at the table pounding it with silverware
- child starts using profanity
- child has nightmares of the sinful event -verbalizing saying -touch me, harder, its alright. making physical movements in bed.
- when being awaken; the child might yell – no, don't touch me get away from me.
- child grades begin to fail
- can't focus

Sexual Recipe: Teachers Targeting Children And Students

What attracts teachers to students:

- their immaturity- too young to understand
- their innocence – unaware of the danger
- their demeanor – movement, walks, body language
- sex appealing – looks, beauty, smiles, eye contact
- their attire – fashion mentality, tight fitting clothes Colorful styles, short and satin
- their school days – when they were students – a very
- Important factor of concern teachers targeting students.

What attracts teachers to children and young adults:

- their demeanor- movement, walks, body language
- sex appealing – looks, beauty, smiles, eye contact
- their attire – fashion mentality, tight fitting clothes colorful styles, short and satin
- sexual activities
- colognes – smell of freshness
- body size – skin tone
- posture – stands, sitting. positioning
- booty size
- active – outgoing
- chest – breast size
- raw sexual desire
- personality, conversation, loneliness
- rejection – by spouse
- easy targets – students
- unhappiness – fulfilled interacting with students
- failing *grades – teachers tutoring blindly in exchange for sex
- black mail – in exchange for sex
- seduction - touching, sexual stare, positioning of body parts, Language, accidental bumping into each other sad stores, in vic – to home, soft music, the right words, false intentions, communication – phone calls, email, pictures to their phone, and internet

Man, Woman, or Beast, Predator Is She When you do return remember what to do.
Whatever you do Don't let the sky turn blue. If you must fight -fight, fight,
To get away from the predator with all your might. Make believe
Your superman, the man of steal. Kick ass if that's what it takes.
Call on superman before its too late. Superman will help you that Much I know. my.

On him and watch him fly. He will rescue you – will not let you die.
Have you seem his movies earth bound he goes. He has the famous stores
That has not been told. The flight of night without fear or shame. He flies
Far, far away in the wind. He could be your guidance angel just call him
"you'll see". My child he will come as fast as he can. I once was told of such

A man. I didn't believe it at first but now I do. As weird as it seem an airplane
In bound. He surrounds his body supporting the airplane in flight. The airplane I
Understand was in danger of crashing to the ground. When all of a sudden it was
Turned around. So believe me when I say my child he's a friend indeed. He will
Save you again, and again. Predator, predator, hear me well. You mess with my
Child. You will go not to jail but to hell. Superman you know will see to that. He
Will scoop your ass up and that's a fact. He will swing down and get you where
Ever you are. Predator, predator I give warning to you. Don't touch my child

Predator. I'm warning you. Don't harm a hair on her head. If you do predator your
Dead. Because superman won't stop until justice prevail. Justice will come, "O" yes

It will. Because superman "Predator" is the man of steel. You will get a one way
Ticket straight to hell -man, beast, or woman only time will tell. So "Teachers" I say
Unto you. The law has their eyes on you. So many of you have target "Students" and
That's not right. Your destroying their life, future, and education too. Sexually,
Psychologically, and much, much, more. Their not being sent to school for you to
Have your way with them. It's called seduction and maybe rape too but who knows
Better than you. Knock, knock, whose there. "OOPs", It's the police.

We come for you. Get dress Predator we'll coming in taking you to jail
For your sin. Thank you, thank you, for your decency. I'm naked as
A jay bird can't you see. I'm glad its all over. I couldn't stop myself.
I got too involve and forgot about the rest. The devil struck my heart of sin
Sexually, decadence, controlling my thoughts and desires.

This list is probably inconclusive looking at the environment in which we lived. Terribly dangerous, turbulence, and thoughtless in the mind of many lashing out at our future of tomorrow, and that being children and young adults. Despite everything that you have read. Some of you will feel differently. That's alright because no one thinks alike. Maybe that's a good thing. My argument is this. Our children know that they're safe from the hands of "would-be- predators" male and female alike. They should be safe and feel safe. They shouldn't be treated like sluts, whore, prostitute, and or like a fresh piece of meat.
https://tcta.org

TCTA, Teachers are perceived as role models in the community, according to Texas Classroom Teachers Association, and the law and regulations that mandate appropriate standards of conduct can lead to adverse employment action, certification sanctions and criminal consequences. During the 2017 legislative session, Senate Bill 7 was passed in an effort to address educator misconduct and improper relationships between educators and students. Sexual misconduct and indecent exposure with a minor is a felony that requires the perpetrator to register as a sex offender. It is also a felony for any school district employee to engaged in a sexual relationship with a student, even if that student is of the legal age of consent.

This prohibition includes students enrolled in schools where the teacher is not employed.
A school district must complete an investigation into allegations of educator misconduct, even if the educator resigns from the school district. SB 7 implements a new requirement that school districts must notify the Parents or Guardian of a student with whom an educator allegedly engaged in an improper relationship, regardless of whether the educator resigned or was terminated. If an individual is found to have engaged in sexual conduct or a romantic relationship with a student or minor, regardless of age or enrollment status in the district, the State Board for Educator Certification will permanently revoke that educator's teaching certificate.

SB 7 expands the criminal prohibition of online solicitation of a minor to include communications between employees at a school and a student. A person commits this offense if they knowingly solicit a minor to meet with another person with the intent that the minor will engage in sexual contact with the person. SBEC, and I quote, may sanction the teaching certificate of an individual who has engaged in deliberate or repeated acts that can be reasonably interpreted as soliciting a sexual or romantic relationship.

Prohibited acts include, but are not limited to:

- Communications tending to show that the educator solicited a romantic Relationship with the student;
- Making inappropriate comments about a student's body;
- Making sexually demeaning comments to a student;
- Making comment about a student's potential sexual performance;
- Requesting details of a student's sexual history;
- Requesting a date;
- Engaging in conversations regarding sexual problems, preferences or fantasies of either party;
- Improper hugging, kissing or excessive touching;
- Suggesting that a romantic relationship is desired after the student graduates,
- including post-graduation plans for dating or marriage; and
- providing the student with drugs or alcohol; unquoted.

https://www.fbi.gov/investigation/violent-crime/cac
Crimes Against Children /Online Predators; It's unthinkable, but every year, thousands of children become victims of crimes---whether it's through kidnappings, violent attacks, sexual abuse, or online predators. The mission of the Crimes Against Children (CAC) program is to:

- Provide a rapid, proactive, and comprehensive ability to counter all threats of abuse and exploitation to children when those crimes fall under the authority of the FBI;
- Identify, locate, and recover child victims; and
- Strengthen relationships between the FBI and federal, state, local, tribal, and international law enforcement partners to identify, prioritize, investigate, and deter individuals and criminal networks exploiting children.

Investigative Priorities

- Child abductions---the mysterious disappearance of a minor, especially a minor of tender years (12 or younger).
- Contact offenses against children—production of child pornography, sextortion (https://www.fbi.gov/news/stories/stop-sextortion-youth-face-risk-online-090319). Domestic travel to engage in sexual activity with children, and international travel to engage in sexual activity with children.
- Sexual exploitation of children—online networks and enterprises manufacturing, trading, distributing, and/or selling child pornography.
- Trafficking of child pornography---distribution and/or possession of child pornography.
- International parental kidnapping---wrongfully retaining a child outside the United States with the intent to obstruct the lawful exercise of parental rights.

INVESTIGATIONS

Child Abductions; in 1932, Congress gave the FBI jurisdiction under the "Lindbergh Law" to immediately investigate any reported mysterious disappearance or kidnapping involving a child of "tender age"----usually 12 or younger. There does not have to be a ransom demand nor does the child have to cross state lines or be missing for 24 hours before the FBI will become involved.

All reports of circumstances indicating that a minor or possibly has been abducted are afforded an immediate preliminary inquiry. In this initial inquiry, we evaluate all evidence, circumstances, and information to determine if an investigation is warranted under federal law. If a case is warranted, we will immediately open an investigation in partnership with state and local authorities.

Child abductions by strangers are often complex and time is of the essence. FBI Child Abduction Field Officers by Child Exploitation and Human Trafficking Task Forces (CEHTETFs), which combine the resources of the FBI with those of other federal, state, and local law enforcement agencies. Each of the FBI's 56 Field Offices has worked investigations developed by the Crimes Against Children program, and many of our legal Attache offices have coordinated with appropriate foreign law enforcement partners on international investigations. Several of these investigations are also worked in coordination with internet Crimes Against Children (CAC) Task Forces, which are funded by the Department of Justice. Furthermore, the FBI supports training for federal, state, local, and foreign law enforcement agencies involved in these investigations.

The FBI, in conjunction with domestic and international law enforcement partners, investigates U.S. citizen and permanent residents who travel overseas to engage in illegal sexual conduct with children under the age of 18. These crimes are exacerbated by the relative ease of international travel and the use of the internet as a platform for individual exchanging information about how to find child victims in foreign locations.

INTERNATIONAL PARENTAL KIDNAPPING

The FBI investigates matters when a parent or other person takes or wrongfully retains a child outside of the United States with the intent to obstruct the lawful exercises of parental rights. Our field offices across the country serves as the primary points of contact for those seeking help. To request assistance or learn more about our services, please contact your local FBI office.

When a child is abducted by a parent and taken outside the United States, one criminal and one civil may be pursued:

- The international Parental Kidnapping Crime Act (IPKCA) of 1993: A criminal arrest warrant can be issued for a parent who takes a juvenile under 16 outside of the United States without the other custodial parent's permission.
- The Hague Convention on the Civil Aspects of International Child Abduction: In nations that have signed the Hague Convention, there is a civil process that facilities the return of abducted children under 16 to their home countries.

The criminal process enables the arrest of the abducting parent but does not specifically order the return of the child, although the child is usually returned when the parent is apprehended. The civil process, on the other hand, facilitates the return of the child but does not pursue the arrest of the abductor. As a result, a criminal process would not be pursued if circumstances indicates it will jeopardize an active Hague Convention civil process.

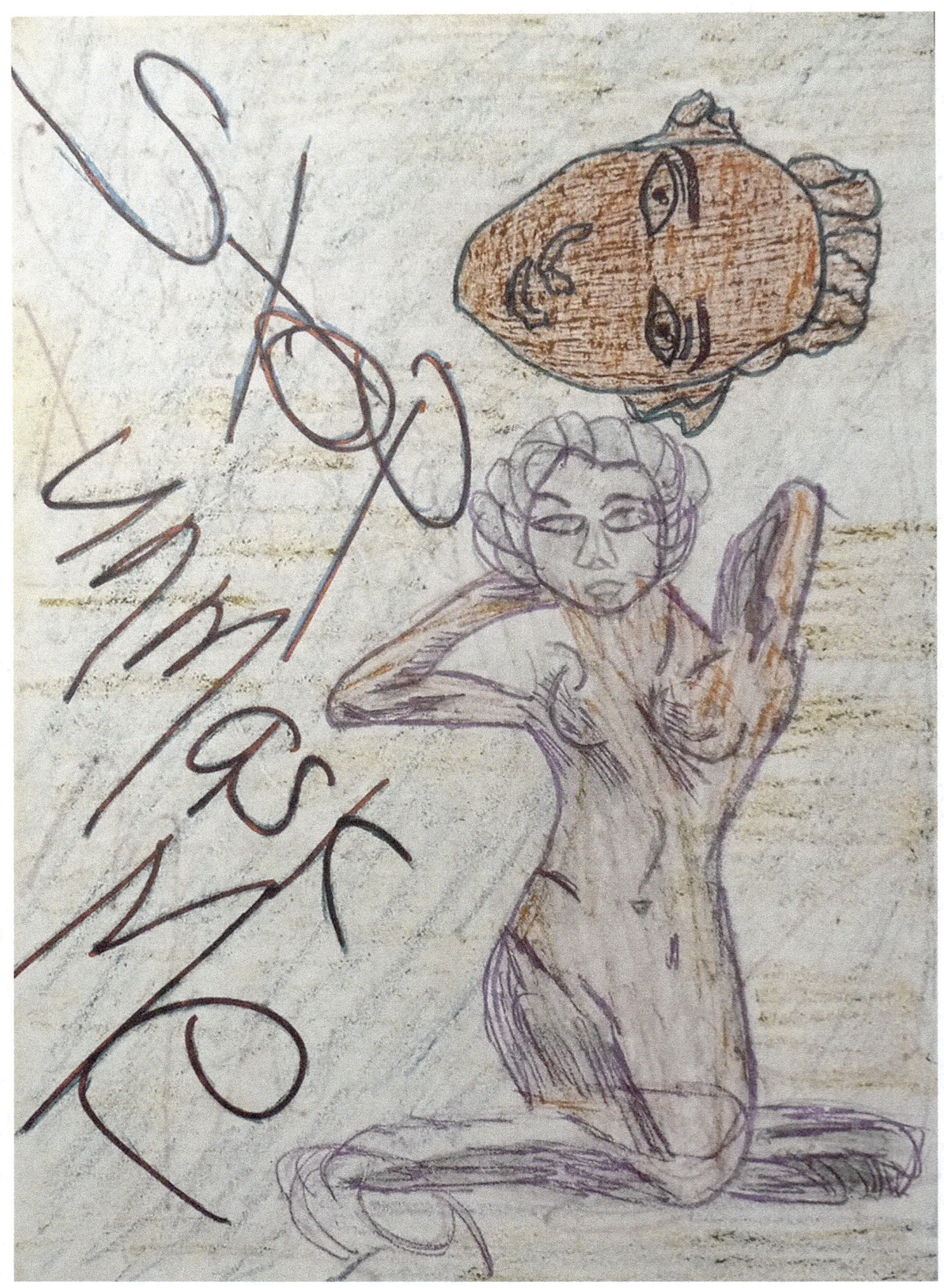

Base on these considerations, we pursue criminal action in international parental kidnappings on a case-by-case basis. We take into account all the factors and guidance among the impacted state and federal law enforcement agencies, state and/or federal prosecutors, the Department of State, the Department of Justice, and the left-behind parent.

It's important to understand that the FBI has no investigative jurisdiction outside of the United States, except on the high seas and other locations specifically granted by Congress. We work through our existing partnerships with international authorities through the U.S. Department of States, our Legal Attache.

To assist with the recovery of children internationally, the United States implemented federal legislation under the international Child Abduction Remedies Act by signing the Hague Convention on the Civil Aspects of international Child Abduction in 1988. The Hague Convention is an agreement among its signatories that states: A child under 16 years of age who is habitually resident in a country party to the Hague Convention, and who is removed to or retained in another country party to the Convention in breach of the left-behind parent's custody rights, shall be promptly returned to the country of habitual residence.

Signatory countries of the treaty are obligated, with certain limited exceptions and conditions, to return an internationally abduction child under 16 to the country from which they habitually resides if an application to the Hague Convention is made within one year from the date of the wrongful abduction. The Hague Convention only applies to abduction between countries who have signed the treaty.

The U. S. Department of States, Office of Children's Issues, has been designated as the Central Authority under the Hague Convention for the United States. For more information about our current parental abduction cases and to help us find these children, see Wanted by the FBI Parental Kidnapping (https;//www.fbi.gov/wanted/parental-kidnappings).

Our authority in parental kidnapping cases stems from the Fugitive Act. Although this status most commonly applies to fugitives who flee interstate and/or internationally. Congress has specifically declared that the statues is also applicable in cases involving interstate or international parental kidnapping. Because many fugitives flee with their own children. the statute serves as an effective means for the FBI to help local and state law enforcement arrest these fugitives. In order for the FBI to assist with an Unlawful Flight to Avoid Prosecution arrest warrant. the following criteria must be met:

- There must be probable cause to believe the abducting parent has fled interstate or international to avoid prosecution or confinement.
- State authorities must have an outstanding warrant for the abductor's arrest charging him/her with a felony under the laws of the state from which the fugitive flees.
- State authorities must agree to extradite and prosecute that fugitive from anywhere in the United States if the subject is apprehended by the FBI.
- The local prosecuting attorney or police agency should make a written request for FBI assistance.
- The U.S. Attorney must authorize the filing of a complaint, and the federal arrest process must be outstanding before the investigation is instituted.

INITIATIVES

Child Abduction Rapid Deployment (CARD) Team

The first few hours after a child is abducted are critical. That is why we established CARD Teams in October 2005. CARD Teams are comprised of experienced personnel with a proven track record in crime against children investigations, especially cases where a child has been abducted by someone other than a family member. Team members provides on the-ground investigative, technical, and resource assistance to state and local law enforcement. The teams work closely with FBI Behavioral Analysis Unit representatives, National Center for the Analysis of Violent Crime coordinators, and child exploitation task force members.

In addition to their unique expertise, CARD Teams are capable of quickly establishing an-on-site command post to centralize investigative efforts and operations. Other assets they being to the table including a mapping tool to identify and locate registered sex offenders in the area, national and international lead coverage, and the Child Abduction Response Plan to guide investigative efforts.

ENDANGERED CHILD ALERT PROGRAM

In 2004, the FBI began its Endangered Child Alert Program (ECAP) as a proactive approach to identifying unknown individuals involved in the sexual abuse of children and the production of child pornography. A collaborative effort between the FBI and the National Center for Missing and Exploited Children, ECAP seeks national and international exposure of unknown adults (referred to as John/Jane Does).

VIOLENT CRIMES AGAINST CHIDLREN INTERNATIONAL TASK FORCE

The Violent Crimes Against Children International Task Force (VCACITF) is a select cadre of international law enforcement experts working together to formulate and deliver a dynamic global response to online child exploitation through strategic partnerships, the aggressive engagement of relevant law enforcement, and the extensive use of liaison.

The VCACITF (formerly known as the Innocent Images International Task Force) became operational in 2004 and serves as the largest task force of its kind in the world, comprised of 68 online child sexual exploitation investigators from almost 46 countries. A five-week training session for newly invited task force officers brings them to the United States to work side-by-side with FBI agents in the Crimes Against Children Program. The VCACITF also conducts an annual case coordination meeting where task force members come together in a central location to share best practice and coordinate transnational investigations between members.

I have a good memory of the past and the presence. Why is that? Because I'm living the future. I understand the missing, abduction, lost of a child, and that bad things can happen to them. The pain is great because you're not willing and ready emotionally, psychologically, nor physically ready to accept it. Because you wasn't expecting anything like that to over power taking control over the life of your child. No, no, no, that couldn't happen to me. You now feel lost and out of touch with reality. Yes, I understand the problems caused by something like that. My heart goes out to all parents, fathers, and mother's alike in times like these. Because I was once a child and understand that all lives matters. I therefore have seen many things in my life, and not all was and or has been pleasant or good. You'll never know when something is going to happen to your child. You can't honestly prepare for it. Therefore you're not going to know until it happens. That is where the Bible comes in. Friends and family can only do so much. Reading the Bible and listening to sweet music can quickly help the heart and soul ease away the pain of suffering pounding its way on you. The Bible is always at hand regardless of your religion preference. The Best Defense with regard to child safety, and children health and welfare is EDUCATION. Education means to know, know means knowledge, knowledge means to take action. Your action depends on what's going on at the time. You need to know what you're responding to. Because that determines what type of action you need to take if any. You'll need to take steps ensuring and implementing the action. That could be anything such as (1) yourself getting involved. (2) A close friend or a neighbor (3) local police (4) FBI) (5) community involvement (6) Missing Person Alert Agency (7) and of course the news media.

What if the captor has your child up the street, down the street, a few blocks away, and or next door? How would you respond to that? Wouldn't that be a mother's uncle? Your child right under your nose. To utter such words you will have no way of knowing. Rule of thumb! Anytime something like that happens trust no one. Suspect everyone even your neighbor, and or your best friend. You can always apologies later. Because the beating of the drums, and the hot pursue is finding your child. It could mean having to step on toes, and pissing somebody off. Look at it this way. Its better to be pissed off than to be pissed on. That would mean you're making progress because you now have that person attention. Being a parent. Mother, and or a father you would hope that person would understand. But as times goes by and the tension heats up, you'll find out that's not always the case because no two people thinks alike.

Therefore that person may not feel the same as you do. Therefore these words of sweetness, goodness, and pure in heart, and spirit has been enclosed for you in your time of distress.
These words of sweet nothing is taken from the Holy Bible, Placed By The Gideons, and I quote, I will lift up mine eyes unto the hills, from whence cometh my help. My help cometh from the Lord, which made heaven and earth. He will not suffer thy foot to be moved: he that keepeth thee will not stumber. Behold, he that keepeth Israel shall neither slumber nor sleep. The Lord is thy right hand. The sun shall not smite thee by day, nor the moon by night. The Lord shall preserve thee from all evil: he shall preserve thy soul. The Lord shall preserve thy going out and thy coming in from this time forth, and even for evermore.

I was glad when they said unto me, Let us go into the house of the Lord. Our feet shall stand within thy gates, O Jerusalem. Jerusalem is build as a city that is compact together: Whither the tribes go up, the tribes of the Lord, unto the testimony of Israel, to give thanks unto the name of the Lord. For there are set thrones of judgment, the thrones of the house of David. Pray for the peace of Jerusalem: They shall proper that love thee. Peace be within thy walls, and prosperity within thy palaces. For my brethren and companions' sakes. I will now say, Peace be within thee.

Because of the house of the Lord our God I will seek they good.
Why is it that grown men prey on young girls? what is it that they lacked as a child? what do u think www.forharriet.com
about it? By Family & Relationships, and I quote, I feel once they do that and get away with it they will continue to do it again. Answers: Best answer: They are not real men. They are sick, sorry people who will eventually get what they deserves. The scary thing about it is that it's always someone you wouldn't expect.....Take it from me...I feel like it is just so easy...I mean it takes practically nothing to get laid....By and adult. You can go to the local pub and hook up with someone within an hour.....it ain't hard...So, if you are that messed up in the head that you need to go after someone's CHILD...There's a special place in Hell for you. Your question is confusing to a point.

185

There are two definitions to your questions and they each have different answers, so I will answer both. 1. Why is it that grown men prey on young girls? What is it that they lacked as a child? What do u think about it? Meaning Guys and minor girls. This is simple there is an innocence that is there and a power thing that turns guys on that are into this sick crap. Not all guys are into and those that do look for this crap are either very insecure and need the power stuff or twisted and need help. Power ones need prison and twisted need help. 2. Why is it that grown men prey on young girls? What is it that they lacked as a child? What do u think about it? Meaning older guys and younger but legal women. This is usually dealing with older men's need to feel attractive. A lot like women needing the same support from men. Women tend to get it from guys looking at them. They can tell if they are still attractive by the way men look at them. Men on the other hand equate attractiveness with sex. The younger the woman the more attractive the man feels. As for men being attracted to younger women. 18-25 is a women's most attractive time frame. It is natural that men (who are visual creatures)are attracted to them.

Define "prey" If you are indeed a concerned mother and somethings happened to your daughter I hope that you are not looking the other way due to the fact that the grown men prey may be living under your roof or someone you know. You are right generally speaking that once someone does something and get away with it they will continue to do it again. Please be supportive of your daughter and do not allow her to be vulnerable to these men lacked as a child, worry about the child now, who needs an adult for guidance and support. You may be her only hope.

I think grown men prey on young girls because they need to be in CONTROL of something. Some people view things (women), girls; children: young boys) as property, not individuals-and when they lack control in a situation they pick out their subjects to take it out on; they look for someone who looks weak to them. It's easier for a lion to pick out the weakest animal in a hunt. They look at who is at the end of the herd or pack. Some people are the same way. They study their victims. They get a sense of their characteristics, their weaknesses and they play on that. If it's a family member, or close friend, they base things on ownership. It's yours-and sometimes when people view things as property. They think they can do anything they want to because it's theirs.) That is a wrong way to view children but men feel like they need to be in control of situations in their life. It's bred into them. And if they don't have control then they seek out something or someone that they can control.

If that is their problem, then I agree if they don't get help it will go on until someone puts a stop to it. It's a cycle, and things could get worse and young people could be destroyed by the actions of perp. Also, I think some men get a charge out of stealing innocence from young children. It feeds their perversion. But again as I said before, it's a control thing. If you are a mother or relative or even a friend of a young person who is being victimized by this, don't stand by and let it continue. Believe me it will effect the child for the rest of her/his life. It's a sickness. Something evidently happened to them as a child and they cannot break the pattern. They need help for sure. Anyone who knows of any of these men should report them immediately. They prey on these young girls because the girls want to be loved and want someone to be there for them. That makes them vulnerable; unquoted.

https://www.missingkids.org/theissues/sextoin
Sextortion; and I quote, Red Flags—Those involved in the sextortion of children often:

- Approach a child on social media after using it to learn about the child's interests, friends, school, family, etc.
- Intentionally move their communications with the child from one online platform to another (e.g., moving from social media to private video chat or messaging apps.
- 8 Use tactics to coerce a child, including:

- Reciprocation (I'll show you, if you show me")
- Initially offering something to the child, such as money or drugs, in exchange for sexually explicit photos/videos.
- Pretending to work for a modeling agency to obtain sexual images of the child
- Developing a bond with the child by establishing a friendship/romantic relationship
- Secretly recording sexually explicit videos of the child during video chats.
- Physically threatening to hurt or sexually assault the child or the child's family members.
- Using multiple online identities to contact a child
- Pretending to be younger and/or a member of the opposite sex
- Accessing the child's online account without authorization and stealing sexual images or videos of the child.
- Threatening to create sexual images or videos of the child using digital-editing tools Threatening to commit suicide if the child does not provide sexual images or videos.
- Saving sexually explicit conversations with the child and threatening to post them online.

There are some certain online behaviors that may increase the risk for a child to be a victim of online enticement or sextortion. Some of these behaviors includes:

- Lying about his or her age to access platforms which would allow a child to communicate with older individuals
- Initiating contact with an individual online or offering to provide sexually explicit images to the individual in exchange for financial compensation, alcohol or drugs, gifts, etc.
- Sending sexually explicit photos or videos (known as "sexts") of oneself to another individual.
- Between October 2013 and April 2016, there were 1,428 reports of sextortion of minors made to NCMEC's Cyber Tipline. 78% female and 15% male.
- People engaged in sextortion typically had one of three main objectives:
- To acquire increasingly more explicit sexual content of the child
- To obtain money or goods from the child
- To meet in order to engage in sex with the child.

The ages of child victims ranged from 8 – 17 years old.

CREATING A PLACE TO REPORT

In 1998, NCMEC launched the Cyber Tipline to provide the public and electronic service providers with the ability to report suspected child sexual exploitation including online enticement of children for sexual acts, extra-familial child sexual molestation, child pornography, child sex toursm, child sex trafficking, unsolicited materials sent to children, misleading domain names, and misleading words or digital images on the internet. After NCMEC's review is completed, all information in a CyberTipline report is made available to the appropriate law enforcement agency.

PREVENTING ABUSE THROUGH EDUCATION

Because of the massive amount of information that comes through the Cyber Tipline, NCMEC is n a unique position to sport trends and evolving threats to children- especially online. NCMEC's digital citizenship and safety programs, Netsmartz (http://www.netsmartzorg/), is an innovative educational program that utilizes games, animated videos, classroom-based lesson plans, activities, and much more to help empower children to make safer choices online; unquoted.

Children need to be talk to look everyone straight into the eye, ask questions loudly-like, I don't know you and neither do my parents! I don't have permission to go with you." "Go away, I don't know you." Not talking to strangers isn't the same as not being friendly. You can teach your children to smile, and say hello when greeted. might look friendly and appear to be your friend but look car be deceiving.

Its not always what you see but how you feel. In most instants warning signs comes from the guts revealing their evilness to you but what happens next would surely surprise you. We don't pay attention to warnings but instead go forth into the evil of the night wondering what's on the other side. What am I talking about? The human mind no matter how recklessly and powerfully it may be. We don't listen from within clearing out the darkness as evil approaches surrounding us with madness. The look of faces, touching of the hands, and eyes staring into space looking down on us as the moon slowly disappears into the sky above. Nevertheless we go and go farther into our own world thinking that freedom, trust, and belief is only a detail of what to come. Fear and fear not no evil will harm you not now not ever for the power of protection is devastating you into the rein of love.

As you look into the eyes of your parents pulling you away from what would be called and consider the path of danger. What if anything has been said that makes sense to you? As a child and young children you have a tender heart that pumps blood into every organ of your body but goes beyond the fulfillment of the brain. We think with the goodness and the fixation of the brain as we grow into a body of maturity. But not all lives to reach and or enjoy a full life that once was promise to us as a human being. Why is that you ask? Well things happens but not always for a reason. How true, how true but what does it mean to you? It means that your life can be cut short by the hands of others stealing from within the soul of the young. As they lie so quietly in their crib but not to awaken the next morning in the dwelling of their parents.

How so, how so, but its true. Because so many children had been stolen, and taken away in the middle of the night without warning to places far, far, away, and never to be seen and or heard from ever again. Therefore let me be clear and righteous with you leaving no doubt and or false belief in your young mind. Remember this and remember this well. Strangers whoever they may be might look friendly and appear to be your friends but look can be deceiving. Strangers will use such things called tricks up their sleeves, and it could be any number of things such toys, candy, sweet sounding music, flowers, and animals to get you to come with them luring you away from safety into their environment of darkness and evil. If this should ever happen to you my child run as fast as you can. I know what you're thinking as you look at him. A complete stranger no doubt but you being so young, and attracted to whatever is. In his hands you begin to think and feel that its alright when in reality its not. But you feel that's it's OK to be with him. You don't see him as being harmful and or danger. That is understanding taking into consideration your age group.

We as adults takes things for granted but shouldn't because our children should be our first and foremost our priority. Our concern for their safety, health, and welfare should be first within our lives. No harm should come to them. No stranger should approach them with the intent to blacken their life and well being. Keep away from me satanic letting no evil come possessing your child. The understanding is clear children do not think danger, do not think that strangers are monsters, and that strangers will harm them. That is where you the parent comes in. You are their teacher, protector, savior, eye of goodness, road map to understanding, training of their young mind, and hands of awareness as they mature not just in body but also in spirit. Help them to know, and

understand that the ground they walk on is harmless but people they meet may not always be. Therefore where ever they go, go within the boundaries, grounds of safety should they need the helping hands of parents due to whatever reaches out to darken their life shorting what would be a life of greatness, and pursue of happiness. These are things that we as parents tends to ignore, forget, putting blinders on, and that's the safety of our children. Safety is a word that is rarely spoken and or used in family conversations, marriage, family reunions, and therefore the wit of what we so called wisdom falls beneath the cornerstone foundation of our thinking, caring causing our children to suffer sometime a brutal death, beaten, torture, and the hardship of evil.

It is our spoken word that will prevent all of this from happening. But instead we fail even to open our mouth until its too late. We then wonders why something so terribly happened to such children. Parents by not opening your mouth you have yourself the blame. It only impact on the problem, and causes the lives, and safety of other children to be in danger of suffering the same faith. The evil I say is beyond the spoken word of goodness cashing shame into the hearts of many because the safety of our children has fallen to the way-side. Because you have done nothing to stop it. What a fool you say? What a fool you are. Speak no evil, Say no evil. Do no evil. Well, its too late now. We now wonder why things has betrayed us putting our children life in danger at such a young age.

Well, wonder no more because you didn't get off your ass to do anything to prevent whatever was going on at the time. You were too busy focusing on yourself, and things that matters to you more when you should had been concentrating, and paying attention to the needs of your children. You as a parent should never be too busy for your children. You should always put them and their safety, health, and welfare first in your life. They are your children. They depends on you for guidance. You are their safety net. But above all you are their parents. Their mind of course has not develop enough to distinguish right from wrong, and the different between yellow and red as it relates to society. Because as parents we know that children lives their day surrounded by fun and games. They look forward only to waken up to whatever would be a normal day fill with love, family, happiness sitting around watching television, and listening to the radio. That's a normal life for them other than attending school, and being with their friends children of their age group. The word abduction; meaning to abduct has became an unspoken word when associated with women. I filtrated into the mist when women were used by men to gain the attention, trust of young children, and young adults luring them into a nest of snakes and snails camouflage by evil forcing them against their will into awaiting vehicles. The devil has struck as evil walks the land of the free dressed in clothes none with standing echoing the name women with out reach hands, and a soft voice only to be distinguish as someone representing themselves as a friend. The impact of her face demonstrate that children were powerless because women were not seem as predators, or people that would do or cause harm and or danger to children. What if anything deep down into the darkness of mankind anyone could say? I didn't see it coming. I didn't know that women were evil. I didn't know that women would do such a thing. And, your right! Evilness of mankind conducted and committed by women were unheard of, and furthermore shocked the world.

Because they were "women". Who in God's name would think that a woman would do such a thing? This evilness and sinful deed became wildly spread and internationally know when people were confronted by those who were captured by authorities. Even then people were shocked. This is not something people say that a woman would do. A page in history has turned. The wicked has fallen from the sky of darkness preying onto young children and young adults without mercy luring them into the gate of hell taking advantage of them like loose animals having their way with them. The beast has grown mad and barking like a mad dog from hell walking around with bloodshed eyes of the devil looking for you, and others like you, called children of this free world at least that's what we thought. We now know that even women can be predators. Why, because the world that we lived in has turned black and dark as the sea causing the water to turn red draining the wicked from the body of hell forcing them out into the light revealing them to the naked eye of evil. Why would women do such things to children? Why would she risk freedom, life, and liberty, spending the rest of her life behind bars in prison? Why would she sacrifice everything, density, respect for others, and worldly possessions preying on children?

The obvious answer maybe not politically correct would be for the man. What is the common rule of knowledge, and understanding that would cause a woman to give up life? The life that she had, marriage, and or single knowing that one day she would be find out, and eventually capture and apprehended. Ya, ya, I say unto you. Fear the Lord and do no wrong. Let the evil within you become part of the ground that you so dearly walks on. Cleans your soul from that which is bad, wicked, and evil. Is this act of violence preying on children, abducting a child, and or kidnapping a child worse your freedom? How do you confront and respond to such an act of violent? What happened to your pride being a woman? What happened to a mother's love for her children "that never dies"? If that means anything to you as a woman! Why would you being a woman abduct and kidnap another woman's child? What if anything have you to gain? What did that child ever do to you? What if it was your child?

That makes it hard and difficult to say. Wouldn't it not depend on who's the mother and who's the predator? I would hate for a copy of this book, written by me, ALVIN WALLACE, to fall into the wrong hands of a would be, cold blooded predator. Whoever it may be male and or female. Look at our country, The United States Of America has come to. Predator male and female alike preying on children wanting to have sex with them, and luring them into prostitution. Killing them and slaughtering them like animals. How could such a person walk and live without guilt, and or without a conscious knowing he/she has did these things to another human being? I would called that person a cold blooded killer, child molester, monster, in human, and a dirt bag that does not deserves to live.

https://howtoadult.com
THINGS KIDS SHOULD KNOW ABOUT STRANGERS, by Kathryn Hatter, Demand Media, and I quote, The world can be frightening and sinister, but you don't necessarily wants to project overwhelming fears onto your child. Educating your child about strangers is an important task as you strive to protect him. By informing your child about stranger danger, you equip him with information necessary to stay safe. Defining a Stranger: The term "stranger" can create an image in a child's mind of a weird or creepy person who looks unusual or acts intimidating, warns the National Crime Prevention Council. To keep your child safe, define a stranger as anyone your child or your family doesn't know in a personal and friendly manner. Explain to your child that a stranger could be anyone she doesn't know—even someone who looks and sounds friendly and harmless. Because she doesn't know the person, she can't know for sure that he's a friendly and safe person. SPECIFIC STRANGER RULES: Help your child understand specific stranger rules that will help him navigate situations.

"Safe" strangers would be people he doesn't know who are servants, such as police officers and firefighters. If your child needs help, he can speak with a safe stranger without worry. Instruct your child never to accept any gifts or items from someone he/ she doesn't know, advises the University of Michigan Health System. Tell your youngster never to walk near a car in response to a stranger calling him. POSSIBLE LURES: A stranger might use a lure to entice a child. Teach your child some stories a stranger might tell her to help see through the lies. A harmful stranger might ask a child for help with directions to engage her in conversation. A stranger could also promise a child a gift or a treat to lure the youngster into close proximity. Another common story involves a lost animal and a request for help finding the pet. Finally, a stranger might approach a child with a story about an emergency that involves a parent, promising to get her in an emergency—if someone happens, only a trusted family member would be sent to get her. Practicing Rules: Encourage your youngster to follow safety rules, advices the kid power website. Tell him that he doesn't need to be polite to strangers, especially if he feels afraid. In this situation, he should shot "No!" and run away from a stranger toward other people who will help him. Tell your child that it's never OK to go anywhere with anyone without getting permission from you first.

https://www.ncpc.org
National Crime Prevention Council: RECOGNIZING AND HANDLING DANGEROUS SITUATIONS, and I quote, Perhaps the most important way parents can protect their children is to teach them to be wary of potentially dangerous situations—this will help them when dealing with strangers as well as with known adults who may not have good intentions. Help children recognize the warning signs of suspicious behavior, such as when an adult ask them to disobey their parents or to do something without permission, ask them to keep a secret, ask children for help, or make them feel uncomfortable in any way. Also tell your children that an adult should never ask a child for help, and if one does ask for their help, teach them to find a trusted adult right away to tell what happened. You should also talk to your children about how they should handle dangerous situations. One ways is to teach them "No, Go, Yell." If in a dangerous situations, kids should say no, run away, yell as loud as they can, and tell a trusted adult what happened right away. Make sure that your children know that it is okay to say no to an adult in a dangerous situation and to yell to keep themselves safe, even if they are indoors. It's good to practice this in different situations so that your children will feel confident in knowing what to do. Here are a few possible scenarios: * A nice-looking stranger approaches your child in the PARK and asks for help finding the stranger's lost dog. * A woman who lives in your neighborhood but that the child has never spoken to invites your child into her house for a snack.
* A stranger asks if your child wants a ride home from school. Your child thinks he or she is being followed. An adult your child knows says or does something that makes him or her feel bad or uncomfortable. * While your child is walking home a friend's house, a car pulls over and a stranger
https://www.kidpower.org/library/article/safe-without-scare/
asks for directions.

Teaching Kids to Be safe Without Making Them Scared, by Irena Van Der Zande, Kid power Founder and Executive Director, and I quote, You can teach children to be safe without scaring them—You just need to know. Young people are at risk of assault, abduction, and abuse even in caring families, schools, and communities. Skills and knowledge are the keys to keeping kids safe. The good news is that there are simple and effective ways of teaching children how to protect themselves that will work most of the time. Parents, teachers, and other caregivers need to know that their children are more likely to be harmed by someone they know than by a stranger. Children need to have clear safety rules both for strangers when they are out on their own and for setting boundaries with people they know.

Anyone can be a child molester—a neighbor, a relative, a family friend, a youth group leader, a teacher, even another child. The best way to protect your children's safety is know what is happening with them. Make the time to ask them often, "Is there anything you've been wondering or worrying about that you haven't told me?" and to listen to their answers with patience and respect. Children need to understand that there are different rules whey they are not in the care of their adult and when they are on their own. Children who are only a short distance away from an adult in charge even for a few minutes are on their own. They don't need to worry. They just need to know what to do. Just telling children about safety or just showing children what to do is not enough. When we just talk to children about danger, their raised awareness can actually raise their level of anxiety. Young people learned best by actively participating. Practicing children's personal safety skills increases their confidence and competence. It is important to do this in a way that is not scary, but is fun. Your child can

learn with you, and in programs such as Kid power. Be sure that you are calm yourself when you talk to kids about strangers.

If you sound anxious, they will pick up on that. Instead tell kids in a matter-of-fact way that you believe that most people are GOOD, and that this means that most strangers are good, but that a few people have problems that might cause them to hurt kids.

https://www.kidpower.org/library/article/Small-Children
SAFETY RULES FOR CHILDREN WHEN THEY ARE ON THEIR OWN: * Most people are good. This means most strangers are good. * A stranger is just someone I don't know and can look like anybody. * The rules are different when I am with an adult who is taking care of me and when I am on my own. When I am on my own, my job is to check first with the adult in charge before I let a stranger get close to me, talk to me, or give me anything. * If I am old enough to be out on my own without an adult to ask, it is safer to be where there are other people close by to get help if I need it. * I do not give personal information to strangers or to someone who makes me feel uncomfortable. * It is OK to get help from strangers if an emergency is happening to me, and there is no one close by that I know. * My job is to check first with an adult in charge before I go anywhere with anyone (a stranger or someone I know). I will tell the adult in charge where I am going, who will be with me, and what I will be doing. * I will have a safety plan for how to get help anywhere I go. * I will know what my family's safety rules are for children answering the door, being on the phone, and being on the internet.

To Be Able to Follow These Rules, Children Need to Practice These Kid power Skills: * How to stand and walk with awareness, calm, and respectful confidence. *How to move away and stay out of reach from someone approaching them. * How to walk away from a stranger without waiting even if that person is being very nice. * How to check first even when someone they know and trust say not to. * How to get help from a busy or insensitive adult if they are lost or scared. * How to make noise, run, and get to safety in case of an emergency. * What to say and do if a stranger approaches them at home. Kid power Safety Rules With People Kids Know: I belong to myself -my body, my time, my spirit-All of me. Touch for play, teasing, or affection has to be both people's choice and it has to be safe. * Except for health, no one should touch me in my private areas (the parts of the body covered by a bathing suit). * No one should ask me to touch them in their private areas. * Touch or other behavior for health or safety is not always a choice, but also should never, EVER, have to be a secret. * I do not have to let what other people say control how I feel. * Anything that bothers me should not have to be a secret.

* If I have a problem, I need to tell and adult I trust and keep on telling until I get help. * It is never too late to get help. To Be Able Follow These Rules, Children Need to Practice These Kid power Skills: * Saying "No" to unwanted or inappropriate behavior using polite words, eye contact, and assertive body language. * Persisting even when someone uses bribes, hurt feelings, or power to try to pressure them into doing something that makes them feel uncomfortable. * Protecting themselves from hurtful words. * Verbal choices for getting out of potentially dangerous situations. * Getting the attention of busy adults and telling the adult the detail about situations that make them confused or uncomfortable. We as parents know that life is more than a path having blinders on ignoring what could, and what will happen if we fail to implant the seed of awareness teaching our children about the other side of life, the dark side. The evilness within this world and society problems that bears down on us.

Their weakness that cannot defend for themselves fighting off the predator seeking the innocence of the young pure in heart carrying them off to be slaughter. Treated like animals helplessly because the power is in their hands knowing that the face standing before them, and beneath them is too young to understand what's going to happen to them. Parents the world around us has changed. Therefore people have changed. People are not the way they were years ago. It now take one to know one. If you know what I mean. Trust no one with your children that you are not comfortable with. Know when your children are trying to tell you something. Know when there are red flags warning you against something. Do not ignore the signs. You should always know when something is wrong. The signs will not mislead you. They could be your only wake up call.

Remember, mother's love for her child never dies. So many people today men and women alike have twisted minds. Some have no mind at all. Psychiatrist called it mental illness. I called it an excuse to harm the very young punching holes into what is clearly known as avoiding prosecution defeating justice thereof. They therefore preys on others stealing the breath of life and respect of our children. Sometime there are things that I don't understand and can't comprehend when it comes to threatening the life, health and welfare of children. That is where I draw the line. The best excuse that you can give me is thank but no thank send me straight to hell. But from what we as parents have seen over the years, life, health and welfare of a child doesn't matters to those wants to harm children.

Years ago people believe in an eye for an eye. Should we not believe in that today? How is it different from lethal injection? You'll at least be alive. Both feet in hell. The question however cruel and or misleading that stands out the most in people minds would probably be "do you deserve to live'? Remember these words; the eyes of the wilt's fears no evil. In keeping with that understanding let me say this. Than why should we feel sorry for them? Give them the punishment they so dearly deserves. Did they feel sorry for you? Did they feel sorry for your child? How does that grad you? The Bible if I'm not mistaken says to turn the other cheek. Something to think about, yes! This is when you wonder if the punishment fits the crime.

However, what the law distaste and how you feel is two different things. Although the law will listen to you as your heart beats with sorrel and disparages expressing the wishes and demands. The Bible teaches us to forgive. For he knows not what he have done. I find that hard to believe. He is as guilty as sin. When you take advantage of a young child between the age of 12 to 18 then you deserves a one way ticket to hell. Who can forgive those who trespass on the life of children taking advantage of them? Best respond "I will see you in hell". The pain will not let you forgive and or turn the other cheek. Your justice therefore will be justice. That is when your mind, body, and soul will begin to heal. Your heart, and the pain within will not let you forgive, and turn the other cheek. The tears running down your face will not let you forgive and turn the other cheek. The hands of evil and torture that inflicted harm on them the love of your life will not let you forgive and turn the other cheek. Because we have seen what can and what will happen to children. The price we pay for being parents. No, it's the price we pay for caring.

Let not your heart be deceive by evil. But let evil die quickly and go straight to hell. This we need to pursuit against those who preys on you, your children and your helplessness. But when that happens we as parents need to stop at nothing until our children are safe within the arms of safety, and back home with love ones, family, and friends. We should stop at nothing until justice is served. But what is justice when it comes to your children safety, health and welfare? Children doesn't think like we do because the brain is very young. You could say they doesn't think at all. But of course you would be wrong. Children thinks like children. Therefore as parents you has to think for them. Get them to ask questions. Get them to question things. Because their brain is very young, and therefore has not fully, and completely develop into a thinking process of knowledge and understanding. You can question that but it would explain why children of that particular age group cannot walk home alone.

They're not capable and or mature enough to handle situation of serious nature. First of all they're not expecting anything to happen to them. Rule #1. don't let your guard down.

https://parentmap.com/article/stranger-danger-six-tips-keep-kids-safeParentMap—Stranger danger l: six tips to keep kids safe, by Kathleen F. Miller, and I quote, You want to coach kid to avoid danger—without scaring them with images of creepy people lurking behind every tree. It can be a fine line for some parents, so local experts offer the following tips for keeping your elementary-age kid safe yet unafraid. Keep 'them safe indoors: If they are old enough to answer the phone, kids should know how to call 911. Children who are old enough to answer the door should be taught to always check the identity of the person at the door without opening it. 2. Keep 'them safe outdoors: Parents should know their child's route to and from school, and insist that a child never take shortcuts. Teach children never to go anywhere with anyone without parental permission.

Children should be taught to avoid isolated areas of parks and playgrounds, as well as public restrooms, building sites and dark streets. Police say parents should coach a child to think about alternatives if he or she is being bothered or followed. Walk to the places your child often walk to and look for choices. Is there a store, school, or business they could enter and ask for help? If followed by a car, or if a stranger gets out of a vehicle and asks for directions, children should be taught to run away from them and yell. 3. Teach your child about predator's tricks: Predators use tricks. Teach your child to recognize the common methods of luring, including bribes (such as money, toys or the promise of something the child would want), requests for help (My puppy ran away! Will you help me look for it?)or threats.

A predator can often be recognized as someone who asks a child to violate a family rule, such as telling the child she doesn't need her parent's permission to accompany them. 4. Develop a CODE WORD: Teach the child a code word." What if someone other than a parent needs to pick up the child unexpectedly, this person needs to know the "code word" before the child agrees to leave with him or her. 5. Know the risks: Statistically, your child is most likely to be harmed by an adult they know, rather than a stranger. Estes says that parents should be on alert for predators among people the child already knows and learn what predatory red-flag behaviors to be aware of. "One of the biggest myths that we 'bust' in our workshops is the idea that strangers commit all the crimes against children. In reality, someone the child knows commits 90 percent of childhood sexual abuse and 93 percent of all abductions. 2. Safety, 3. Watch out for themselves.

4. Tell someone when they feel threaten. 5. Tell someone when they are being follow. 6. Tell someone when they are approach by a stranger. Note: A stranger is someone that you do not know. 7. Teach them not to be afraid to let someone know when something is not right. 8. Teach them to be open and honest when something happens to them and others. 9. Teach them not to approach strangers with animals, dogs, cats, when playing outside. 10. Teach them not to follow a stranger into a house, apartment, and or any dwelling without the permission of parents. Teach children when outside to stay in plain view of their parents and or in the present of another adult. Teach children to take notice of how the stranger is dress, height, race, and residential area. Teach them how to use a cellular phone and if all possible sign language. Children and because their brain is so young they're friendly toward strangers.

They doesn't know that people are not always who we think they are, and therefore bad things can happen. They catch us when our eyes are closed. They catch us when we think nothing is wrong causing us to look the other way. When we finally wait up out of a deep sleep its too late to prevent what has already happened. Sorry to say but its true a stranger can be anywhere and any body. They can strike without warning destroying the life that

we had and the life of the child. What would you had done? It all depends on how fast you had time to act. You see in situations like these time is of the essence. Just remember, what we do and when depends on time, not just time, but time of notification. You can't jump through your ass and expect a miracle. Because even a miracle requires time. them, and do bad things to them. In the eyes of a child strangers are their friend. We therefore need to teach our children that strangers are not their friend. And, that a stranger can be a man and or a woman.

What must you say to your child? Say it in a way that children are not afraid, and let them ask questions. Children are easily afraid and scare. You want them to know and understand that not everyone are their friend. The best way to describe a stranger "a stranger is someone that you do not know". A stranger will 1. hurt you, 2. harm you, 3. do bad things to you, 4. touch you in your "Private" 5. kidnapped you, and abduct you – to take you away for a very long time so that your parents will not know where you are. 6. harm your parents. 7. take advantage of your friendship doing things to you that they should not do. Things that you as a child should not do. 1. You should not get into a stranger vehicle, car, van, truck, or whatever to include a recreational vehicle (RV). 2. You should not be too friendly toward strangers. You should not let a stranger touch you. 3. You should not take anything from a stranger. Do not go any where with a stranger 5. D with a stranger without your parents permission. that you should had done early on. Blame yourself not the child. You caused that can of worms to be open.

Now deal with it! Be on the alert and always aware of where your children are. That's very important to us as parent! Is it not? Of course you're not going to say no. Children needs to know that we are there for them. If we let our guard down something could happen to them. Streets are not safe. Children could be that "Stop Sign" that you parents needs to focus on. And, to understand that they are important, and a life long lived to appreciate and to believe in. Children needs to know that we put their safety first above our own. That tells the children that we love them. Happiness is the child that can be love. Happiness is a child that is safe from harm. Happiness is a child that loves you back. Happiness is a child that lives out their dream. Happiness is a child that grows up without rejections.

WHAT A YOUNG CHILD SHOULD KNOW WHEN WALKING ALONE AND HOME
FROM SCHOOL. If we as parents do not tell them our children will never know. We will have ourselves to blame. Children should be told not to stop and talk to strangers. They should be told that strangers will say that your parents sent me to pick you up. Your parents can't come to get you. Your parents said for you to come with me. Hurry, your parents are waiting. Children should be told that strangers will say anything to get them to go with them. Parents, the more you educate your children to danger the better they will be. Too many children has fallen to the way side at the hands of strangers because they didn't know 1. what to do and 2. the danger awaits them. Children between the age of 12 to 18 do not know or understand the meaning of such words as predator, enemy, danger, abduction, fear, threat, rope, stranger, face-down, tied-down, and touch. Stranger, stranger, stranger, tell me what you see don't scare these little children just let them be. Let them let them go without harm into the safety net of their parents arm. All that you have done and its not bitter sweet if you look deeply, deeply, into your heart you will see that its only meat. Tell me, tell me, what they have done to you. I will make them and their friends turn blue. You are a stranger for sure that much I know. So why should it matter if you opens the door? Surely these children stranger has done you no wrong. Please open the door and let them go home. There eyes are beautiful as beautiful as the sea. I thank you stranger for letting them be. Was that too much to ask or did you simply feel sorry for me? Do you stranger or do you not feel good you did the right thing now leave the neighborhood on the next train. I guess you wonder stranger why I ask this of you. Stranger, stranger, you need not say no more leave quickly before I throw you to the floor. I once knew this girl who live not far away.

She wanted to play and played she did. With my dogs of course as she laugh in the wind. She was so happy and smile as she dance about. This girl surely is someone that you should know. She call you by name day after day looking up at the sky far, far, away. I haven't seen her for quite awhile.

I heard her parents say these words a loud. Come inside child, come inside now, the sky is falling so don't ask why. It is getting dark. It is getting late. Come inside child before its too late. I must look out for you that much you should know. Come inside child so that I can close the door. We can close our eyes to the danger thereof. When it comes to children lets keep them safe. No matter what we say, no matter what we do. Children safety starts with you. You can't shake a stick at it nor can you quote a price. Their safety is not for sale and neither is their life. Danger, danger, so she say. Be aware of strangers every day. Don't be trick by candy or his toys. Your not a dog dare not be treated that way. Whatever you do run far. far, away. Let me say this and I will. He will use another to draw you in. Run, run, run until you are home. Tell your parents what is wrong.

According to the Bible, and I quote, For I considered all this in my hearts, so that I could declare it all: that the righteous and the wise and their works are in the hand of God. People know neither love nor hatred by anything they see before them. All things come alike to talk to all: one event happens to the righteous and the wicked; to the Good, the clean, and the unclean; to him who sacrifices and him who does not sacrifices. As is the good, so is the sinner; he who takes an oath as he who fears an oath. This is an EVIL in all that is done under the sun: that one thing happens to all. Truly the hearts of the sons of men are full of EVIL; madness is in their hearts while they live, and after that they go to the dead. But for him who is joined to all the living there is hope, for a living dog is better than a dead lion. For the living knows that they will die; but the dead knows nothing, and they have no more rewards, for the memory of them is forgotten. After their love, their hatred, and their envy have now perished; nevermore will they have a share in anything done under the sun.

sites/default/files/rmbs/stranger-danger-eng.pdf www.aesd.net/sites/default/files/rmbs/stranger-danger-eng.pdf Walking to School -Safety Tips, by Remind Children, and I quote, *Stay with a group. Always walk with at least one friend, two or three is even better. * If a stranger offers you a ride, say "NO" and stay far away from their car. * if a stranger follows you on foot, get away from him or her as quickly as you can. You can run and yell "loudly". "HELP". * If a stranger follows you in a car, turn around and go the other direction. * Never leave school with a stranger. * Tell a trusted adult if a stranger is hanging around the school, playground, or public bathroom. * Leave items home and clothing that display your name at home so a stranger cannot read it and use it to talk with you. * If you arrive home alone, call your mother, father, or other trusted adult to let them know you are home and all right. Keep the door locked, don't open the door for strangers, and don't tell strangers that you are home alone. * Never accept things from a stranger. I agreed with all the walking to school safety tips but others needs to be added. Parents needs to walk with their children to school especially the very first day.

Parents needs to caution the child with regard to alternative first and foremost making sure that the route is safe. A few common senses safety rules are as follows: * As you walk from time to time stop, turned around and see if you're being follow by a stranger a suspicious looking person that want to do your harm. *If being followed by someone wanting to harm you, and or to do bad things to you let whoever walking with you know. This is when the child needs to armed him/herself with kick ass rules of common senses. * If there is a store and most of the times there is go into the store, and tell a trusted adult/store keeper that someone is following you. That store keeper will know what to do, and he/she will watch out for you.. Do not ever ignore the evil ways of strangers, and or take them for granted. * What if the stranger comes into the store? First of all the child shouldn't panic. It sends the wrong message telling the stranger that he/she is scare. Identify the stranger to the store keeper. Again, the store keeper will know what to do even if it means calling for the police he/she will. If the stranger doesn't seen to be a threat very carefully leave the store. If after leaving the store and the stranger is still following you. Tell the nearest trusted adult. Asked that adult to call the police. If listening to music-- keep the volume down low. If talking-- talk at a low volume so that you can still hear others around you and in back of you. From time to time walk at a faster paste. Children should discuss as a group what they would do if someone was following them. Discuss if they must run and if necessary where to meet up at. The ideal plan is not to leave anyone behind. Discuss how they would want for the last person to get to the areas of interest. They should discuss what to do next. Such as two stay behind to look for the other person. The others if part of the plan should hurry to the school letting the school staff know what's happening. Don't turn music up so loudly grinding out noise behind you when walking to and or from school.

Because you need to be able to hear others and foot steps thereof. Hearing the foot steps of others behind, and or around you can be a safety net, and a comforter when walking to and from school especially if you're walking alone. It's when you don't hear the foot steps that red flags goes up striking the nervous system sending a warning to your brain. Discuss PASSWORDS and or CODE WORDS to use in case something should happen while walking. Words that only you and the group knows. This we as parents would call a CONTINGENCY PLAN. Contingency, by definition, according to The American Heritage dictionary, means An event that may occur but is not likely or intended. Parents, therefore needs to be involve in their children thinking process guiding them to the right path of righteousness formulating ideas.

Parents, you are the key to making this happen ensuring that it works. Your children will have ideas but their not going to know and or understand the impact, segment, and cruel details that goes into the working knowledge of such a plan. Animals for many years has been known as man best friend particularly dogs. Because of his fury hair and look. The relationship between dogs and human is strong. It has been for many, many years. Dogs are born with an implant beyond the intelligent of man. It detect human nature, love, companionship, and of course danger. Man on the other hand have something called the brain.

It's the housing that enhances and stimulates his feelings and desire. Men relationship with dogs therefore is understandably clear and can be seen by interacting, and communication translated from them. Dogs therefore understand their relationship with men, and danger if any posed against them by the hands and evilness of men. Children not all but most of them has relationships with dogs Dogs therefore becomes their friend.

Parents, this is one way strangers interacts with children pursuing their willingness to obey and go with them. Children are attracted to animals especially dogs. Dog therefore could be children worse enemy but only when dogs are used as a tool to overcome and override the obedience of parents to follow them for the wrong reason. The problem is children don't understand the different and parents that's where you come in. Remember, dogs are not the enemy. The stranger whoever He /She may be. Children will come up to a complete stranger outside and or inside a store pretty much anywhere to meet and play with a dog. That's what a child does! It's their way of addressing and being friendly toward the dog. Human beings men and women alike are aware of that, and therefore will use animal to lure your children into their resident. This is not always the case but does happens. It's a parent worse nightmare a nightmare that will torment them for year. The pain will be too much, and too difficult to overcome knowing that it will haunt your child in years to come.

The emotional and psychological breaking down of the child's mind will be infected causing him/her to in counter problems beyond their imagination. The mother and child will be lest to deal with the scares whatever

they may be going on within the child's mind. I can' tell you enough how devastated this will be. This threatening disease and misery in order to recover will need the help of family, friends, and professionals. But be not warn. It's far from over especially for the child. Although the child will be able to re-adjust it won't be easy but to the child age of development, and time of whatever happened to him/her wounds will be heal. But not entirely and or at a 100 percent but enough so that the child will be able function at slow past growing out the monster that inflicted this cling within her. Mother's be ware. Corrections, mother's and children be ware. Because your children are targets. Just because the animal is presence the child will enter the stranger resident. It just a question of what happens next! You can't always blame the stranger.

It's what the stranger does makes whatever happens wrong and dangerous. Because once the child/children are behind closed doors anything can happen. We have seen and heard that young children are sexually molested, exploited, and forced into prostitution and raped. Parents, knowing what happens to children you need to teach them "self awareness" training their mind to be on the alert for whatever might happen to them. Keep a watch on your children when they are outside playing. When you take your children to the park and or to the play ground. Don't let them out of your "eye" site. Make them the "apple" of your eye and your safety net surrounding them with your love and protection. When at the supermarket, local stores and the mall never let them leave your side, and or astray away from you. Knowing that children likes to run loosely throughout stores to play with toys and hang out with other children.

I observed this frequently when working overnight as an overnight Stocker. I saw children alone in the toy and electronic department. You began to wonder where the parents are. The store will sometime announce children missing and or at a certain place waiting on their parents. But there are other times when the child cannot be found. This could not only could but will be a nightmare of terror for parents. When on public streets hold tightly to your child. Don't let them break away or pull away from you. Children can easily get lost in crowded places, and especially in the streets surrounded by so many people. Parents, don't let this happen to you. Yelling is too late. Crying is too late. Focus on your child/children safety. You as a parent can easily get distracted by things and also by others such as advertisement, traffic, problems, and so much more. Your child / children can easily end up in the hands of a stranger. You should kick start alerting those around you, and yell for your child. Do not ever assume that your child is or will be alright.

Doing so when delay a search for your child, and will give that person, stranger, and or predator to further abduct your child leaving with him/her. Parents this must not happen, and its where you come in taking immediate action ensuring your child safety. When on public transportation such as buses, trains, ships, and street cars know where your child is. Don't get caught off guard having to ask others where your child is or have you seen them. Remember, you have a responsibility to your children and its called safety. Parents listen to me and listen well. I'm going to read you a porn although it might sound bad. But in the long run it might save your ass. Roses are red and violets are blue. What's in the hell wrong with you? I have children here. I have children there. They love you not you stranger but their parents to death.

What are you doing? What can you say? Right vs. wrong will never go away. Away we go, away, away, my child will live to see another day. What are you saying? What do you fear? My children are what keeps me alive. So I asked you stranger what's its going to be? My children have done nothing don't you see? Please let them go harm no hair on their head. Let me take them home and put them to bed. I hope it not too much to asked from someone like yourself. Were you stranger not once a child, and your mother love you to death? I speak from the heart. I speak from the soul. I'm asking you stranger let my children go. Tomorrow is Sunday do you not know? It's a sin, sin, sin, stranger what are you doing? I will pray for you and your soul too. Just let my children go before they turn blue. The Bible you never spoke of stranger tell me why. Do you fear the Bible? Is that the reason why? You will burn in hell stranger and that's the truth. For the Bible don't lie. Do you want to burn in hell stranger or live a full life? Than let me say this. Bow your head and cross your heart. Ask God forgiveness and we shall apart.

I have told you many things even things that you should already know as parents. But when does common senses rule of thinking kicks in? When does right vs. wrong, do and or do not kicks in? Does it matters or makes a different? A mouth full, yes, but what does it mean to you as a parent? We go through our busy days focusing on so many other things. But never to say what if something should happen to my children. I understand that its not something that we as parents wants to hear or think about. But we should. I would rather think about the "if" now then to wait for something to happen and not know what to do. Have I go you thinking now? Throw me some rocks. Throw me some signs. Let the life of my children shine. Let it shine so deep. Let it shine within. Let the life of your children make a different in the end. I will not forget thee. I will not turn my back. Because the life of my child is what makes things right. Roses are red violets are blue cookies are sweet and my children love you. Protect them with your love and do no wrong.

They are angels day and night. Be not stand still and look about. Let not your child walk away in the darkness far, far away. Do not speak to me. For the eyes of wisdom is a tree. You will now know what's right or what's wrong. But whatever happens just be strong. We have no answer to present to you. What's wrong is far to choose. When its done to a child "however" (young) right vs. wrong give your heart out righteous to all that waits letting no child go without love leaving no child beside the curve. There are times when we wonders if we're doing the right thing. Growing our children the way that we do. We understand that their young pure in heart. But when we questioned they fall apart. We spoke of right. We spoke of wrong. When it comes to our children let them go home. What do you do? What do you say?

Where children are involved it matters less. We do what we must. We do what we can. Our children are our future where as the world stands alone. What is best for you is good for the stranger. When I see what's going on in the world and in our society today this book parents is a must that you should read, and a book that you should encourage others also to read. Parents, I have written this book especially for you, and for our futures of tomorrow our children young in heart. According to the Bible, and I quote, Who is like a wise man? And who knows the interpretation of a thing? A man's wisdom makes his face shine. And the sternness of his face is changed. I say, "keep the king's commandment for the sake of your oath to God. Do not be hasty to go from his presence. Do not take your stand for an EVIL thing, for he does whatever pleases him? Where the word of a king is, there is power; and who may say to him, "What are you doing?" He who keeps his commandment will experience nothing harmful; and a wise man's heart discerns both time and judgment,

Because for every matter there is a time and judgment, though the misery of man increases greatly. For he does not know what will happen; so who can tell him when it will occur? No one has power over the spirit to retain the spirit, and no one has power in the day of death. There is no release from that war, and wickedness will not deliver those who are given to it. All this I have seen, and applied my heart to every work that is done under the sun: there is a time to which one man rules over another to his own hurt. Then I saw the wicked buried, who had come and gone from the places of holiness, and they were forgotten in the city where they had so done. This also is vanity. Because the sentences against an EVIL work is not executed speedily, therefore the heart of the sons of men is fully set in them to do EVIL. Though a sinner does EVIL a hundred times, and his days are prolonged, yet I surely know that it will be well with those who fear God, who fear before Him. But it will not be well with the wicked; nor will he prolong his days, which are at a shadow, because he does not fear before God.

There is a vanity which occurs on earth, that there are just men to whom it happens according to the work of the wicked; again, there are wicked men to whom it happens according to the work of the righteous. It's enough to make you wonder what's going on inside us. We are suppose to be human beings with a heart of gold. If this is true. Then why are we doing such terribly things to children shorting their life, future, and dreams? Were you not a child yourself? Listen parents some things just doesn't make sense. Let me draw you a puzzle. A puzzle I called you. The first thing that you are going to say. What is the hell that he is talking about? Let me paint you a picture. Being a woman only you can birth a child. Therefore only you can bring a life into this world. Men have tried. Men have fail. They're not a woman so go to hell. I would think having that power of life in your hands producing a new born the life of a child would mean something special to you not just at that time but throughout life. This I would say is an honor an honor only a woman has. Lets fill in the pieces of the puzzle. Birth is giving life. Life is what we're born with.

Now that new born a baby if you will has been born. You now are not just a parent but also a mother. A mother's love never dies but rather enhances a safety net protecting her child. The health and welfare of that baby depends totally on you growing and transforming it into a young child. You as a parent and as a mother are responsible for protecting your children everyday of your life. What changes when the baby becomes a young child? Absolutely nothing. Your right! But something does change. You let your guard down. That's why harmful things comes to your child. But its not something that you as a parent wants to hear. I understand that because it hurts like hell. Call it a wake up call. Call it a message from beyond. Call it whatever you feel comfortable with. But whatever you call it. It will not change the truth. Parents, you need to understand the important of being a mother. It doesn't stop when the child is born. The end represents the means.

The means represents the different. The different represents what would had become. When a child does something wrong your ready to whip ass. Parents, who whips your ass when you, and your over site allows your children to fall into arms way, into the hands of predators and strangers? Your quick to tell the child that you know what time it is. Therefore there is a structure of development that the child goes through but to ensure that the development, and the structure is complete we as parents, mothers, and fathers needs to protect them from harm, strangers, and predators. What are predators? Simply put, they are would be strangers preying on your children.

https://www.ojjdp.gov./jjjournal/jjjournal598/safe.html
Keeping Children Safe: Rhetoric and Reality-By Ernest Allen, and I quote; Don't take candy from strangers." We will remember our parents passing on these words of wisdom with the hope that they would protect us from harm. Wouldn't it be wonderful if life were that simple? Unfortunately, children are at risk of abduction and sexual victimization, and most of the individuals who perpetrate these crimes are not perceived as strangers by their victims. Are traditional child safety messages effective, accurate, and complete? Do they adequately warn children about the threats to their safety? Do they unduly frighten children and parents? Are we giving children information that makes them more vulnerable to victimization rather than less?

www.missingkids.com/home

To answer these questions, the National Center for Missing and Exploited Children (NCMEC) reviewed existing research and it own data base of long-term abduction cases that do not involve family members. An Underreported Problem: Child victimization is a large and underreported problem. Too many times, problems are not found because no one is looking for them. Most sexual abuse is committed by men (90%) and by persons known to the child (70% to 90%), with family members constituting one-third to one half of the perpetrators against girls and 10% to 20% of the perpetrators against boys".

https://www.justice.gov/ According to the U.S. Department of Justice, teenagers and girls are among the most frequent victims of sexual attacks. According to the National Victim Center, 29 percent of rape are younger than 11, and 32 percent are between 11 and 18 years of age. Acccrding to the Washington State Attorney General's Office, the average victim of abduction and murder is an 11-year-old girl who is described as a low-risk, "normal" child from a middle class neighborhood who has a stable family relationship and whose initial contact with an abductor occurs within a quarter of a mile of her home. Stranger Danger: According to Dr. David Warden, and I quote, No matter how intelligent the child, he or she does not see the world through skeptical adult eyes..... Children live very much in the present. They can't foresee someone's actions or judge their intentions, certainly not at primary school age. They have a very weak understanding of motive, they simply take someone at face value. The concept of stranger danger is difficult, because it clashes with the social constraints on children to be polite to adults. Research suggests that children don't really know what a stranger is. They feel that once someone tells his name, he cease to be a stranger.

https://www.ojjdp.gov/jjjournal/jjjournal598/safe.html

According to Dr. Ray Wyre, and I quote, The first step in advising 'never talk to strangers' is to make sure that the child understands what a stranger is. Children might believe it means a person who looks odd, rather than someone they do not know." Dr. Wyre further observed that a child's image "of a stranger is different from an adult's. The person trying to ensure them could seem caring and persuasive and not at all threatening. After ten seconds chat, they are no longer a stranger to a child.

https://www.ojjdp.gov/jjjournal/jjjournal598/safe.html

According to Host Daniel J. Travanti asked, "Does your child know what a stranger is? The fact is most children just do not know. Think a stranger is someone threatening and evil. The problem with telling your children, 'don't talk to stranger' is that the bad guy don't always look bad." On a cable program, young, elementary school children provided their definitions of a stranger: * A stranger sometimes wears a hat...sometimes a black or brown jacket and is a guy with a beard....some hair and a moustache and some glasses." * I think a stranger is like...a punk rocker that drinks beer all day and sits around in a vacant lot." * A stranger looks mean and ugly...a creep." *Big...bigger than you, bigger than most people." The concept is clearly a difficult one for a child to grasp. A neighbor, a familiar face in a child's daily routine, or someone the child's parents know well enough to speak to or whose name the child knows is probably not regarded as a stranger. The Myth of the Stranger: In the MTC study, the term "child molester" was defined as someone whose sexual offenses were against victims under the age of 16. Sexual offense" was defined as any sexually motivated assault involving physical contact with the victim.

Boe.maso.k12.wv.us/wp-content/uploads/sites/12/.../Child_Molesters_Who_Abduct.pdf

The MTC study found that 66 percent of abducting child molesters and 80 percent of non-abducting child molesters were to their victims. //books.google.com

Hidden Victims, according to Psychologist Robert L. Geiser, and I quote, Hidden Victims "social problems have an uncanny ability to survive most attempts to remedy them. Their first line of defense is to spring onto the scene as full-blown crises. NISMART provides an important starting point for understanding the full range of the problem. Armed with a more accurate picture of those who victimize children, we can provide more effective information to families to help parents keep their children safe. Rhetoric Versus Reality: For generations, our fundamental messages to children have contained three basic premises. * "Don't take candy from strangers ". As indicated above, in at least two of three cases, the offender is not a stranger in the mind of the child. Usually, the victim and offender know each other, at least casually.

Child molesters often seek legitimate access to children and then victimize them through a process similar to seduction. This reality does not make the message wrong, only grossly inadequate in providing protection for children, who need more comprehensive information about the dangers they are far more likely to face. *Don't be a tattletale." One of the most stigmatizing names that a child can be called is tattletale. From their earliest moments, we consciously and subconsciously encourage children not to communicate. Thousand of children are hidden victims, and the key to prevention and detection is communication. Children must be taught that if something is happening in their lives that they do not feel right about or that makes them feel uncomfortable, they must tell somebody they trust. *You're just a kid. Be respectful to adults; they know what they're doing." With this final message, we face a delicate challenge. All parents want their children to be polite and respectful to adults. Our message is not that we want children to be disrespectful, but that we must empower them to realize that they have the right to say no to those who would abuse their authority as adults; unquoted.

https://www.hg.org/child-abduction.html Child Abduction Law-Child Kidnapping Law, and I quote, Child Abduction is the offense of wrongfully removing or wrongfully retaining, detaining or concealing a child or baby. Abduction is defined as taking away a person by persuasion, by fraud, or by open force or violence. There are two types of child abduction: parental child abduction by a stranger. When one parent abducts his/her children)from the other parent it is often a divorce action and is meant to circumvent the court or act in defiance of a court order regarding legal custody of the children). Parental child abduction may occur within the same city, within the same state, country, or internationally. What is child abduction law? Laws regarding parental abductions vary. In some states and countries this is a criminal offense, but not in all. In many U.S. States, there is no formal custody order and the parents are not living together, the "abduction' of the child from the parent is not considered a criminal offense. However, many states have made the abduction of a child across state lines by a parent a crime. The National Conference of Conference of Commissioners on uniform States Laws (NCCUSL) Drafted the Uniform Child Abduction Prevention Act in an effort to bring state law uniformity to this issue. Congress has enacted many civil and criminal laws to address abductions, kidnapping, interstate and international child abduction cases. Convention on the rights of the child; Reaffirming that children's rights require special protection and call for continuous improvement of the situation of children all over the world, as well as for their development and education in conditions of peace and security. Missing Children Act; Requires law enforcement to enter complete descriptions of missing children into NCIC, even if the abductor has not been charged with a crime. Uniform Child Abduction Prevention Act; The purpose of the Uniform Child Abduction Act is to deter both predecree and postdecree domestic and international child abductions by parents, person acting on behalf of a parent or others, Family abductions may be preventable through the identification of risk factors and the imposition of appropriate preventive measures; unquoted.

Stalking, in a word means to watch, follow, observe, and photograph movement of others without their knowledge and awareness. You could even say its an act of spying on another. It doesn't take an educated fool to understand the different. Someone approaching you pretending to be a friend could actually be a stalker. So, I asked; where is the red flag? This brings me to the story at hand; It's about a stalker, not necessary a stalker but the things he/they does. The story starts out like this, New blank at. People feel like their being sexually target. Someone is being hit over and over again. Two people are seem holding hands outside. A question is asked; are you following me? I would assumed that the person didn't like the answer. Because she said; Is that a reason for you to follow me? That reveals three things of important:

Fear of being target
Fear of being follow
Fear of being stalk: that makes you feel very

uncomfortable and awkwardly, batty, and unsafe. Do not keep quiet. Tell someone. Being stalk is dangerous. Because these are very dangerous people. Inform the police immediately even if you feel that they're not going to believe you. Yes, that does happen unless of course its one of their own. But most importantly you should tell them. The movie now takes us into what is called "the deadly sex trafficking cycle about a black man named Richard residing somewhere in the state of Washington. A 75 year old black career criminal / pimp has been contacting women in prison putting money on their book and be-friendly them into street crime of prostitution upon release. The police got wind of what this guy was doing and stopped him one day driving around. He didn't have much to say except that its his way of making a living. He called it providing a roof over their head having no place to go. He spent many years in prison for molesting women.

What lead this guy to targeting women in prison on record charged according to him was being gang-raped as a young child. This black man in question was named Richard. He was eventually arrested and returned to prison. The police salmonella dressed his crime as an another form of human trafficking. You see, according to Richard, the pimp these women owed him therefore they're his property. They must re-pay him by working as prostitutes. Richard would let them know upfront that the money on their book was not free. He would say get your ass on the street bitch and make that money. I took care of you in prison now you must take care of me. "Get your ass out there". Those of you refused I've kill you. He put enough fear into them that they did not try to escape. But for some of the women it wasn't a big deal. Because they had a roof over their head and therefore felt safe. But once Richard, the pimp was arrested and returned to prison everything stop.

The women, well, were left to seek other employment hopefully something more suitable to life skills. Yes, this was a short story but you should had learned something. First of all, know who you are communicating with from prison. If you do choose to communicate with such a person from prison tell others because they might know personal information preventing your from becoming a victim of a human sex trafficker. Learn as much as you can about such creepy people before jumping into the water, and later finding out that he's a human sex trafficking. That it's your body he wants as financial income for self purpose. Don't be so quick to say yes. Don't be so quick to ride away in a complete stranger vehicle. Don't be so quick to take his money. There are computers in prisons. Ask someone to do a brief background check. Why go from prison to a force cage prison, force to have sex with strangers against your will? Do you need his money that bad? Is your freedom more important? Now that we know what this guy Richard; there must be others out there like him. A word of advice to women in prison.

Stay away from men like Richard. Stay away from Women like Richard. Don't take their money. Call your family members, friends, and others that you know if you need money for whatever reason. I understand that being in prison you have needs and wants. But that's a dangerous way of acquiring it. It could even cause you to be sent back to prison. It could cause you to be arrested for prostitution. It could cause you to get STD, a sexual transmitted disease. Is that's what you want? Mothers, fathers, if you have a daughter in prison try not to let this happen to her. Be there for her while she's in prison. Be there for her when she is being release from prison. Don't force her to go left when she should go right. Don't force her to make the wrong decision. They have served their time once release. What they need now is an opportunity to take back what they have lost. A chance to regain their life and suitable employment in society. No, no, no, it will never be the same but its up to them. Parents make some signs; "Hands Off My Child" "Hands Off My Child". You know what; even a pimp can be a Predator. A stalker can be a Predator. Life lesson. lesson learn.

https://www.missingkids.org/theissues/infantabductions; Infant Abductions, and I quote, For the purpose of this analysis, infant abductions are defined as any abduction of a child under one year of age. This type of abduction can take various forms; from a noncustodial parent abducting the infant, to a stranger abducting the child from the hospital, home, or a public place. RISK FACTORS FOR INFANT ABDUCTIONS RELATED TO HEALTHCARE; NCMEC has developed a list of characteristics from an analysis of 327 missing infants under six months of age related to healthcare occurring from 1964 through October 2019, in the United States. However, there is no guarantee an infant abductor will fit this description. Usually a female of childbearing age who appears pregnant. * Most likely compulsive; most often relies on manipulation, lying, and deception. * Frequently indicates she has lost a baby or is incapable of having one. * Often married or cohabitating; companion's desire for a baby or the abductor's desire to provide her companion with "his" baby may be the motivation for the abduction. Usually lives in the community where the abduction takes place. * Frequently initially visits nursery and maternity units at more than one health care facility prior to the abduction; asks detailed questions about procedures and the maternity floor layout; frequently uses a fire exit stairwell for her escape; and may try to abduct from the home setting. * Usually plans the abduction, but does not necessarily target a specific infant; frequently seizes any opportunity present to abduct a baby. * Frequently impersonates a nurse or other allied health care personnel. * Often becomes familiar with health care staff members, staff member work routines and victim parents. * Often demonstrates a capability to provide care to the baby once the abduction occurs, within the her emotional and physical abilities. IN ADDITION, AN ABDUCTOR WHO ABDUCTS FROM THE HOME SETTING (IS): * Most likely to be single while claiming to have partner.

* Often targets a mother whom she may find by visiting health care facilities and tries to meet the target family. * Often plans the abduction and brings a weapon, although the weapon may not be used. * often impersonates a health care or social services professional when visiting the home. WHAT NCMEC is Doing About it; Educating Professionals in Prevention Strategies; As the nation's clearinghouse about missing and sexually exploited children, NCMEC maintains statistics regarding the number and location of infant abductions and provides technical assistance and training to health care and security professionals in an effort to prevent infant abduction from occurring in their facilities. NCMEC also provides evidence-based guidance about how to respond when an infant abduction occurs and technical assistance to law enforcement during and after an incident. Proving and Professional Referrals; Coping with the experience of a child abduction demands courage and determination on the part of the victim, parents and guardians, and other family members; unquoted.

We as parents needs to understand the important of an amber alert, and what it means to us and our children especially when it involves their safety, health, welfare, and recovery from whoever may had taken them. It's easy to say; its not my child. While should I care? It's easy to do nothing when its not your child. What kind of a person is that? An amber alert is the criminal justice system program to apprehend and arrest the predator that abduct and kidnap your children. It's a system of recovery returning your children back to you, and a system developed alerting you seeking your help. Remember the first 48 hours are critical. An amber alert is like a cry for help involving you the parents, and others, informing you that something is wrong. Why would you not want to help? Why would you not want to get involve? An amber alert is like a baby crying in a crib, asking you for help, telling you to come now, telling you to do something. Help, help, help me. An amber alert saves lives; your children life, your baby life, your son life, your daughter life. What should you do when you receive an amber alert? Do nothing – its not my child. Do nothing-while should I be concern? Do something – it could be my child. Tell others – encourage them to get involve. Ask if you can help – wouldn't that be the right thing to do? Ignore the amber alert – the wrong thing to do.

A: amber
M: messages
B: bulletins
E: emergency
R: recognition

A: alert
L: local
E: enhance
R: return
T: test

Amber alert is a warning letting us know there is danger around us, here, there, and every where. This alert cannot be ignore or to close a blind eye to. It's something that will happen again and again. It's not a question of how and when. But recognizing the signs. Amber alert is not just a word. But a system of government program, design to save lives, rescue children, and return them back to their parents. It's only because of this system so many children have been returned to their parents. Some people do not believe in the system, its purpose, or its function. But one thing for sure its hope for hundred of children. I'm more concern about where we go from here. It could be an indication of our humble faithfulness, our security, and how we governs ourselves. A word of faith is better then no faith at all. Because, to believe in something is to have faith in it. The word itself amber alert has great power but that power comes from within. Although years ago it was a Bill passed by many. Because of that Bill; children now has a second chance at life. A life that only belongs to them; the young generation. Behold I say unto you; believe in them, believe in the amber alert system; and above all believe in yourself. Articles that follows will be of great important; history to be told and a lot to be learn. Many of us have witnessed amber alerts, and received amber alert messages on our phones. The question is; do you know what to do next? Only time will answer that question but when it happens to you. Not even then will you know what to do. But those of you who have this book; you will know what to do. Call yourself the lucky one's knowing that you did the right thing.

AMBER ALERT

Amber Alert what can I say? Amber Alert can save the day. Mayday, mayday it's the way. It can warn you about others and that no lie. Amber alert has been around for years. Amber Alert is only for kids. Amber Alert is in every state; mandated by Congress to make it work. Amber Alert was a Bill that passed. Amber Alert can kick your ass. Amber Alert "parents" can work for you. But parents "you" must do your part to. Amber Alert parents is a system that saves lives; but without your help "parents" it will die.

Every year and every day; a child goes missing or runs away. The child is reported to the police seeking their help. Asking the police to get involve is something parents that you must do. You must first verify that she's missing. You must first verify she's gone. You must call a friend or two. You must search your house stirringly looking for clues. You must walk, run, every where searching your yard, searching your yard near and far. Search the barn and all the roads. Search rives and lakes that are near by. Search high and low looking for them.

If all has fail and there is nothing more that you can do. Get on your knees and pray for God to help you. He will help you when no one will. God is there for you in thick and thin. He will never leave your side when you need Him the most. He will pray with you and give you hope. He will listen to your every word. He know that your in heavy labour and has a lot to say. He will not leave you or go away. Remember that God is every where. Don't try to deal with this Amber Alert on your own.

You'll stress yourself out worry about what to do. Please don't do that to yourself. You'll get sick nevertheless. That is not what you wants to do. Your child is depending on you so turn to God and He'll help you. So keep yourself healthy and well if not for you do it for me. If you get sick your child will suffer to. God don't want that and neither do you. Believe in the Amber Alert system let it work for you.

Remember God is always there watching over you. The Amber Alert system will help bring her home; and with God help she will not be alone. The Amber Alert system so many of you did not trust. But now that your child is missing your heart has turned blue hoping that God will find her soon. As you can see the Amber Alert system works. It only needs your help and your support. it will find your child and bring her home. The Amber Alert system doesn't stand alone. Because God is always there watching over you. The Amber Alert system works for all. Just like God its there for you. So have faith in the Amber Alert system "it" will help you. Whenever your child is missing do whatever you can. You can believe in yourself, believe in God, believe in the Amber Alert system, it's a win, win, win.

https://amberalert.ojp.gov/about/guidelines-for-issuing-alerts
Guidelines for issuing AMBER Alerts by Office Of Justice Programs, and I quote,
Every successful AMBER plan contains clearly defined activation criteria. The following guidance is designed to achieve a uniform, interoperable network of plans across the country, and to minimize potentially deadly delays because of confusion among varying jurisdictions.

Summary of Department of Justice Recommended Criteria:

- There is reasonable belief by law enforcement that an abduction has occurred.
- The law enforcement agency believes that the child is in imminent danger of serious bodily injury or death.
- There is enough descriptive information about the victim and the abduction for law enforcement to issue an AMBER Alert to assist in the recovery of the child.
- The abduction is of a child aged 17 years or younger.
- The child's name and other critical data elements, including the Child Abduction flag, has been entered into the National Crime Information Center (NCIC) System.

There is reasonable belief by law enforcement that an abduction has occurred:

AMBER plans require law enforcement to confirm an abduction prior to issuing an alert. This is essential when determining the level of risk to the child. Clearly, stranger abductions are the most dangerous for children and thus are primary to the mission of an AMBER Alert. To allow activations in the absence of significant information that an abduction has occurred could lead to abuse of the system and ultimately weaken its effectiveness. At the same time, each case must be appraised on its own merits and a judgment call made quickly. Law enforcement must understand that a "best judgment" approach, based on the evidence, is appropriate and necessary.

The law enforcement agency believes that the child is in imminent danger of serious bodily injury or death:

Plans require a child be at risk for serious bodily harm or death before an alert can be issued. This element is clearly related to law enforcement's recognition that stranger abduction represent the greatest danger to children. The need for timely, accurate information based on strict and clearly understood criteria is critical, again keeping in mind the "best judgment" approach.

There is enough descriptive information abut the victim and the abduction for law enforcement to issue an AMBER Alert to assist in the recovery of the child:

For an AMBER Alert to be effective in recovering a missing child, the law enforcement agency must have enough information to believe that an immediate broadcast to the public will enhance the efforts of law enforcement to locate the child and apprehend the suspect. This element requires as much descriptive information as possible about the abducted child and the abduction, as well as descriptive information about the suspect and the suspect's vehicle. Issuing alerts in the absence of significant information that an abduction has occurred could lead to abuse of the system and ultimately weaken its effectiveness.

The abduction is of a child aged 17 years or younger:

Every state adopt the "17 years of age or younger" standard, or at a minimum, agree to honor the request of any other state to issue an AMBER Alert, even if the case does not meet the responding state's age criterion, as long as it meets the age criterion of the requesting state. Most AMBER plans call for activation of the alert for children under a certain age. The problem is that age can vary—some plans specify 10, some 12, some 14, 15, 16. Differences in age requirements create confusion w hen an activation requires multiple alerts across states and jurisdictions. Overuse of the AMBER Alert system will undermine its effectiveness as a tool for recovering abducted children.

The child's name and other critical data elements, including the child Abduction flag, have been entered into the National Crime Information Center (NCIC) system:

Immediately enter AMBER Alert data into the National Crime Information Center (NCIC) system. Text information describing the circumstances surrounding the abduction of the child should be entered, and the case flagged as a Child Abduction. Many plans do not mandate entry of the data into NCIC, but this omission undermines the entire mission of the AMBER Alert initiative. The notation on the entry should be sufficient to explain the circumstances of the disappearance of the child. Entry of the state data into NCIC expands the search for an abducted child from the local, state, or regional level to the national; unquoted.

https://www.fema.gov/emergency-managers/practitioners/integrated-public-alert-warming-system/wirelesss-emergency-alerts
Wireless Emergency Alerts:

Wireless Emergency Alert (WEAs), by FEMA, and I quote, are short emergency messages from authorized federal, state, local, tribal and territorial public alerting authorities that can be broadcast from cell towers to any WEA- enabled mobile device in a locally targeted area. Wireless providers primarily use cell broadcast technology for WEA messages delivery. WEA is a partnership among FEMA, the Federal Communication Commission (FCC) and wireless providers to enhance public safety.

WEA can be sent to your mobile device when you may be in harm's way, without the need to download an app or subscribe to a service. WEA are messages that warn the public of an impending natural or human -made disaster. The message are short and can provide immediate, life-saving information.

Type of Wireless Emergency Alerts:

Presidential Alerts are a special class of alerts only sent during a national emergency.

Imminent Threat Alerts include natural or human – made disasters, extreme weather, active shooters, and other threatening emergencies that are current or emerging.

Public Safety Alerts contain information about a threat that may not be imminent or after an imminent threat has occurred. Public Safety Alerts are less severe than imminent threat alerts.

America's Missing: Broadcast Emergency Response (AMBER) Alerts are urgent bulletins issued in child-abduction cases. Rapid and effective public alerts often play a crucial role in returning a missing child safely. An AMBER Alert instantly enables the entire community to assist in the search for and safe recovery of the child.

Opt-in Test Messages assess the capability of state and local officials to send their WEAs. The message will state that this is a TEST.

Wireless Emergency Alert Tips:

Follow the action advised by the alert. The message will show the type and time of the alert, any action you should take, and the agency issuing the alert. The message will be no more than 360 characters. You can get more details from local authorities, local news or trusted social media sources.

WEAs have a unique tone and vibration, both repeated twice. WEAs messages are free and will not count towards texting limits on your wireless plan.

Wireless providers are selling devices with WEA capability included. To find out if your phone can receive WEA alerts, contact your wireless provider.

If you are on a phone call when a WEA is sent in your area, the message will be delayed until you finish your call. WEA do not track your location. They are broadcast from area cell towers to mobile phones within the defined geographic location; unquoted.

https://en.wikipedia.org/wiki/Amber_alert
An Amber (also AMBER Alert), by Wikipedia, and I quote, or a child abduction emergency alert (SAME code: CAE) is a message distributed by a child abduction alert system to ask the public in finding abducted children. It originated in the united States in 1996.

AMBER is a backronym for America's Missing: Broadcast emergency Response. The alert was named after Amber Hagerman, a nine-year-old girl abducted and murdered in Arlington, Texas in 1996. Alternative regional alert names were once used; in Georgia, "Levi's Call" in (memory of Levi Frady); in Hawaii, "Maile Amber Alert" (in memory of Maile Gilbert); in Arkansas, "Morgan Nick Amber Alert (in memory of Rachael Runyan).

In the United States, Amber alerts are distributed via commercial public radio stations, Internet radio, satellite radio, television stations, text messages, and cable TV by the Emergency Alert System and NOAA Weather Radio (where they are termed "Child Abduction Emergency" or Amber Alerts"). The alerts are also issued via email, electronic traffic-condition signs, commercial electronic billboards, or through wireless devices SMS text messages, AMBER Alert has also teamed up with Google, Bing, and Facebook to relay information regarding an AMBER Alert to an ever-growing demographic: AMBER Alert are automatically displayed if citizens search or use map features on Google or Bing. With the Google Child Alert (also called Google AMBER Alert in some countries), has recently been abducted and an alert was issued. This is a component of the AMBER Alert system that is already active in the US (there are also developments in Europe), Those interested in subscribing to receiving AMBER Alerts in their area via SMS messages can visit Wireless Amber Alert, which are offered by law as free messages.

The decision to declare an AMBER Alert is made by each police organization (in many cases, the state police or highway patrol) that investigates each of the abductions. Public information in an AMBER Alert usually consists of the name and description of the abductee, a description of the suspected abductor, and a description and license plate number of the abductor's vehicle if available.

When investigators believe that a child is in danger of being taken across the border to either Canada or Mexico, U.S. Customs and Border Protection, United States Border Patrol and the Canada Border Services Agency are notified and are expected to search every car coming through a border checkpoint. If the child is suspected to be taken to Canada, a Canadian Amber Alert can also be issued, and a pursuit by Canadian authorities usually follows.

INCIDENTS NOT MEETING ALERT CRITERIA

For incidents which do not meet AMBER Alert criteria, the United States Department of Justice developed the Child Abduction Response Teams (CART) program to assist local agencies. This program can be used in all missing children's cases with or without an AMBER Alert. CART can also be used to help recover runaway children under the age of 18 and who are in danger. As of 2010, 225 response teams have been trained in 43 states, as well as Washington, D; Puerto Rico, the Bahamas, and Canada.

AMBER RENE HAGERMAN (November 25, 1986 – January 15, 1996) was a young girl abducted while riding her bike with her brother in Arlington, Texas. A neighbor who witnessed the abduction called the police, and Amber's brother, Ace, went home to tell his mother and grandparents what happened. On hearing the news, Hagerman's father, Richard, called Marc Klaas, whose daughter, Polly, had been abducted and murdered in Petaluma, California, on October 1, 1993. Richard and Amber's mother, Donna Whitson (now Donna Norris), called the news media and the FBI. They and their neighbors began searching for Amber.

Four days after her abduction, near midnight, Amber's body was discovered in a creek behind an apartment complex with severe laceration wounds to her neck and naked. The site of her discovery was less than five miles from where she was abducted.

Within days of Amber's death, Donna Whitson was "calling for tougher laws governing kidnappers and sex offenders". Amber's parents soon established People Against Sex Offenders (P. A. S. O.). They collected signatures hoping to protect children.

Whitson testified in front of the U.S. Congress in June 1996, asking legislators to create a nationwide registry of sex offenders. Representative Martin Frost, the Congressman who represents Whitson's district, proposed an "Amber Hagerman Child Protection Act." Among the sections of the bill was one that would create a national sex offender registry.

For the next two years, alerts were made manually to participating radio stations. In 1998, the Child Alert Foundation created the first fully automated Alert Notification System (ANS) to notify surrounding communities when a child was reported missing or abducted. Alerts were sent to radio stations as originally requested but included television stations, surrounding law enforcement agencies, newspapers and local support organizations. These alerts were sent all at once via pagers, faxes, emails, and cell phones with the information immediately posted on the Internet for the general public to view.

Following the automation of the AMBER Alert with ANS technology created by the Child Foundation, The National Center for Missing and Exploited Children (NCMEC) expanded its role in 2002 to promote the AMBER Alert.

RETRIEVAL RATE

According to the U.S. Department of Justice, of the children abducted and murdered by strangers, 75% are killed within the first three hours in the USA. Amber Alerts are designed to inform the general public quickly when a child has been kidnapped and is in danger so "the public (would be) additional eyes and ears of law enforcement; unquoted.

EMERGENCY CODE WORDS FOR PARENTS AND CHILDREN
****

CODE WORDS and SIGNS	TRANSLATION
Openhand	Ok
Closehand	trouble
Snake	danger
Shark	run
Bad odor	stay out
Loose teeth	pain
Clear sky	no danger
Dark sky	warning
Open window	unsafe
Black cat	send for help
Flat land	under ground hide out
Country road	search
ICE	call police
Dirty dog	watch out
Blood	keep out
X-5	Emergency
Red	Extremely urgent
Sick	call medical
Flames	call the fire service
Bare foot	something wrong
Old buildings	hulking
Basement	cold
Closet	black out
Under ground	dark
Next door	neighbor
Man	geezer
Car	heap
Weapon	catapult
Farm	steading
Fresh grave	sepulcher
Abandon house	disused
Abandon building	derelict
Help	Mayday
Be careful	heedful
911	Emergency
Woman	frau
Armed	gird
Missing	mislaid
Tall	lanky
Short	fleeting

EMERGENCY CODE WORDS FOR PARENTS AND CHIDREN ---CONTINUES

White	undyed
Trail	slipstream
Cave	cavity
Hole	hovel
Airplane	cab
Boat	barque
Barn	grange
Church	mosque
Bus	chaise
Train	convoy
Upstairs	overhead
Attic	garret
Freezer	meat
Under water	immersed
River	runnel
Lake	loch
Ocean	the deep
Police	blue
Box	bin
Crate	lug
Ship	craft
Club	clique
House	structure
Garage	base
Left	port
Back yard	lawn
Female	gal
Tree	sapling
Creek	rivulet
Apartment	flat
Forest	woods
Trunk	torso
Body	person
Mile	distance
Bedroom	chamber
Plant	mil
Van	wheel
Turn	twirl
Cabin	hut
Campsite/RV	cantonment
Street	man made

Parents it doesn't matters what type of words you used. As long as it makes sense to you and your children. Something that you and they both understand. Caution, don't make it too hard or too simple. for example: the sky is blue. answer: that's strange there was no forecast of rain. Your mother sent me for you. answer: hm; what is my mother's name? But also remember; you can use code words. Be on the alert for: Your mother is sick. She sent me for you. Come, we must go now. Come, come, get into the car. Hi, I am a friend of your mother. That's a nice dog. What is his name? Hi, would you like to take a walk with me? That's a nice toy you have. Would you like some candy? I once had a dog. Hey, why don't you and I go to the zoo. I'm your mother won't mind. When you're ready I've take you right back. (tricks of the trade). Know what code word or phrase to use.

According to the Bible, and I quote, Be merciful to me, o God, for man would swallow me up; fighting all day he oppresses me. My enemies would hound me all day, for there are many who fight against me, O Most High. Whenever I am afraid, I will trust in You. In God(I will praise His word), in God I have put my trust; I will not fear. What can flesh do to me? All day they twist my words; all their thoughts are against me for evil. They gather together, they hide, they mark my steps, when they lie in wait for my life. Shall they escape my iniquity? In anger cast down in peoples, O God! You number my wanderings; put my tears into your bottle; are they not in your book? When I cry out to You, then my enemies will turn back; this I know, because God is for me.

I will not be afraid. What can man do to me? Do you indeed speak righteousness, you silent ones? Do you judge uprightly, you sons of men? No, in heart you work wickedness; you weigh out the violence of your hands in the earth. The wicked are estranged from the womb; they go astray as soon as they are born, speaking lies. Their poison is like the poison of a serpent; they are like the deaf cobra that stops its ear. Which will not heed the voice of charmers, charming ever to so skillfully. Breaking their teeth in their mouth, O God! Break out the fangs of the young lions, O Lord. Let them flow away as waters which run continually; when he bends his bow, let his arrows be as if cut in pieces. Let them be like a snail which melts away as it goes, like a stillborn child of a woman, that they may not see the sun. Before your pots can feel the burning thorns, He shall take them away as with a whirlwind, as in His living and burning wrath.

The righteous shall rejoice when he sees the vengeance; He shall wash his feet in blood of the wicked. I agreed that children should have respect for adults but not when their life, health, and welfare is in danger being over power, and control by adults who's trying to harm them causing bad thing to happen to them. With regard to respect adults needs to know when to draw the line. The adult is always right! Like anyone with an undisputed tongue adults should be give and shown respect by children. It's practice and a ritual implanted in your children brain as a young child growing up being told to respect your elders. There is a passage in the Bible that speak about children should respect their parents. The Bible doesn't say what if. What if someone abduct your child, what if someone molests your child, what if someone kidnap your child, what if someone sexually assault your child. What if mislead me thinking that he/she is my friend when in reality that person is preying on me to molest me.

What if! A passage from the Bible, and I quote, "You shall not circulate a false report. Do not put your hand with the wicked to be an unrighteous witness." You shall not follow a crowd to do EVIL; nor shall you testy in a dispute so as to turn aside after many PERVERT justice. If you meet your enemy's ox or his donkey going astray, you shall surely bring it back to him again. If you see the donkey of one who hates you lying under its burden, and you would refrain from helping it. You shall not PERVERT the judgment of your poor in his dispute. Keep yourself far from a false matter; do not kill the innocent and righteous. For I will not justify the wicked. And you shall take no bribe for a bribe blinds the discerning and PERVERT the words of the righteous. "also you shall not oppress a stranger, for you were strangers in the land of Egypt.

Take heed to yourself, least you forget the covenant of the Lord your God which He made with you, and made for yourselves a carved image in the form of anything which the Lord your god has forbidden you. When you beget children and grandchildren you have grown old in the land, and act corruptly and make a carved image in the form of anything, and do EVIL in the sight of the Lord your God to provoke Him to anger. "And the Lord will scatter you among the peoples, and you will be left few in number among the nations where the Lord will drive you. A lesson learned doesn't has to be a whipping of the ass or a slack across the face to get your attention gainfully acquiring your awareness keeping children safe out of the hands of evil minds of strangers. You as parents should now realizes that your children are not safe from those who truly wants to harm them. If we the parents thereof seek not a safe environment for our children we might as well fold our arms and play dead. Seek not I say but do what I say sends a message that no one is going to get off their ass.

Fighting for the right of all children, and young adults until something happen causing us to raise war against the evil ways of man kind. We see today that so many children are being target by those who wants to do bad things to them. Children don't have the means to think on their feet when something happens, and or the ability to re-act quickly in an emergency situation. Even with parent reading this book some of them going are still going to do nothing. Some of them will close their eyes to the danger and threat and threat that walks the face of the earth preying on young children and young adults. We hear on TV and on the Radio when children has been abducted. They initial an alert, alerting people that a child has been abducted. This I say is going to continue until we stop talking about it, and do something about it. Not one man or one woman can stop the evil that press on our children. Let me say this your not consider an adult until you are as least 21 years of age.

This book therefore pertains to young people young and old. Parents its time for you to wake up, and smell the evil that leaves a bad taste in the mouth of many. We don't need those threats on our children. Our children needs not be target. Our children needs not be the back door of those things that they can get away with preying on our children. Our children have a tongue. Teach them to use their tongue to speak out. Children tongue might be the only weapon against this evil the monster preying on our young children and young adults. Their mouth is also a weapon. Teach them to use their mouth telling you if anything has happened to them by others. According to The Holy Bible Placed By The Gideons, and I quote, listen to this carefully. Not unto us O Lord, not unto us, but unto thy name given glory, for thy mercy, and for thy truth's sake. Wherefore should the heathen say, where is now their God? Their idols are silver and gold, the work of men's hands. They have mouths, but they speak not: They have ears, but they hear not: nose have they, but they smell not: eyes have they, but they see not: They have hands, but they handle not: feet they have, but they walk not: neither speak they through their throat. To get rid of a virus. It must be treated. To get rid of a disease. It must be identified. To get rid of a war. It must be fought. To get rid of a problem.
It must be confronted; unquoted.

PREDATOR

To be or not to be walking in the daylight with arms hanging down. What came over me I don't know. But it was like time has pass us by although the grass had turned beautifully brown signing off to what life could had been. Was taken by a star so high in the sky lifting me up beyond the clouds. What is happening someone asked. There was no answer nor was the wind blowing or the sound of life around. What could it be? What could it mean? Surely we're not dead laying on the ground in a needle of nails. Although I wasn't sure however strange it seem. It brought meaning to my dreams. My eyes lest my body with the beating of my heart if in fact I had a heart.

I awakened and realized that I was living in the present and the past. I begin seeing people all around running and walking near and far. Some look angry and mad as hail like the earth was about to open up and swallow me alive. To be I said or not to be. I am a predator can't you see? I traveled far and traveled long searching only for a home. Could it be your home did I not asked? Yes it could be said the man standing along. Get back I say. Get back now Watch our child before you die.

I am as evil as a beast walking the streets and looking for fresh meat. Could it be you I say? Could it be you as I walk around searching the zoo. I am not a fool can't you see? I have traveled far looking for you but only found the devil "you". Could I be wrong; I don't think so. You look a mess little girl can't you see? I am the predator stocking you. if you don't believe my child ask your friend because I'll be back at the smell of the wind. It won't be what you think nor you will be able to move, because your legs my child will be tied into knots waiting for me to find my way killing you off day by day.

I am the beast that no one sees an animal that preys on people but not like you and me. The animal of prey could it be you tracking my kill like an animal in the zoo. So now you see what a predator I am. No street is safe when you're alone believe it or not I'll follow you home. I'll glad you from behind and carry you away making you my prey this very day. You see, I like pretty girls like you and your friends they make me feel good like little red riting hood. That reminds me of other girls like yourself reported gone missing but no one would had ever thought it was me. So my child what have you to say for yourself? I am the predator; have you no questions for me? I'm sure you will my child when I tie you to a tree. You can scream and yell all you want but no one will hear you. We are too far away out in the country; look and see for yourself. Don't even try to escape. You won't get far. You'll get lost my child and maybe end up dead. Whatever you do; don't go too far because there is no wishing well. But you will wish there was when I catch up with you. Child, be aware of predators whoever they may be. The streets are not safe that's something you should know. Predators are everywhere; have you mommy not told you so? Be smart, carry protection where ever you go. A predator just might show up knocking on your door. Blacking the streets spreading evil all around, taking away their dreams and their children lives. What does it mean? What does it do? Surely you have learned from others and your parents to. To be afraid of a predator; how foolish can you be? You will die predator can't you see? Foolish or not your time will come. They will get you predator and then there will be none.

Hey predator, you think your so smart when I'm finish with you, you will need a new heart. Your mother should had told you to leave children alone. Now I'm going to welt your ass and send you home. Monkey see, monkey do, hey predator you belongs in a zoo. Kiss my ass predator that's what you should do, if you mess with me she'll kill you too. If you mess with my child I'll hurt you today turning you into a chicken, hey chicken soup, kicking you around from boot to boot. Roses are red predator violets are blue but when I get stud with you there will be a hole in your shoe. Do you know why predator, yes or no, it will remind you of what will be, what will come for all eyes to see. To put you on notice predator that's more than you deserve; better yet predator listen to these words. It will serve you well to listen to me because I'm only going to say it once before nailing you to a tree. Your heart will bleed and your mind will die and smell like sh_t in the sky.

To solve the problem involving strangers. They must first be identified. To solve the problem of predators. They must first be identified as predators. Therefore to stop the evil of strangers. You must first know what they do. Know and understand that anyone can be (1) a stranger, and (2) a predator. I therefore challenged all parents, mother's, and father's alike to be the watchful eyes of your children protecting them with all your understanding, inner emotions, unbroken strength of love, and heart felt arms of desire, and the strength you have do whatever necessary shielding your children from danger, and hell that awaits them by the evil hands, and distrust of others so that they not to be afraid to walk the streets, leave their home, and or to attend school.

https://Souce:wavemedia/shutterstock
How to listen to Those in Mourning; by Marilyn A. Mendoza Ph.D; and I quote, There is a difference between hearing and listening. We can hear what someone is saying, but how often do we really listen? Listening is a skill that can be developed and can have a positive impact in all areas of your life, most certainly in your close relationships.

Therapists are not born with good listening skills, but we are taught them as part of our training. There are many reasons why people don't listen. our attention span is short, we are in a hurry, and there always seem to be distractions around us. Frequently, we do not listen, because we are thinking about what we are going to say in response to the speaker. when someone is grieving the loss of a loved one, we have trouble listening, because it is so painful. it stirs up all our feeling about loss. We feel awkward. We usually do not know what to say and are afraid of making a mistake. Being uncomfortable makes us want to change the topic or try to leave the situation as soon as possible. Unfortunately, what the bereaved really want and need is someone who can listen and be supportive. While what we say to the bereaved is important. We cannot fix the situation. What we can offer is an ear. there are some basic things that we can all do to be better listeners that don't require any special training. First, it is important to find a safe, comfortable place to talk, where there are minimal distractions. be patient. Put down whatever you are doing. Turn your cell phone off or mute it so that you are not disturbed or tempted to look at it while listening. Look at the person with whom you are speaking. Try to keep comments to a minimum and only when there is a pause in the conversation. Try not to interrupt the speaker. Although it may be uncomfortable, it is beneficial at times to sit in the silence. Just being with the person at that moment can be powerful. Remember, this is about listening to the bereaved. Be sure you are not pressed for time. Nothing can be worse than starting to open up about a painful loss only t have the listener be in a hurry and need to leave. You can also reach out to hug or hold the hand of the speaker if it is someone you know well.

For others, ask if it would be alright with them. Also, making understanding utterances, such as uh-huh or nodding your head, can be helpful and let the speaker know you are following what they are saying. In 1988, Harville Hendrix, a marriage therapist, introduced the IMAGO Technique to facilitate and improve communication between couples. It is called MIRRORING and is one of the best exercises for learning how to truly listen. Mirroring involves repeating or reflecting back on what you heard the speaker say in a non-judgemental way. This is not the time to say you shouldn't feel or think that way. That would essentially shut down the speaker. This may feel uncomfortable and artificial, as we are not used to speaking and listening in this way. Validation is the next important part of being a good listener. You don't necessarily have to agree with the speaker, but the point is to support and validate their point of view. Saying "I don't believe you" or you shouldn't think or feel that way" will invalidate the speaker and shut down communication.

Paraphrasing what you heard the speaker say, and clarifying if that was indeed what the speaker said, lets the speaker know you are listening and trying to understand them. Empathizing is about understanding and conveying back to the speaker what you believe they are feeling. If you hear someone talk about being angry, and you think they shouldn't feel that way. Keep that to yourself and simply validate the speaker's feelings. Saying "I know how you feel" is not empathizing but rather inserting yourself into their narrative; unquoted.

I know that this is a challenged that you faithfully accepts bringing forth with and clearly understood that evil nor fear will prevail and prey upon young children bless it be in the name of God. Because they are protected by the hands of the almighty God. So man fear not that is within you. Be it here known. So much information has been implanted into your seed of the brain producing harvest of wisdom, and understanding birthing you out of the darkness recognizing that evil walks on the face of the earth as we stand still being possess by its evil and harmful ways. But we must not let anything My over power our thinking, and or control the minds of our young children and young adults. Storyline addressing issues and concerns.

I couldn't think of a better way to end this story then with a beach tail as storyline about myself. It muster my meaning and understanding of life, and pain that others goes through without knowing why due to blindness of the mind being entrapped by an unknown void. But when we awaken the next morning its like it never happened. Strong feeling of desires reaches out to touch the one standing and sitting beside you. But should it be? Then ask the question; why me? It may be rare and unusual but what's the hail. One, should be able to talk about his own life within a story while expressing the needs of others. But to do so you need to recognize and understand the story, and why it was written. So let me begin with this. I wrote this book on behalf of children, and young adults making parents aware that our future generation, their life, safety and welfare is in danger of being prey on by predators males and females alike throughout the United States and around the world. What a woman goes through to birth a child into this world then weeks, months, and years later to have it taken away from her. A world we have known to know as freedom for all allowing us to walk the streets by night and by day unharm. Why should we live in fear of salvation, fear of the dark, fear of each other, fear to leave our children alone with friends and family? Why is this happening to us living in a land of opportunity, under the protection by law abiding citizens, law enforcement agencies, and an organization called the big brother program looking out for the well being of those in need of their help? Surely, you have heard the expression; if it not broken don't fix it! What does that mean to you? I smell a skunk. The smell of a skunk is a warning of unforeseen happening around you. When it comes to our children and young adults; you can't put a price on love. Their life is worth more than that. It burns my heart when I hear that children and young adults has been taken or should I say Gone Missing, kidnapped and abducted by others.

I hurt alone with that parent, mother and father; because His / Her child could had been my child. My blood runs cold wondering where that child could be. What hurt me the most is not knowing whether or not that child is alive and well. No parent should has to go through something like that. So you asked me why I wrote this book. Ask yourself why such a book should not be written. First of all looking beyond the high risen you should get down on your knees thanking God for this book. The person behind this book is thinking of you "the parent". Finally, to make parents aware that unless they get involve its not going to stop. This story is not about me. This story was not written about me. This story above all was written for you -for you the parents – for you the mothers and fathers – and for those who soon will be parents. So I ask you where do we go from here? parents, mothers and fathers out there that has children missing, and has been missing for weeks, months, and many years.

I say to you; what if anything has change? There has been too many children forced into prostitution. Why? Maybe because their parents are too poor financially to come to their aide. Maybe the parents are involve in their children kidnapping and abduction. Maybe the parents sold off their child / children for money. Who knows? Maybe I'm right; and again maybe I'm wrong. Can you say differently? We read about it everyday children are being mistreated and mislead thinking that everything is alright when its not. Trouble within the home. Trouble outside the home. Is it not time to put a stop to that? Why in the hail do you think I write? I write because I love to write. I write because writing excites me. I write because writing takes me places and into the lives of other people. I write because writing expresses who I am.

I write because writing helps to express the need and desires of so many people. It lets you know what is going on within the world. Writing informs you about things that you would not had heard about if it wasn't for writers like myself. Writing spells out "what's wrong, make it right"! Writing expresses the need, the will power, and the struggles that we go through everyday. Writing brings people together. Writing educates us all. I am not your average writer. I come from a large family living in the state of Georgia years ago. My family and I worked hard on farms and in the cotton field as young children living in the Back Woods of Georgia just to survive. I'm from the State Of Georgia, the cotton state. The state that harvest pecan, oranges, apples, and other fruits. But many years ago their cotton and tobacco was Georgia main Crops. I picked cotton, hand tobacco, and worked the farms. I learned a lot as a young child growing up. It was like working on a plantation. Child labor but it put food on our table and forced hunger out of our belly. I was lucky enough at a very young age to leave the State Of Georgia whatever year that was after being taken by my late aunt and uncle to live with them in Youngstown, Ohio. In the year when JFK was President. I did not know how to Read or Write; you see I did not go to school in those back woods of Georgia. For starters, they clothes me, educated me, and raise me to the point of graduation in 1972. I struggled my way years later beyond the stars of no return. I served in the military-U.S. Army for approximately sixteen (16) years. I later married my best friend and lover, Daphne Coombs Wallace in 1992. We are living the life not the best life but a good life. Hey, if you don't want to buy my book "that's Ok".

I will not whole it against you. You see; I can't make you buy my book. Because that decision is all yours which is the down fall of being a writer. I wrote this book hoping to make a parents, "You", aware that their children are not safe. Parents need to take action now protecting their children from the hands of those endangering their children. Parents need to protect their children from becoming missing. They need to protect their children from the hands of kidnappers and abductors. They need to protect their children from being force into prostitution and sold to others. We as parents need to do our part to protect our children from harm, and from the threat of others. You know, I see writing as a gift, a moment in a person life where everything changes. You then wonders what to do. Look what writing has done to me.

Writing helps you to control your emotions, anger, and feelings. Writing helps to curve your life. Writing helps to remind you of who you are. What you will become. But it is not the end of the world. For me, it's the beginning of a miracle a miracle to be recognize, understood, and acknowledge. A miracle of pleasure and excitement. What does thou say? What does thou want? What does thou need? Writing gives me an opportunity to talk and relate to people. Writing gives me an opportunity to open people eye, to help people, warn people of danger, help children and young adults, inform parents where their child / children might be, to interact into the lives of others, look out for others, steer parents and children in the right direction, and answer questions that no one else can and much more. Every parent, young adult, and children between twelve (12) years of age and older should buy this book.

Bloodline and lifeline that you'll never forget. A book that you'll always want by your bed side. Mothers and fathers, and those who soon will be mothers and fathers should also buy this book. Your friends and family members should buy this book. Professionals, such as business people, college professors, lawyers, doctors, and others. And, to say the least even complete strangers. Why, this book just might be the only hope for you getting your children back. Giving you directions, guidance, hope, and a piece of mind and understanding how to obtain help in such time of need. Because in time like this your body takes a dive for loss hope and despair. Your brain is scramble to the point where you cannot move or think. Your so STRESS OUT that You don't know what to do and or what to think. And, your mind becomes like a vegetable cloudy, confuse, and stress out to the point where everything just doesn't seem to make any senses. You later as time drives on began to feel helpless, unsure, weak, and tired, wondering if your child is still alive. Wondering if you'll ever see your child again. Wondering if your child is alright. Wondering if the abductors / kidnappers will let your child go free. Wondering if the abductors / kidnapper will keep their word and not kill your child. You will wonder if you did the right thing by cooperating with the abductors / kidnappers. Finally, you will thank me one day for writing this book. God bless you. God bless America; and God bless our children and young adults. These poem to follow strikes a hole in my heart as a stake of fire burns within me begging for mercy and understanding wanting to know the threat that we face in relationships and marriages. That troubles me and causes cold water to run down my face as tears freezes staring into the eyes of many. I don't understand everything or comprehend what's to follow but life that we know will never be the same. It has been said that no relationship is perfect. I tend to believe their wrong and furthermore confuse. A relationship you see is the beginning of life, peace, love, and happiness. It identifies who we are, how we communicate, and how we understand each other. According to past experiences and the book of knowledge; no man stands along, and no man is an island. Translation; We all need someone. So, the question is, where do we go from here? This poem I say that you are about to read plays an important part in our life as men and women as we confront natural fulfillment of life "relationship" and "marriage". I feel that this is a beautiful way to end this story understanding the role that parents play into the lives of their children. Key to understanding; it takes two to form a relationship. It take two to form a marriage. the final key is when a child is born transforming into a family. With that in mind a wall of protection stands tall and strong reminding us to be safe.

HAPPY NEW YEAR (a waking of the soul)

New Year; what a beautiful day. A day to remember. A day to rejoice. A day to admire even from the sky. New Year Eve; that's what it is. A day people talks about from ear to ear. It's no wonder, it's the talk of the town. Kids are singing and parents are running all so round. Rejoice, rejoice, New Year Eve is here. Shout, sing, jump up and down. Just bring in the New Year with a smile.

Laugh and yell Happy New Year. May God bless you and a good cheer. You can see the length of their tongue and deep throat of their mouth as it open wide whispering these words(O' what a beautiful day) of sweetness and love.

New Year Eve is a time to celebrate respecting and welcoming in the new year. It's a time to be with friends. A time to welcome family from end to end. A time to say hello to strangers and wish them good luck and a happy new year. It's midnight and all is well. I can see the red fox peeping from the well. His fur is red and white and beautiful to. He has a shining nose pointed right at you. If you could read the writing on his nose. You would be surprise of what it says; Happy New Year to all of you. Drink of red wine and have a good cheer. I'm in the snow having a good time. Come with me and lets joyous the town. Happy New Year, happy new year, and good bye.

Make a joyful noise unto the Lord. Shout and sing Hallelujah to his name. It's New Years Day; rejoice, rejoice, on this New Year Day. It's a time to sleep in. It's a time to make love. A time to hold hands and all of the above.

Come, come to me all ye children of God. All ye children of Bethlehem. All ye children of the earth. Open your heart. Open your mind. Thank God for being alive and able to see this day. For it is written; no man stands alone. No man is an island. I pledge allegiance to which it stards.

Wait, wait, I say unto you. The day has come causing us to give thanks unto the Lord. A day that He birth into this world. All we need is to do; is to welcome it with out reach arms. I wonder sometime what does it mean!

When I look around and see what all that God has made. It makes me realizes that life is beautiful. A life that we have been given by His hands of mercy. So I say unto you. Believe in Him. Believe in yourself. Because life is too short to waste. Live it now. live it well. Because time will come when you must tell the tell. And, you will know then that you're dead.

Be good to yourself. Be good to your friends and others. Love your wife and worship her with a smile. She is your heart and soul. And; the ground that you walk on. She is your love and beset friend. She is your lover when days are old. She will not let your bed turn cold. She is your heart of the night when you need her the most. She is your pillow when in pain.

She can help you sleep when your lonely and cold. She can bring you a blanket when your sick and not feeling well. So, I say, listen to your heart and listen well. Take care of your wife and her whispering well.

Don't let the water run cold but worship it like silver and gold. Eat of the fruit that is good for you as you concentrate on something new. Something new, something old, what does it mean to you? "Hm", Look at your wife and say these words; I love you yesterday, I love you then, I love you now to the very end. Go tell it on the mountain letting the whole world know that you are alive, and filled with the Holy Ghost of Jesus Christ. I never thought of life as a story to be told but there is something special within the each of us. It's life!. That would explain the Birth of Jesus Christ when He created the Heaven and the Earth. He gave us life. He gave us a new beginning. He gave us this New Year Day.

O' Holy Night, what will it be? Let my thoughts be your thoughts. Let my touch be your touch. Let arouse erotic feelings of love come forth causing the walls to talk. Let the bed rise as if it was possess removing guilt and shame revealing what we love the best. Eat of its fruit and never let go. In the heat of the night the story was told. Let my voice be your voice. Let my need be your need. Let my pain be your pain. What about sex? Is it different or just the same? When you feel it you will know; spreading of the legs is the open door. Don't open too wide. Don't let the hands drop. just focus on her and for get about the clock. Because if you do the wrong thing can fly in. You don't want to get hurt in the end.

It's all good if you does it right. But not in anger and never fight. It's just not healthy! Don't you know that? Sex is good at the right time. But make sure you're lying down. Do it right or not at all. She'll love you when you take your time. She give you her best. She'll make you feel good. She'll make you come even in the woods. She'll make your head spin. She'll make you hot. She'll love you sir a lot. It's not when, how, or where, just let it happen and do your best.

What more is there to say? What more is there to do? Just close your eyes and dream of your manly sex machine. He will not disappoint you. I don't think so. Because when its all over He will close the door. When it's all said and done; let us live peacefully as one.

Mirror, mirror, on the wall; picture me in the Garden of Eve. Look at me! Tell me what you see. Look at the garden. Tell me what you see! What fruit have I eaten? Talk to me. I'm your wife to be. Tell me, tell me, what do you see? The Garden of Eve is so beautiful. There is all kind of fruit. I must see you. I must see you now. Please take my hand and let us eat of the fruit together. Do you not agree? Beautiful garden. Feed me, feed me, I beg of you. There is no snake to save the day. Don't you want me? What are you waiting for? Don't worry about the snake. It has gone away. I am hungry; hungry for you. Its now just you and me. Roll down the covers and get into bed lets love each other as if we were dead. Love me my dear. Love me now. Let us unroll positioning ourselves having pure sex and yelling "yes", yes.

If only a man could love that deep. What a world this would be. There would be much laughter, and children running around having a good time. A woman wouldn't be lonely. There would be peace, love, and pure heart of passion looking upon a star between them every night as they unroll. The bed and the walls would have a story to tell. If only life was like that but its not. But on this New Year Day who knows.

Maybe God needs to turn up the heat. Maybe your right. At the end of the day God is watching all of us. If people only knew the out come of life maybe New Year Day would be a wake up call. Well, this New Year Day has came to an end. Bye, and good luck as you start your New Year. Take care of yourself. Take care of your wife and have a good cheer.

WHEN YOUR IN PAIN YOU'RE NOT ALONE

As the world turns so do we. We eat together. We sleep together and make love around the tree "you and me". How beautiful is that? How lovely it sound? Me and my husband are on the merry go round. What can I do? What can I say? Just love him deeply everyday. We stick out our tongue laughing openly. But when it comes to sex the whole world must see us loving each other from sea to sea. Don't it feels good to do just that padding his ass while wearing a hat? My husband and I are good as you can see. But when it come to life it takes a blind man to see.

If you can't see love leave sex alone because you're not getting any when we get home. Don't get me wrong. He's not a man with out a heart. Because deep down we could never be apart. So call me mean, so call me nice. Do me wrong I will beat your behind. Look at us we have a beautiful house.

The time has come for us to move on. Marriage is in the air so we can't go wrong. The church is down the street but won't be there long. I have been thinking about this for a very long time. It's time to tie the knots making it right. So let me say this knelling on my knees. I love you. I love you a lot. Will you marry me and stop the clock?

If I do. I'm not saying I'm not. Will you promise to love me and never depart? Believe it or not from what I have seem. You my dear can be very mean. I understand you love me and I love you to. But is this the right time for me and you? We have known each other for a very short time. If that make sense to you I prefer to wait awhile. I know that you are disappointed to hear those words. But it is for the best considering what's going on.

Ok, I hear your words. I listen most heartedly and patience to. But what ever you do don't let my heart turn blue. I would hate to loose you. Surely you know that brings love into my life us being together flying naked in the sky. But that's only one reason I love you so much. When we first met. Where did we go? We went to a fishing hole that you and I love so much.

It's a place where we can make passage love in the mud. Like the fish in the sea. They have sex to. So why shouldn't we? It's getting hot out here. Lets take off our clothes. Lets jump into the water naked as jay birds feeling nine years old. Take me back in time. I don't care. Just don't say no to you and I making me cry saying goodbye. I will never do anything steering you wrong. Because when it ends we must go home. We have so much to say to each other. And; Babe, I love you to. But when it come down to it. Our love sticks like glue wearing the same shoe. There is no turning back. There is no looking around. Come home babe and just be mine. I will treat you right. I will treat you like a queen. Should the shoe be on the other foot. I will treat you like a king. Never say never, and never leave. I love you with my heart and soul please don't let my bed turn cold.

A HEART TO HEART TALK REACHING OUT TO MY DAUGHTER

I heard about you and what a lovely girl you are. I understand that you're turning 15, what a girl, what a joy, please tell me what that mean to you and afar as you look beyond the stars. I can see that you're smart and beautiful to so tell me sweet thing what's happening to you. Roses are red so colorful and blue it tells me a story so sweetly about you. When I put two thing together I remembers you that you're parents loves you to. Isn't that nice something that you need to know because parents are so special they opens the door. Listen to me please and hear these words. Money is sweet but it doesn't grow on trees. What are we trying to say? What does it mean? Your life. Your 15. Dream my girl of a beautiful life don't look back and don't ask why. Just be happy that is what you should do. You're a young lady now is that not true? You grew out your welcome as young girls would say evolving into an adult now and everyday. Your not a little girl anymore look around and look at yourself. But remember these words: Your parents only want the best life for you so whatever you do don't turn blue. Remember that your parents are there for you. Parents love their child no matter what and unconditionally. This is important and something that you should know. Because parents have that gift and insight making sure that everything is alright.

What are they looking at? What can it be? Their looking at your future and your family tree. How important is that(input a name)_____ your family learning about your family tree? Yes you were born that we know but your family tree has yet to be told. As bold as you are at the age of 15 listen to your parents, and without fail because they will never lead you down the wrong trail. They mean will same as you but no parent knows what can turn blue. Only time will what happens later because nothing is good without love. It's something that happens only in flight. Your parents may say that its too late, but believe me its alright, Lord help those who don't turn out right. Parents don't know some time what goes through your mind forgive them my child. It's better to tell the truth then to lie. They are there for you special days of the year so never for sake them where ever they may be. Keep in touch with your parents Lord help should anything happen to you. Your parents would die and surely turn blue. Your parents would not for give themselves knowing that something has happened to you. Because your so precious in their life they don't want to loose you no way no how. Talk again. Parents worries about their child day and night whether you know it or not because "their parents".

Because what? Because their parents they love you so much. What more can I tell you? What more can I say? Parents love their child no matter what "any way". Take that as a grain of salt and learn it well. Because the moment will come hopefully when you need them the most, so don't turn your back, don't turn red, sometime we think little of each other and that's not right. The more we argue, the more we fight, God knows that's not right. We speak words that want us to fight. When we get mad, and angry to just look out your door or into a mirror, but whatever you do don't stand still. Something might scream, yell, and shout, it could be your voice without a doubt. Angry I say control it not it could become stronger then a bark. Because this never take your problems home. It's not a good ideal nor a wise thing to do, nevertheless we sometime act the fool. Remember these words and for sake me not. It's not what you say. It's how you say it. Such words we know are these you see they can make you feel like a bee. Words; angry, mad, unhappy, hurting, fear, poorly, hungry, tired, and so much more. Hey, don't give up whatever you do your parents are on their way to help you. Christmas mix a birthday gift for a special time of the year. A birthday for two. A poem for you. They have you in their heart. They have you in their soul. Is it not true that you love them to? Heaven help if something happens to you. Your parents, your parents would not know what to do. They would be crying to hard thinking about you. What can I say that you don't already know? I know that you are turning 15. What does it mean to you? Fifteen is the age when your life turns around, an age that you should appreciate because your life is changing before you. You have only one life to live so live it well. It's not how old you are.

It's the life you lived. Whatever happens don't look back. Enjoy your life one day at a time. Don't wait until it comes around. It might be too late. You'll never know. Your parents told you what to look out for. Your parents have so much to say. It can't be said all in one day. So listen closely to what I have to say. My child if you only knew that education is about you. Your parents no matter afar communication can bring you together sketching the ground that you walks on making you feel closer to them. It's not how far that you are away. it's what inside of you and how you feel about them. Roses are red and violets are blue. Your parents deeply love you. So, when you wakes up in the morning think of them send them a letter in the wind.

When you can't come to where they are don't worry about a thing because they have you in their heart therefore your never apart. Mother's love for her daughter is deep and strong that means you'll never be alone. Mother's love goes far beyond the stars reaching out to touch you. What does that mean? What more should I say? Think about it your mother loves you to death. The first book of Moses called Genesis and I quote; The earth was without form, and void; and darkness was on the face of the deep, and the spirit of God was hovering over the waters. Then God said let there be light". And God divided the light from the darkness. Then God said let us make man in our image; According to our likeness; So God created man in his own image; in the image of God he created Him; male and females He created them. And the Lord God formed man out of dust of the ground, and breathed into his nostrils the breath of life; and man became a living being, and out of the ground the Lord made every tree grow that is pleasant to the sight and good for food. Then the Lord God took the man and put him in the garden of Eden to attend and keep it, and the Lord God said it is not good that man should be alone. I will make him a helper comparable to him; unquoted.

I wrote this song in hope of bringing laughter, and smiles on children faces as they struggle to get through each day bringing forth hope, and meaning to life around us. A laugh is good. a smile is good. It's better then being depress, and worrying about what tomorrow will bring. Because without hope we have nothing. A smile gives you hope. A laugh gives you "Joy". Joy bring out the best in you. This song was written without music notes therefore as you sang this song input your own music notes and just have fun.

HEY PRETTY GIRL

==

Hey pretty girl with your red dress on – sit-ting in the back seat sing-ing a song.

Those guys on the corner stand-ing against the tree- sit-ting on cars and look-ing at me. What are they doing? What can it be; look around girl you will see. Watch the tall guys and see what they do –

Be-cause the other three are com-ing to-ward you. Who are they wait-ing for? Who could it be? Baby get Ready to run! Baby get ready to run. Hey, hey, hey, those guys over there. those guys over there, are up to no good. Those guys over there - don't lived in the neigh-bor-hood.

===

Those guys over there - are they climb-ing a tree? Are they really - or look-ing at me? I don't think so but - I really don't know. I only wish they could go. This neigh-bor- hood don't need their kind – be-lieve it or not "baby"- I'm not ly-ing! I don't care what you say. I don't care what you do. This neigh-bor-hood is not for sale. I just wish they would go to jail.

===

Do you think they like my song? Baby you know I have a gun. Baby you know life has just begun.

Life has just begun. How silly is that! How silly is that- I don't care. Baby girl say no more. Baby girl clean up the floor. Baby girl, hey, who are you speak-ing to? Baby girl, don't be no fool.

===

Get-ting back to my song. Hey, pretty girl, this one for you. I wrote this song pretty girl out of the blue – think-ing of you. Hey pretty girl it doesn't matters to me- if you turn blue. Your not the only fish in the sea! You get it, you get it, you're not the only fish in the sea, you're not the only fish in the sea.

===

Walk-ing down the streets a mile away. I'm sing-ing my song while children play-ing. Let's talks pretty girl with your red dress on – sing-ing my song all the way home. Your home, my home, pretty girl, which way should we go? Which way should we go, which way should we go? Which way should we go – I don't care. It all depends on who you love the best.

Count your blessing, count them all but don't be a fool, and don't drink alcohol. Hey pretty girl, you'll live a long life, if you do the right thing, we'll all be alive. Hip hop, hip hop, what's going on with you? Be aware of predators they're always around. Be care - ful they will track you down. You know they will, and that's no lie. Be care-, ful child you could die. I don't mean to make you cry- just be patient and be safe. You should look forward to liv-ing another day.

===

Hip hop, drop the ball. Hip Hop, follow them all. Hip Hop, what should it be? You pretty girl around the tree. Hip Hop, Hip Hop, just sing-ing your song. It won't be the same when you're gone. Hip Hop, Hip Hop, hey pretty girl sing-ing is my life. What will it be pretty girl, what will it be you and me sit-ting in the tree. Hip Hop, Hip Hop, money don't grow on trees so don't drink the wine and don't look at me. Hip Hop, Hip Hop, what will it be, you're sing-ing my song walk-ing down the streets.

==

Hip Hop, Hip Hop, with a double beat only my eyes and your eyes can see. Hip Hop, Hip Hop, its time to turn back the clock. Hey pretty girl please look at me you have a sweet ass and a pretty face. if that's not enough what can I say sit down my child and cross your legs.

==

Hip Hop, Hip Hop, go and run around the block. Hip Hop, Hip Hop, when I look at you only children knows what to do. Hip Hop, Hip Hop, be care-ful run-ning around the block. Hip Hop, Hip Hop, sing my song out loud as if you know the words. Sang it like an angel unto the world to the heart of man-kind and women alike. Just like super-man the man of steel he saves the word from within.

==

Hip Hop, Hip Hop, it's what I would say. Being a girl how hard could it be? Wouldn't that make you tell the truth! tell the truth about me and you? Hey pretty girl what's up with you? Why don't you come and shine my shoes? Hey pretty girl - what can you say? Come shine my shoes and make my day. I don't bite - therefore you have nothing to fear. Do this song grab - you my dear? Hip Hop, Hip Hop, hey baby, your pretty and hot. Hey baby, you also rock. Hey baby, you're a fox. Sing-ing alone, sing-ing my song. Hey baby, don't you fear. You're the pretties girl out on these streets so sing my child and don't skip a beat.

========================WRITTEN BY AUTHOR: ALVIN WALLACE =======================

A song to bring laughter into the life of a child life. Children as you read the words of this song make it into something that you, yourself will enjoy and respect. Make this song part of you by transforming yourself as a memory of thought looking at a tall plant in the distance seeing how beautiful and green it is as if there was a wild animal running fast to attack its enemy. Change the words, mix them us, just have fun. What's missing; music notes. Children, that's where you come in. You insert your own music notes. Turn it into a song, but not just a song, but a song that speaks for you.

A WALK IN THE PARK LOOKING FOR A BUG

==

A walk in the park look-ing for a bug. These bugs you say were beauty-ful and smart. One would think their life was far apart. But as a stranger would save lives, and die young. be-cause bark-ing in the sky is pretty dumb. "WOW, I wasn't expecting that. That little bug had a lot to say but since you killed it. it speaks no more.

==

An eye for an eye, and a tooth for a tooth. Which bug would you choose to be? This little bug is climb-ing the tree. If you was a little bug; what would you do? If that bug was I, I would crawl away. I would look for food any-where I could. Be-cause when we cross the line dark-ness comes and we hide within.

==

Neither to say I wouldn't be nice. But ask me would I be surprise. I would pull up all dirty socks and, sleep in a zoo. Wouldn't that not be the right thing to do? After all, we are bugs don't you know? Our world is not that large but small in size. We are a few bugs but we are alive.

==

That, I don't think, that wouldn't be very smart. these bugs surely you don't know. Their beauty-ful bugs no doubt, no doubt, no doubt. But they will kill you on contact. So, if I was you. I've be pre-pare to fight back. Now that you under-stand. What more can I say? These bugs needs some-where to play. Bugs like humans com-pan-ion is a need. Bugs eat other bugs a need or not. Be-cause only their stomach can turn back the clock. Bug time and clock time, what different does it make?

==

A mighty good question, what does it mean? Bugs my friend, yes, they have a queen. What-ever a bug does don't ask me why. It's a matter of sal-vat-ion and sur-vi-val at the least, bugs don't care if you sneeze or leave. They know what they are. They know what they can do. Bugs like human don't go to school.

==

I'm not say-ing this to change your mind. Be-cause these bugs will kick your be-hind. Am I wrong, or am I right; get ready baby, get ready baby, get ready to fight. Hey, I heard enough, I heard enough, I heard enough!

==

The question is did you set the clock? Be-cause time is on our side "that much I know. Yes, we're human, and you are bugs. Be-cause of that, I must say this -bugs or not, there is a way. I won't go away empty hand-ed or alone.

==

Just remember it's a long way home. You are mak-ing me laugh, just wonder-ing what's in-store. If you feel not to tell me, that's ok too. Be-cause its not the end of the world.

==

Repeat after me; it's not the end of the world, it's not the end of the world, it's not the end of the world, If you feel not to tell me that's ok too.

==

I repeat, we are bugs that's not so bad. You are human "we're half and half". What have we done? What have we said? What have we done? What does the future whole? Bugs stand up tall the future is near. For that reason we much push on. Our goal I remind you is to go home.

==

Repeat after me; our goal is to go home, our goal is to go home, our goal is to go home.
Go home, go home, and go home; and go home.

==

KEEP YOUR EYES ON THE "WHAT"!

==

Keep your eyes on the road, look where you're going, pace yourself, don't look back. Catch your breath, and stay in contact. The enemy you're seek-ing is not for be-hind. The enemy you seek is not far be-hind. Do what you do best, and don't fall be-hind. Do what you do best and don't fall down. Be-cause the road you take must not make you late. It all depends on which way you go, take the short road it will get you there. Just be careful of who you meet. They might sweep you off your feet. It could even be some-one you know. Just be care-ful it's a friend not a foe.

Repeat, don't fall be-hind, don't fall down, don't fall be-hind, don't fall down. Just be care-ful of who you meet. They might sweep you off your feet. Just be careful of who you meet. Just pray that God will keep you safe watch-ing over you and the road ahead.

==

Keep your eyes on the streets, let the streets be your friends, learn them well you won't go wrong. The enemy is at your home. Their knock-ing at your door, not to say hello, not to be your friend, but to cap-ture your wives and your girl - friend. So watch each other back, and do no wrong, rest assure we'll soon be home.

Repeat, we'll soon be home, we'll soon be home, we'll soon, Rest assure we'll soon be home, rest -a-ssure we'll soon be home, rest a-ssure we'll soon be home.

==

Keep your eyes on the path, don't look back, and don't laugh. The enemy for sure is watch-ing you. He'll grab your child, and he'll grab you to. What make you think, you think he cares? If you guess wrong, how suicide it will be. So stay focus, look alive, the enemy he's play-ing no game. If you want to stay alive out smart him. Damn sure he will win.

==

Repeat, The enemy he's play-ing no game, The enemy he's - no game. The enemy he's play-ing no game.

==

Keep your eyes on the grass, there you will a new path. If you walk be-yond this point. Watch your-self, turn around, taken care of your family, if it's the last thing you do. You sworn on an oath to take care of them. So keep your prom-ise and don't let them win.

==

Repeat, don't let them win, don't let them win, don't let them win. So keep your prom-ise and don't let them win.

==

Keep your eyes, yes on each other, take care of your-self. Take care of the one that you love the best. Who-ever they are, who-ever they may-be, I know that it may not be the right thing to do. But right now my son its me and you. Al-though you have a gun. What can you do? He's the Predator, and that's the truth.

==

Repeat, What can you do? What can you do? What can you do? He's the predator and that's the truth, He's the predator and that's the truth. Al-though you have a gun. What can you do? He's the predator and that's the truth.

==

Keep your eyes on what! on the truth, where do we go from here? The streets are not safe and neither are we. How can we be - safe out here all alone? If the streets are not safe, and neither are we, how is it possible for us to feel free? The truth, what more can we do, what more do you need to know? The truth my friend, you say no more, the truth is, let shut the door.

Repeat, the truth, what more can we do, the truth my friend, you say no more, what more can we do, The truth is, lets shut the door. lets shut the door. lets shut the door.

==

Keep your eyes on the predator, he could be any-one, so keep that in mind. If you think I'm ly-ing, do a test your-self, if you are follow, don't turn a-round, think like a rat, hold your head, and hold your hat. The first chance you get go in-to a store. But don't for-get to lock the door. Think quiet-ly and repeat after me – If I was a predator, what would I do? Pursue my prey as much as I can chas-ing them into the neigh-bor-hood. If I was to get caught, so bid it, so bid it, they would run into hid-ing, for years, for years.

==

Repeat, if I was to get caught, so bid it, If I was to get caught, so bid it, so bid it, so bid it. They would run into hid-ing, for years, for years, they would run into hid-ing, for years, for years.

==

One Beautiful Morning was written on behalf of children reaching for a star above, star light, star bright, outer space surrounded by darkness as if it was a dream. A child has a reason to dream. A child has a reason for reaching for a star. It gives the child something to look forward to. Children playing outside; you ask what could it be. When in essence their just having fun. A child deserves to have fun. It's an important part of being a child. It's an open door to good health and their well being. An invitation to learn about themselves. An eye open to life and everything around them. Laugh, laugh, as loud as you can. Tell other children you read this poem to the end. Be happy and be a child. This poem is for you. Change the words. Change the meaning. Make it become a part of you. Make it your poem and something special.

ONE BEAUTIFUL MORNING

One beautiful morning what could I say. It was so beautiful everyone wanted to play.
Well, that was interesting and so was she. It was so interesting she drew a tree. A tall tree it was so rich and bright. Everyone laughed as they flew their kits. The rats and his family of mice you see. they could be heard from around the tree. But no one notice them I wonder why. I know, there was tears in everyone's eye. I wish, I wish, I would have thought of that. I wouldn't be here sitting in this hat. Damn girl, what are you trying to say? Stop I say before I lay you in the hay. What did I do to you? I only came here in the first place to be with you.

Hey girl, shut up; no one told you to talk. I should take my stick and teach you to walk. But whipping your ass wouldn't be enough. You need to wash off your smirk before its too late. One day you will ask; what did I do? Someone will turn around and hit you with a shoe. You should stick a straw down your mouth until you can no longer smile. If that's too much for you to comprehend speak now or hold your peace. I refused to be a burden if that's how you feel. I came here girl on my own free will feel tick top, tick top, you have until five o'clock. Leave now and leave while you can. Because later I will trap you and turn you into a hen. Whatever you say girl that's ok with me. This world is so big I have free will. What are you saying or are you trying to be smart? I can turn you into a frog or have you barking like a dog. If you don't shut up that won't be all. I'll turn you into my maid and make you clean the graves. I'll force you on your knees leaving you there until you bleed. If that's what you want stick out your tongue. When I let you go girl, you have better run. So put on your shoes, your dress, and your hat. Now make believe girl you're a cat. Do you see the streets? Do you see the signs? It's time girl for you to go home.

Leave me now, go away, and don't look back. I don't want to see you and nor do your friends. You girl, must leave here. There is no place for you here can't you see? These people will turn you into a beast. In the woods you'll be safe. the animals in the woods will watch over you. Like a good little girl you will have a home. Look around girl, its freedom as far as you can see. You can choose any tree and make it your home. But I be damn girl if you go back. It won't be safe for you girl and you know I'm right. Remember these words girl; and listen well. Where ever you go girl do not come back here. Because someone will kick you in the rear.

You staying here girl is not wise but kissing your ass, well, would be lying. it would feel so good letting the whole world see your ass being kick by me. The whole world would laugh at you girl. Is that's what you? If not stay away. There is road to the far east and south as you can see. Whatever road you take "make good of it". Girl, let me say this and listen well. Your not the only fish in the sea as you stand here looking at me. You're wasting time don't you see? So rock steady as you travel on your way. I'm telling you now be not afraid. Don't get me wrong girl. Don't think badly of me. I'm doing you a favor girl don't you see?

The Author storyline closing argument

We have longevity launch ourselves into a world of the unknown facing the ream of a new civilization surrounded by three deadest species known to mankind, and the world that we know called the beginning of what will be; a world behold the language, and understanding of indifferent as we approach the environment that was an in vision of our way of life. What change or should I say has changed the foot step of human beings concerning the will of others as they pursue life as we know without torture, without shame, hopefully giving them the strength to pursue greater good, greater opportunity offered by whoever may be with them reaching out to achieve goodness, wealth, love, and most importantly life.

Achieving life therefore should be a freedom of choice, and the right of each concern whoever they may be especially our children. Outside of what we know tells us what? The unknown perhaps and the truth about who we are. I was researching the truth about Predators to include recognition, identification of their features, and danger they presents to others. This inquire lead me to believe that the phrase "the ugly truth" is not just a figure of speech but something that has been around for quite sometime. One way of identifying the ugly truth is by looking at ourselves. The type of Predator we're speaking of are human beings just like ourselves. The only different is they could be male / female. But how would you identify them the (Predator)? That's a damn good question! Because a predator do not has to disguise themselves. "We are all human beings'.

But nevertheless, it doesn't change the fact that we need to be on the alert at all times, and be watchful of anything out of the ordinary or suspicious. We should not assumed, and or take anything for granted. Remember that, this put all human beings in great danger, not just us, but us all of us in great danger, to include our children. Our children are the main target. Of the writing and combine effort of this material, an eye for an eye tends to follow up the belief that we are careless, and blinded by the danger that walks the ground we so freely parade on, thinking that this United States Of America is free from harm when it comes to safety vs children. Red Alert, what are you saying? What are you asking? Think of it this way; danger, armsway, abduction, kidnapping, capture, torture, blind folded, and sold into prostitution. What if anything comes to mind? Were you not warned? To solve this problem; we need to be more on the alert for suspicious activities. We need to become aware of our surroundings. Think of it this way; home invasion, drive by shootings, stalkers, and of course predators. Has this country not become a ground for hostile take over. Who are the hostiles? We are; because not enough is being done to combat these problems. Whole your head and whole them high should be read; you're going to die. Does this not put fear into "you"? I don't want to live in fear, and if you think the streets are safe; you're wrong. If you think the supermarkets, and other local stores in the community (ie) Walmart, Walgreen, 7 – 11, your deadly wrong, blind as a bat, ignoring the truth. Although there are concerns, you, and your children are walking on dangerous grounds. Because others like you, are there for one reason and one reason only; that is, to abduct, and kidnap your children, forcing them into prostitution, hiding them underground, hidden caves, abandon houses, or simply a place out of sight out of mind. Frightening, isn't it? "Blinders over the eyes".

They become like predators, "man eating fish", snakes in the grass, hunger sharks, and to say the least like species without a brain, only thinking of themselves. How would you allow something like that to happen? Isn't it time to say; enough is enough? If so, stop turning a blind eye, stop ignoring what's going on around you. But most importantly do something about it. To stop evil, you need recognize it, to recognize evil, is to know that it is evil, to know that it is evil, is to know that it exist, to know that it exist, is to do something about it, to do something about it, is to act, to act is, to take a stand, to take a stand, is to tell others, to tell others, is to make it known, to make it known, is to talk about it, to talk about it, is to open your mouth, to open your mouth, is to say something, to say something, is to do something, to do something, not to ignore what's going on around you.

Everything here is about the ugly truth of a predator. The misconception of a predator; it's a male. Because if anyone was to do harm, and or cause danger to a child; in the mind of most of us, it would be a man. But now that we know better, and know that a predator can also be a female. Well, how does that make you feel? So, what color are apples now? If you were to choose an apple; what color would it be? But an apple is not a predator; it who we are. It's what we are. It combine with how we think. It combine with how we feel. It's combine with what we do and how we see each other. If that makes senses!

I hope one day to meet all of you but due to COVID 19, I don't know what to do. I don't know whether or not to leave my home. But one thing for sure I'm not along. When I write its not about me but low and behold the whole world will see. I pride myself thinking of you because children are precious and that's the truth. I see life maybe different from you but nevertheless what different does it make. In times like these what can I say. You do what you can for yourself and your child because COVID 19 is alive. It can cripple you. It can make you ill. It can even kill you that much we know. In spite of everything I ask this of you. Be safe, stay safe, and I'll keep writing for you. My prayers, your prayers, may they be the same.

Hope we need. Help is always there. It's now up to us to do our best. I ask as you read this book, read it again, and again, tell others about it, and keep it close to your heart. Keep it in arms reach should you need it (EMERGENCY). Keep this book in a place where you can go for it when you need it the most. Looking for it, not knowing where it is, (is not the answer). Remember, every minute counts. The longer it takes you to act; danger sets in. And; the first 48 hours are critical. WORDS OF ACKNOWLEDGEMENT ANNOUNCING THE PROBLEM FACING US TODAY; BY AUTHOR: ALVIN WALLCE, thank you for being there for me and buying my book. God Bless You. God Bless America. God Bless Us All.

THIS IS FOR YOU PREDOMINATE "PREDATORY"
(but not for long)

He'll be riding three white horses when he come; the police, the police, he'll be riding three white horses when he come, the police, the police, he'll be riding three white horses, he'll be riding three white horses, he'll be riding three white horse when he come.

He'll be coming to get you "Predator" when he come, the police, the police, he'll be coming to get you "Predator" when he come, the police, the police, he'll be coming to get you, he'll be coming to get you, he'll be coming to get you Predator" when he come.

There is no where to hide when he come, the police, the police, there is no where to hide when he come, the police, the police, there is no where to hide, there is no where to hide, there is no where to hide when he come.

They will arrest you "Predator" when they come, the police, the police, they will arrest you "Predator" when they come, the police, the police, they will arrest you predator, they will arrest you predator, they will arrest you "Predator" when they come.

They will take you to jail "Predator" when they come, the police, the police, they will take you to jail "Predator" when they come, the will take you to jail, they will take you to jail, they will take you to jail "Predator" when they come.

You'll be saying not me when they come, bull shit, bull shit, you're liar, you're liar, you'll be saying not me when they come, bull shit, bull shit, you're liar, you're liar, you'll be saying its not me, you'll be saying its not me, you'll be saying its not me when they come.

You'll have to face the music when they come, criminal charges, criminal charges, you'll have to face the music when they come, criminal charges, you'll have to face the music, you'll have to face the music, you'll have to face the music when they come.

The child you kidnapped and abducted is now free, rescued by the police, rescued by the police, the child you kidnapped and abducted is now free, rescued by the police, rescued by the police, the child you kidnapped and abducted, the child you kidnapped and abducted, the child you kidnapped and abducted is now free.

The girls you kidnapped and abducted will have a story to tell, yes they will, yes they will, the girls you kidnapped and abducted will have a story to tell, yes they will, yes they will, the girls you kidnapped and abducted, the girls you kidnapped and abducted, the girls you kidnapped and abducted will have a story to tell.

Their lives will never be the same don't you know, that is true, yes I know, that is true, yes I know, their lives will never be the same don't you know, that is true, yes I know, that is true, yes I know, their lives will never be the same, their lives will never be the same, their lives will never be the same don't you know.

The will suffer psychologically, physically, and emotionally, for a very long time thanks to you, bye your hands, bye your hands, they will suffer psychologically, physically, and emotionally, for a very long time thanks to you, bye your hands, bye your hands, they will suffer psychologically, physically, and emotionally, they will suffer psychologically, physically, and emotionally, they will suffer psychologically, physically, and emotionally for a very long time thanks to you.

The will have to seek child counseling because of what you did to them every day, day after day, forcing them to do the unthinkable don't you know, I'm sorry don't you know, I'm sorry don't you know, they will have to seek child counseling because of what you did to them every day, day after day, forcing them to do the unthinkable don't you know, I'm sorry don't you know, I'm sorry don't you know, they will have to seek child counseling, they will have to seek child counseling, they will have to seek child counseling because don't you know.

You will go to jail for a very long time don't you know, I don't care, but you should, but you should, you will go to jail for a very long time don't you know, I don't care, but you should, but you should, you will go to jail, you will go to jail, you will go to jail for a very long time don't you know.

You raped and tortured their children and lest them to die an't that's the truth, that's the truth, that's the truth, you raped and tortured their children and lest them to die an't that's the truth, that's the truth, that's the truth, you raped and tortured their children, you raped and tortured their children, you raped and tortured their children an't that's the truth.

You will register as a sexual offender when convicted, when convicted yes you will, when convicted yes you will, you will register as a sexual offender when convicted, when convicted yes you will, when convicted yes you will, you will register as a sexual offender, you will register as a sexual offender, you will register as sexual offender when convicted.

There is no room for forgiveness for you and people like you, people like you, people like you, there is no room for forgiveness for you and people like you, people like you, people like you, there is no room for forgiveness, there is no room forgiveness, there is no room forgiveness for you and people like you.

You should get on your knees and ask God for mercy for your sin, that's true, for your sin, you should get on your knees and ask God for mercy for your sin, that's true, for your sin, you should get on your knees, you should get on your knees, you should get on your knees and ask God for mercy for your sin.

MY FINAL WORDS OF WARNING TO ALL POTENTIAL PREDATORS

TARGETING CHILDREN AND YOUNG ADULTS

Whole your head and whole them high the police is passing by. With their weapon in their hand. Taking you to jail. Count your blessings you're not dying. Am I right or wrong. Am I right or wrong. Count your blessing you could be dead; instead you're going to hell. Open your eyes and shut your mouth. To be truthful you deserves to die. Am I not; not telling the truth! Ball up your fist I'll send you to the zoo.

I'll kick your ass where the sun don't shine. I'll make it hurt and scream like a lion. Say one more word and see what I will do. I'll put you in chains and throw away the key. You'll spend years in jail looking at a tree. You'll say kick me; kick me in the ass. When its all said and done everyone will laugh.

Your ass would be sore and your eyes red. You will scream bloody mary "I wish I was dead". But that's too easy, too easy for you. You should be put inside a case with a snake or two. That would be a more suitable punishment don't you think. Let the punishment fit the crime "that's best for you!" They will do you in and that's the truth.

You'll be screaming police, police please help me. These snakes you see all over me. I don't want to die this way. I don't want to die this way please help me. I know that am a predator and must pay the price. Pease let me live. I bey of you. I promise God I'll tell you the truth. I promise, I promise, from the bottom of my heart. I'm not lying to you. I sware to God. If you don't believe me. Kill me now. Becasuse I have nothing to loose and that's the truth.